Deceived

Deceived

Facing Sexual Betrayal, Lies, and Secrets

Claudia Black, Ph.D.

HAZELDEN®

Hazelden
Center City, Minnesota 55012
hazelden.org
© 2009 by Claudia Black
All rights reserved. Published 2009
Printed in the United States of America

Library of Congress Cataloging-in-Publication Data
Black, Claudia.
    Deceived : facing sexual betrayal, lies, and secrets / Claudia Black.
        p. cm.
    Includes bibliographical references.
    ISBN 978-1-59285-698-5
    1. Women—Psychology. 2. Men—Sexual behavior. 3. Betrayal—
Psychological aspects. 4. Adultery—Psychological aspects. I. Title.
    HQ1206.B445 2009
    646.7'8—dc22
                                                                    2008046153

Editor's note
While the stories and lives shared in this book are true, names and other identifying information has been changed to provide anonymity.
This publication is not intended as a substitute for the advice of health care professionals.

13 12 11 10   2 3 4 5 6

Cover design by Theresa Gedig
Interior design and typesetting by Madeline Berglund

To the Women of the Lodge—
those who have entered the doors and begun their healing
and those yet to come.

May You Soar

Contents

Preface

I have been truly graced to have been working in the field of addictive disorders for thirty years. Early in my career I focused on alcoholics and their family members, and subsequently I worked with people addicted to prescription pain medications, cocaine, and other drugs. I became recognized for my work with young and adult children of alcoholics before we even had the language of codependency. Over the years my work has expanded to designing and implementing programs for families in a variety of settings. During this time, as the field of addiction has grown, the recognition of sexual compulsivity has become more common. Nearly a decade ago I began to work with my first group of female partners confronted with sexual betrayal. It was this professional experience that inspired me to write *Deceived*.

Early in this work I quickly noticed three things. First, I saw how my previous experience with adult children and childhood sexual abuse survivors would be helpful, as the wives and partners frequently came from addictive, abusive, or otherwise impaired family systems. Second, I realized that the socialization of women reinforced much of the women's behavior in these relationships: *Give the man the benefit of the doubt. Don't trust yourself. Accommodate. Dismiss your needs in deference to the needs of others, particularly his needs.* Third, while there are many similarities between those addicted to alcohol and drugs and those who act out sexually, being the partner of someone who acts out sexually is a more personal, confusing, and shameful affront. The women I worked with experienced consequences that were disruptive on every level of life: morally, spiritually, emotionally, mentally, and physically.

During the group process, I witnessed incredible courage from these women, who were in great angst and despair—courage that was professionally and personally awe-inspiring. I saw them develop community as they shared their many feelings, experiences, and questions along with much embarrassment, anger, confusion, and shame.

In their despair, I saw these women grapple with self-esteem, self-worth, and dignity at a level I had never before encountered in my work. Was this because of the particular women I worked with? Maybe, but I think not. I think the nature of betrayal they experienced and their profound personal histories, coupled with the safety that was afforded them in the group to claim their voices, allowed them to be authentic with each other and be true to themselves. All of these women came together as a force, and they soared. In their anguish, they cried and they were angry—oh so angry. They laughed and they loved; they bolstered one another; they laughed some more. They came to love and support each other in ways they had never previously expressed or experienced. The common denominator was simply that they each had a partner who was acting out sexually. Some of them had partners who became strong in recovery; others had partners who were never serious about recovery. Whatever their individual circumstances, some women stayed in their relationships, some ended up leaving, and some went through a divorce they did not seek. But each moved forward in her life and benefited greatly through the community of other women she found in her healing process.

Although I recognize that men can be deceived by female partners, and men and women in same-sex relationships also experience sexual deception in their coupleships, it was not feasible to discuss the nuances and differences in every type of relationship involving sexual compulsivity. I have no doubt all will find value in this book and it is my hope all will find community in which to begin healing.

This book is for you, the female partner, and I am honored to be a part of your journey. I continue to be in awe of the resiliency and spirit of women who feel so fragile, so vulnerable, and yet are so strong. In reading *Deceived* it is my hope that you will better understand what is happening in your life, that you will garner validation for your experiences, and that you will find a path that offers you clarity, direction, and voice. Welcome to the community of women who came to call themselves "Women of the Lodge."

Claudia Black

Acknowledgments

My heart is so full when I think of the people whose lives came together in a manner that influenced my writing of this book.

My thanks to Patrick Carnes and Ralph Earle for inviting me to lead my first group with female partners of sex addicts. This experience became a professional and personal gift for which I will always be grateful.

Thanks to Diane Dillon, my co-therapist of many years in working with the Women of the Lodge; it was an exhilarating, challenging experience of great joy, humility, and incredible teamwork in an untapped area of psychotherapy. You are a colleague from whom I learned a lot and a dear friend. It was also because of your insistence that I wrote this book.

While there are many fine leaders within the field of addictions and the sex addiction field specifically and I am indebted to you all, I would like to acknowledge the pioneering work of Patrick Carnes and Jennifer Schneider. They wrote the initial books that spoke about the issues of sex addiction and co-sex addiction and offered a foundational framework for the work in this field today.

Over a period of six years, many women came to group; some stayed for several years, some participated briefly, and others only paid a visit. From literally each and every woman I learned so much about co-sex addiction: the pain of it, and the recovery. I witnessed such raw emotion, incredible courage, and triumphant transformation, and in that process I learned more about myself. I will always carry the experiences of shared tears, laughter, touch, and love. I will always cherish our time together and hold you all forever in my heart.

A special thanks to all the women, named and unnamed, who shared their stories for this book. Your contributions are inspiring. And thanks to the men who shared their experiences—you too made an invaluable contribution. Thank you all for trusting me to honor the lives of others through your stories.

Thanks to my longtime assistant, Sandi Klein, who was once again invaluable. She coordinated, organized, and protected the stories as they were shared with me. She typed, retyped, and edited endlessly for a couple of years, giving me feedback and engaging in important dialogue.

And thanks to Jeri Nilson; your conceptual feedback was invaluable. You asked tough questions and prompted me for more; you embraced the stories of the female partners in a manner that allows this book to speak to even greater numbers of women.

I would also like to thank Jean Collins, Maureen Canning, and Marie C., who took the time to offer me very concrete feedback for which I am most grateful.

And I would also like to recognize my wonderful group of women friends—each one of you has been with me in spirit wherever my personal and professional journey takes me.

Thank you to Hazelden Publishing for quickly responding to the need for a book for women who are living with sex addiction, and for enthusiastically embracing my work. My editor, Cathy Broberg, made it a joy to bring this book to fruition. I thank you for your thoughtful approach and respect given to a topic that is emotional and complex.

Lastly, I lovingly acknowledge my husband of thirty years, Jack Fahey. You always believe in me and my work, respecting the time, the passion, the endless dialogue about content and style. You are my greatest champion.

To all who pick up this book, I hope you find a path that leads to greater happiness.

Introduction

If you have picked up this book, it is likely you are scared and upset about some aspect of your partner's sexuality. It could be that you caught your partner in an affair and now you suspect other affairs. It may be his frequent engagement in pornography or the amount of time he spends at strip joints. Or perhaps you've found credit card receipts or emails that don't make sense to you. It could be that his sexual acting out has become public or that he has confessed to sexual behaviors of which you'd been unaware. You may or may not have heard the term *sex addiction,* and while you have not thought of your partner as an addict, you may recognize that his sexual behavior seems out of control.

It is possible that denial is allowing you to normalize behavior that your gut tells you is something more. You need to trust your instincts. As a dear client of mine said, "You need to trust your worms when they are wriggling inside your gut." Even if you don't know the extent of your partner's behavior, and it is very likely you do not, you owe it to yourself to read this book. What you have recently discovered, or possibly tolerated and normalized, is not necessarily "just what men do." In many cases his behavior has become addictive in nature: highly compulsive, repetitive behavior that continues in spite of the risk and potential negative consequences. If his behavior has become compulsive and addictive (and I use those terms interchangeably), it is treatable. But for your healing, as well as the potential of the relationship to be realized, the truth needs to be acknowledged. That truth can begin with you—your truth.

Facing Deception

To live with sexual betrayal is to live with deceit. *Deception* means to cause a person to believe what is not true; to mislead, betray, delude, or dupe. When your partner is engaging in sexual behavior that violates the values of your relationship, he will go to great lengths to conceal his behavior. In that process, his deception involves falsehood or the deliberate concealment or misrepresentation of truth.

To *mislead* means to lead into error, but not invariably with the intent to harm. His behavior is not intentionally meant to harm you. More likely than not he has deluded himself by believing you will never know, and if you don't know, you will not be hurt.

To *betray* implies a faithlessness that brings another to a disadvantage or into danger. This faithlessness puts your relationship on an unequal playing field. Instead of an equal partnership, you are set up for a "one up" and "one down" relationship, with you being the "one down." Without honesty, your relationship is based on an illusion. While betrayal puts your relationship in jeopardy, it can also create physical danger for you with unsafe sex practices and/or the rage that comes from jilted lovers.

To *delude* is to mislead to the point of rendering another unable to detect a falsehood or make sound judgment. Your partner, as if a magician, has become a master of deception.

To *dupe* means to delude another by playing upon that person's susceptibility or naiveté. Time after time your partner has relied on your naiveté, your need to want to believe him, and your fears of what it means to know the truth.

This book offers validation and hope to you, a woman living with sexual betrayal. It normalizes the craziness you may be feeling that comes with suspecting your partner is acting out sexually in some way but not knowing for certain, or sensing something is wrong but you're not sure what. By meeting other women who have walked a similar path and hearing their stories, you will learn that you are not alone, your shame will lessen, and you will realize you don't need to be in a victim role. When you recognize sexual compulsivity as an addictive disorder, his behavior becomes, while not excusable, understandable. You will see that you did not enter into this relationship by accident, and how family of origin issues strongly influence your choice of partner(s) and your behavior. Your urgent questions will be answered, and you will begin to identify skills that will empower you. While there are no guarantees on whether or not your relationship will survive, you will find a path of strength, direction, and support so that whatever choices you make will come from a place of inner knowing and integrity.

The Chapters Ahead: What's to Come

In the chapters ahead, we'll be following the stories of six women who have faced sexual betrayal. In their own words, these women will share aspects of their lives—from their initial awareness of the problem to their present-day recovery. These women were members of one of the first groups I led for female partners dealing with sexual acting out in their relationships, a group whose members came to call themselves "Women of the Lodge." Throughout this book, their voices will offer you validation and hope, as they have also been where you find yourself today. Each of these women, in various ways, found a path of healing and recovery. That path was in a community of other women who were facing a husband's or partner's sexual betrayal and acting out, and who were looking for help. While the stories and lives of these six women are true, names and identifying information have been changed to provide anonymity. In addition to these stories, portions of other women's stories will be offered to provide a broader scope of the recovery experience. I refer to these women as the unnamed *Coaddict*. You will also hear the voices of unnamed *Addicts*. Just as hearing the voices of women in recovery is beneficial, so too is hearing the men—*Addicts*—speak about their addictions and addictive behaviors.

The women you will meet refer to their behavior and thinking as *codependent* and to themselves as *coaddicts* or *cosas*. These are lay terms commonly identified and popular in self-help groups and literature and used by many treatment professionals. These were not labels the women readily accepted and, in fact, many women initially resisted them or were confused by them. In time they came to find these terms provided them with an empowering language.

The word *codependency* came into use in the late 1970s. Initially it referred to the partner of an addict. Over time its meaning broadened to describe behavioral patterns developed when raised in an addicted family. Later it was recognized that those behavioral patterns were also seen in those raised in impaired, shame-based family systems. The labels *coaddict* and *cosa* include the dynamics of codependency but also addresses the more specific issues related to spouses and partners. Think of these labels as both a (verbal) semantic container for your painful feelings, negative beliefs, and self-defeating behaviors; and an opening onto a new path, a direction to transform your negative beliefs to self-enhancing beliefs, an opportunity to realize the gift of feelings and empowering behaviors. The terms *cosa, coaddict,* and *codependent* are meant to support you as deserving of your own healing and recovery, not to blame you for anything, or to shame you. Don't let them be a roadblock to your own healing. You don't have to take on any labels you don't want; for now, simply be open to what may be a new language.

Chapter One: You Are Not Alone

"Why me?" "How could he?" You will be introduced to six women—Therese, Vanessa, Jacque, Sara, Maite, and Jenny—each of whom was confronted with her partner's sexual acting out, ranging from pornography, multiple affairs, and cybersex to prostitutes. In addition to the betrayal of their coupleship, love, and commitment, these women also confronted legal issues, children sired with other women, sexually transmitted diseases (STDs), and how to address their partner's behavior with their own children. Each one of these women is angry, scared, and confused about what this means for her relationship.

Chapter Two: In the Face of Truth

"This can't be happening." Denial, the core of all addictive disorders and one's coaddiction—the self-defeating thoughts and behaviors created in response to living with an addictive disorder—will be explored. You will realize you aren't alone in your rationalizations and minimizing. The common issues and themes of trying to control your partner, the incessant preoccupation that overwhelms your life, rage, sideways anger, and image management are discussed. The roller coaster of feelings you may be experiencing will be explained, and you'll understand how you have been defending against the pain of your situation and the constant state of grief in which you may find yourself. You'll have the opportunity to reflect on ways you emotionally disconnect from yourself. The chronic stress that accompanies living with addiction and often leads to health problems will also be discussed.

Chapter Three: His Behavior Is Not About You

"Why won't he just stop?" A natural aspect of your coaddiction is focusing on the addict and his behavior. For that reason, I chose not to focus on him at the beginning of this book. You deserve the focus. You deserve your recovery, and it is not based on his recovery. This book conveys that you can find answers to your pain by taking ownership of your recovery process. Nonetheless, it is important to have an understanding of his behavior. This chapter will help you to understand how sexual behaviors can and do become addictive for some; their similarity to substance dependence and/or other behavioral addictions; the possibility of multiple addictions and depression; and the neuroscience of addiction. Addiction is defined as a compulsive behavior that dominates someone's life. The person continues the behavior in spite of adverse consequences and becomes willing to sacrifice what he or she cherishes most in order to preserve and continue the unhealthy behavior. None of this explanation is intended to excuse your partner's behavior. I want to help you understand why it is so difficult for him to stop, and why seeking appropriate treatment through a professional or self-help program will make him more likely to be able to stop acting out.

Chapter Four: You Didn't Get Here by Accident

"Why does this feel so familiar?" "What did I do to deserve this?" Let's be clear: You don't deserve this. No one deserves to be treated with disrespect. While you are not responsible for your partner's behavior, it is not coincidental that you are in a relationship with an addict. In this chapter you will come to understand how original family wounding creates the foundation for impaired relationships, and how family of origin issues influence both you and your partner. Abandonment and trauma repetition will be described. You'll have the opportunity to reflect on how the sexual messages you have internalized influence your life today. You will see the natural dance that occurs between an addict and a coaddict, and identify the influences of family script for both of you. By recognizing the need to speak to the past and complete unfinished grief work, you will be free to work on your recovery and be present in your relationships. By recognizing both the basis and the characteristics of your codependent traits, you will find a direction for your healing.

Chapter Five: Learning the News

"Do I stay or leave?" "What does it mean if we have sex?" "Am I crazy to love him?" Learning about your partner's behavior can come in a variety of venues, sometimes as a surprise, other times after a lot of suspicion. This chapter offers you a model for healthy disclosure and discusses the "dribbling effect" (hearing the news in bits and pieces over time). This is a time of great shock and pain for many cosas, and I will assist you in putting one foot in front of the other until you can make more sense of your situation. There are many questions and issues that confront you with the initial discovery of his behavior. I'll discuss the questions of being sexual shortly after disclosure, whether to stay or to leave, and why it is you love him in spite of the situation. I'll introduce the meaning of a therapeutic separation, a means some couples ultimately find very supportive of their relationship. Hearing how others have responded to similar situations and how they found ways to resolve such questions will offer some validation and direction.

Chapter Six: What Do You Tell Your Children?

"How much do my kids need to know?" "What if they already know or suspect something?" If you are a parent, you are probably asking yourself these kinds of questions. Talking with your children regarding sexually addictive behavior is undoubtedly a situation that no parent wants to face. Parents seldom want to share their secrets, their pain, or their betrayal with their children. They want to protect their children from pain. Unfortunately, addiction within a family takes that possibility away. Perhaps you are frightened about using the word *addiction* and how that might be portrayed or interpreted by your child. This chapter provides you with information about how to approach a conversation with children of varying ages about what is happening between you and your partner. It will also reinforce how your recovery influences your parenting skills.

Chapter Seven: Your Time to Heal

"What is the price I am paying by trying to manage and control that which I cannot control?" "What do I have the power to affect?" "What if he relapses and begins acting out again?" "Am I ready to seek help?" I'll further the discussion about the grief process you are experiencing, look at the language of powerlessness and unmanageability, and address boundaries. Boundaries are vital to your recovery process. I'll introduce the concept of nonnegotiable boundaries that can offer you greater safety and security during this vulnerable period and share with you ways to ease the habit of living in your head—being so preoccupied you can't think straight. You will find validation for the vast array of feelings that permeate your life. The Women of the Lodge share their experiences of reaching out to other women and help shine a light and provide some hope when you can't seem to find it. You don't want to do this alone. You don't need to do this alone. There are others who will walk this path with you.

Chapter Eight: Finding Your Serenity

"Can I ever forgive him?" "Do I even want to try?" When you say you forgive but you have not claimed your voice, grieved your pain, or owned your injustices, that is when you talk the talk but don't walk the walk of recovery. You won't get to a place of heartfelt forgiveness without being emotionally honest. The Women of the Lodge and I will talk about what we think forgiveness is, and about how they came to find it for their partners and themselves. These women found that their healing included a spiritual path. Some were already steeped in a particular faith in which they found solace and support, while others had to sort out the differences they found in their religion and their spiritual path. Still others found their spiritual path in nontraditional ways, discovering a greater peace in a connection with a Higher Power. Whether or not you subscribe to a specific faith or set of beliefs, simply be open to what is shared here.

Chapter Nine: The Women of the Lodge

"Trust and give voice to your reality." Recovery is a journey all the Women of the Lodge have embraced. Here they share with you where they are in their recovery and in their relationships. They no longer live in a crisis state; they no longer live in shame. They have found tools that give them the structure and safety to know they are okay irrespective of what their partner's behavior might be. They invite you to come out of your emotional isolation, to shed your secrets and your shame, and to discover the beauty and power in yourself.

Reflective Thoughts and Questions

At the end of each chapter I offer questions and/or thoughts for you to consider. There are no right or wrong answers. You may choose to address them as you finish reading each chapter, or you may come back to them after reading the entire book. I strongly encourage you to respond in writing, as putting your thoughts down on paper frees you of being too analytical or intellectually defensive and allows you to become more connected to your feelings and the truth. These thoughts and questions are also a good structure to use as a format to begin sharing with other women in recovery, or with a therapist.

Recommended Readings

A significant tool in your healing process is reading not only books on sexual compulsivity and coaddiction, but also books related to codependency, growing up with addiction, and sexual or physical abuse. Books about emotional healing and spiritual practices are also valuable. While I offer you a suggested list of reading materials, I strongly encourage you to browse the self-help section of bookstores, ask other women in recovery what was helpful to them, or ask your therapist.

Taking the Next Step

While sexual betrayal and deceit are devastating, those in recovery are eventually able to find meaning from their history and gifts in the process of healing. With an openness and willingness, you too can take the next step and find healing. The emotional isolation and shame you feel will lessen; you will let go of unneeded defenses. False pride and image management won't be needed as cover-ups; perfectionism will go to the wayside. You will be willing to get help for your depression and anxiety and any of your own addictive disorders. It will be possible to let go of defensive emoting and learn to express your needs and feelings with clarity; you will speak from a place of respect and listen with openness. Boundaries will be your lifeline; they will provide you protection and safety. Your self-esteem and self-acceptance will grow; self-love will be your guide to healthy boundaries. You will listen and trust your intuition; you will trust in your knowing. All of this is possible as you find your community. May that all begin with this book.

 **C h a p t e r   O n e**

You Are Not Alone

Why me? How could he?

Doesn't he love me? What should I do?

How can I keep this secret
without going crazy?

Go to any magazine rack, turn on almost any television station, or listen to popular music and you will be bombarded by themes of sex, intimacy, commitment, and betrayal. While being single is portrayed as fun and exciting, the world of coupleship is assumed to be most people's ultimate goal. Yet confusion exists about intimacy and commitment, and sexual betrayal abounds in our culture.

Most couples, whether married or not, have both spoken and unspoken commitments that sex stays within their relationship; they will communicate and respect each other's personal needs and boundaries. Their expectation is for unconditional love, but they know that relationships have conditions that need to be negotiated openly. Unfortunately these commitments and expectations are simply a facade in many people's relationships. Many women are part of a coupleship riddled with deception, lies, and false perception as a result of their partner's compulsive sexual acting out.

Today, in every neighborhood throughout every community, women are being challenged by the addictive nature of their partner's sexual behavior. Perhaps you are a young wife of nineteen who just discovered that your husband was with another woman within days of your wedding. You feel overwhelmed, realizing you don't know your husband at all. Your parents

1

tried to talk you out of the marriage, and now you are thinking maybe they were right.

You may be the mother of two young children whose husband has just lost his job because he was engaging in Internet sex during work hours. Suddenly, you start to put together what you thought was odd behavior with the fact that he has also been doing that at home.

You could be a thirty-eight-year-old mother of two with only a high school education and no work experience who previously refused to believe rumors about your husband's affairs, but now he's been caught in a federal pornography sting and it's all over the front page of the newspaper.

You could be a stay-at-home mom going crazy with suspicions when your husband travels extensively in his work. You know you've heard a woman's voice in the background in his hotel room when you've called him. He says it's just room service. For several months someone has been calling your home and hanging up when you answer. When you question him, he appeals to your insecurity and your past trust issues with your ex-husband.

Or maybe you're forty-seven years of age, you've masked your shame and confusion about your husband's chronic pornographic activity, and now you are horrified because your children are going to find out about their father's voyeurism. You thought he had stopped that behavior, but he has been caught by the police and this time it looks like it will become public.

Or you could be a sixty-five-year-old grandmother of four who's known for forty-five years that your husband has had one affair after the other. There's nothing particularly different about the current affair that you just discovered; it's just the straw that breaks the camel's back.

The truth is you could be any woman. You may have children; you may not. You may have the financial resources to be independent but you stay in the relationship; you may want out but your choices are limited because you're financially dependent on your partner. You could be of any faith. In some cases your faith may offer direction and comfort, or you may feel trapped as a consequence of the constrictions of your religion. Your ethnicity and culture may help you stay in denial and normalize behavior that you find hurtful and shaming. Then again, your culture may be what offers you strength and support at a time of great confusion. Perhaps finding yourself in this situation is a family tradition. Generations of women in your family have denied, tolerated, and rationalized the sexual acting out of their men.

No matter who you are and what your background is, to be in a relationship with someone you love, someone you believe loves you, someone you
have a commitment with, only to realize he has been acting out sexually is
one of the greatest betrayals.

What I want you to know is that you are not alone. There is a path out
of this painful situation. From my thirty years of work experience in the
addiction field, I am convinced you will find healing happens when you
allow yourself the benefit of getting to know others who have walked this
path before you and who will now walk alongside you. As you read *Deceived*
you'll hear the voices of some very brave women who found the courage
to confront their truth, to stop living their life in reaction to someone else's
behavior, and to trust that they deserve better. These women courageously
stepped out of the secrecy to seek direction and, with that, hope. They
represent what is only a handful of people—at this time mostly women, but
periodically a male in their midst—who found the courage and then the
resources to seek out others with whom they could identify. In self-help
and therapeutic support groups they found validation for their experiences,
they found the support to discover their voices and speak their truths, and
they allowed themselves to believe in their worth. Able to let go of their
shame and their pain, these women embraced their own strengths within a
community of other women who had taken similar paths and most often
had similar histories. They would name their community "Women of the
Lodge."

Community can mean many things, but for these women it meant a
place of belonging and connection. They found other women with whom
they could identify; other women who offered a knowing and an acceptance
of their emotional fragility. As with any community, there were a variety of
people and problems, but there was a coming together at a time of crisis for
support and in recovery for mutual celebration. As they individually and
together moved through uncharted emotional and relational territory, they
became each other's safety net. The phrase "Women of the Lodge" meant
different things to the different personalities, but "Lodge" implied they had
come together to be with each other in a place that offered safety through
structure, where they would feel warmth as if it emanated from a fire. In
this safe place, they became empowered to find their strengths. They found
laughter, joy, hope, connection, and a direction to their lives that fostered

their well-being. Their journey to health and wellness began.

You may not know where your community is. Your anger, pain, and shame may be so great that you don't even believe you want a community. But it is my belief that by picking up this book, you too are a very brave soul who wants validation, support, direction, and hope. This is the beginning of community. You can embark on your journey to health and wellness.

Meet the Women of the Lodge

• THERESE •

Five years into our marriage I discovered my husband had been regularly viewing pornography on the Net. I didn't understand why he would do that because I always tried to please him in bed. I remember crying and telling him it wasn't right. Why wasn't I enough? I really tried to shame him about it, and am sure I did, but he just got better at hiding his behavior. I'd periodically find out [that he was still viewing pornography] by seeing an email or a Web site, or something in the car or the mail. Each time I'd get holier than thou and scold him like a punitive mother. I'd call him a hypocrite in the eyes of the Lord, use the bad parent guilt trip, and then off we'd go to church as the perfect family.

I ran our house with an iron fist and always had a smile on my face for the world to see. My children are beautiful and we always went everywhere as the perfect family. My husband had all the criteria for my family picture. He was fun, good-looking, attended church, and never confronted me. It was the "never confronting" part that would be critical to our relationship. Of course at the time I didn't understand this, but I was such a controller. I couldn't handle anyone who challenged me. That was a major threat to me. At work my husband always acquiesced, was the good guy. He was intimidated by authority and just as intimidated by me. I didn't know this because I couldn't afford to really look at us closely or I would lose my picture of perfect. Perfect didn't include being weak or vulnerable.

I also became a source of endless questions. I incessantly asked him whether or not he had been on the Internet, if he found my women friends attractive, what it was that made them attractive, and if I was prettier than his female coworkers. These questions were intended to make me feel as if I was the only one he'd ever want to be with sexually, somehow believing he had no need for anyone else. I would use my sexuality as a tease, but I really controlled our sex life and often used the kids and illness as an excuse to avoid sex.

Then right about the time I would get comfortable that he was not into pornography anymore, he would be back at it. The next thing I knew, I allowed myself an affair—only one, but I felt so self-righteous. I just didn't understand why he did these things. I became really angry and my way of getting back at him was to spend money. I would go on shopping binges and wait for him to say something to me. He never did. I knew he wouldn't. And I knew why.

I can see now that I was a control freak. Image was my whole life. I loved my husband and I wanted my marriage. A lot of our life was good, but we had this secret life. Ultimately, through our church, we found some help with people who knew about sex addiction and it was a relief for both of us to learn his behavior was an addiction. That took away a lot of the shame. But it was his addiction, and I saw the work needing to be done as his. After all, I was leading the moral compass. I was busy with school, church, and the kids. I was happy he was addressing his problem, but it would take some time and a few more relapses before I really understood that I had some

**of my own codependency characteristics that needed
addressing.**

. . . .

While there are a variety of behaviors that reflect codependency,
Therese's codependent traits that interfered with her ability to be honest
were her perfectionism, her need for control, and her sense of entitlement.
In her perfectionism, image was important and Therese perpetually put on
a happy face. She sought control where she could, only to fuel the dysfunction in her relationship. She silently punished and tried to induce guilt; she
engaged in hurtful behavior toward herself and others under her sense of
entitlement. Therese saw everything as being her husband's problem.

Use of the Internet to access pornography and/or engage in a virtual sex
encounter known as *cybersex* is escalating at alarming rates. Some women
claim emphatically that they would accept Internet sex any day over other
behaviors. Yet when the behavior is addictive, women like Therese feel the
betrayal, the humiliation, and the shame as do the other wives and partners
of men who are acting out with multiple affairs, escorts, masturbation, or
pornography.

Culturally, the messages given about pornography and masturbation
vary, creating confusion about what is normal or healthy. Some cultures
view masturbation as a natural pleasure-seeking act, while others have no
tolerance for such behavior. Some view pornography as a normal part of
adolescence and adulthood, while others cast moral judgment on it, recognizing how it can perpetuate the objectification of women. As a result of
these mixed messages, women partners may experience conflicting feelings
when they become aware of such acting out.

Irrespective of bias, what you need to remember is that we are talking
about the compulsivity of these behaviors. In reality, if your partner is compulsively engaging in pornography and masturbation, you most likely feel
just like the women whose husbands are being intimate with other people,
only you don't have a flesh-and-blood person (or persons) to blame. You feel
confused, guilty, and ashamed, and you doubt your own desirability. You
may be enraged and scared.

Like any compulsive behavior, compulsive masturbation and engagement in cybersex warrant attention; there is potential for recovery from

their addictive nature. Masturbation is a fire that feeds on itself. Because there is physical pleasure, the act reinforces itself. People repeat things that make them feel good. Compulsive behavior causes addicts to lose valuable work, family, and social time. The more time a man spends with pornography or engages in cybersex, the more he isolates himself.

C. S. Lewis writes of the man who masturbates as having a harem of imaginary brides. And this harem works against his ever getting out and really uniting with a real human. Think of the tremendous advantages of the harem. It is always accessible, always subservient, calls for no sacrifices or adjustments, and can be endowed with erotic and psychological attractions which no real person can rival. "Among those shadowy brides he is: always adored, always the perfect lover, no demand is made on his unselfishness, no mortification ever imposed on his vanity. In the end, they become merely the medium through which he increasingly adores himself."[1]

• VANESSA •

I met my husband in college, and he was ideal for me. Charming, smart, but most important to me, he adored me, put me on a pedestal, and needed me. I love to help and look after people. He and I made a great team. He was a loner with low self-esteem and I was the face of confidence, popular, top of the class, and going places. He was broken and looking to be rescued and I was always looking for a project to save. He excelled under my tutelage and became more successful than he had ever imagined. We were both thrilled with our results. Sadly, this is no foundation for a relationship and I believe he felt like a fraud and coped, as he always had, by sexually acting out. I took his accomplishments as another boost to my esteem and became even more grandiose. My career was rocketing, my husband project was doing well, and all was good in my fairy-tale world. I had a perfect life.

I lived in the fast lane—working and partying. My work addiction was modeled on my parents, and I was

relentless with the time and energy I poured into getting
to the top. What I did not know, with so much time and
effort expended on my interests and active party scene,
was that my husband, who proclaimed to be ever-swamped
with work and still a loner, was very busy with other
things—namely, other women. For our entire relationship
he had been medicating his own feelings of inadequacy,
believing he was not good enough, by acting out sexually
in every way imaginable. Compulsive daily masturbation,
cybersex, Internet affairs, and infidelity that ranged from
one-night stands to longstanding affairs, from unknowns
he picked up over the Internet to women he worked
with, regular women in multiple cities he traveled to on
business, prostitutes, and escorts. Risky sex, unprotected sex
in public places, sex in our home, bisexual encounters, and
sex with other couples. It was constant and progressive.

All of this was happening and I was happily oblivious,
partly because denial was such a learned coping mechanism for me from my growing-up years, and partly because
I was so caught up in my own addictions of work and
crazy living. As a child I was very quick to figure things
out and with my straight-A marks, compliant demeanor,
and affable personality, I excelled in school. I excelled at
most anything I put my mind to. What was it that drove
me so hard? The need to prove I was okay, the strong
desire for acceptance and approval, the inherent core
belief that I wasn't good enough? The truth was that my
family was foundationally broken. I was raised by parents
in a loveless, work-addicted marriage subjected to controlling silence and terrifying rages. From a young age,
I was set up to believe that I wasn't of value and was
meant to be abused by men. This played out for years
with the duality of my life: a seemingly perfect persona
on the outside and brokenness on the inside, ever driven
by my core belief of being not good enough.

But today I realize I had chosen a mate who was also a master deceiver. We were in the ultimate dance of an addicted couple. So here we were in our dance, me running as fast as I could, living this fun, exciting life, oblivious to the reality of a very fractured coupleship. Then one day before the birth of my son, I was told I had an STD [sexually transmitted disease] that threatened my health and the health of our unborn baby. That was the beginning of my husband telling me about some of his behavior. Fortunately, I was able to have a caesarean and the baby was born healthy, and I was treated as well. Our child created shifts for both my husband and me. We both knew we couldn't go on like this forever and our lives needed to change.

. . . .

Vanessa, whom you just met, and Jacque, whom you are about to meet, are professional women in their thirties. They take great pride in their work accomplishments; work is a primary source of their esteem. Busyness is a common defense that helps women stay in denial. Slowing down would give them time to analyze their feelings and to ponder the nuances of their partner's behavior that are niggling at their consciousness.

Vanessa's work addiction, her partying, and her image of the good life override her ability to recognize that she has chosen to be in a relationship with someone who is already engaged in compulsive sexual behavior. Consequently, she is shocked at the unmistakable realization that her husband has a problem. For Jacque, the signs that something was not okay sexually were blatant on the first date, but she readily doubts herself and gives her partner the benefit of the doubt. Jacque more clearly represents the woman who on some level is aware immediately, has profound moments of shame and fear, but works diligently to ignore them. What both of these women recognize in hindsight is how their original family dynamics influenced their frequently unhealthy coping skills. Partners of sex addicts are often raised in addictive, abusive, or otherwise impaired family systems.

• JACQUE •

"Turn on the TV," a commanding voice in my head said. I didn't usually listen to myself, and I wasn't often home to watch *The Oprah Show*. I always thought people who sat watching that drivel were pathetic, but the voice persisted so I reached over the sofa on my way out of the room to grab the remote and clicked on the TV. My premonition of drivel and pathetic people was immediately confirmed by the whining I heard from the woman describing her husband's affairs, viewing of pornography, and various other tawdry lowlife events. I didn't need to watch this crap. Yet my feet were cemented to the floor and my fingers refused to click the off button on the remote. I found myself leaning on the couch to listen and pretty soon I hopped over the back and made myself comfy, while with unbelieving ears I listened to several couples describe their walk with sex addiction. "Whew," the louder but very unsteady voice in my head said, "thank God this isn't my problem." Yet a quieter, steadier, and stronger voice kept repeating, "This *is* my life." I clicked the show off as it ended, hopped up, and kept hearing the voice that said "This *is* my life." And in my ever-present inability to listen to myself, I walked out of the room saying to myself, ". . . and there is nothing I can do about it."

I had been married for just over eleven years and had accomplished much in my career—accolades and awards galore. Yet I felt no joy. I only felt empty, alone, numb, and afraid. I didn't listen to myself. I looked outside of me to the things I did and the reactions of people around me to know how I was doing and feeling. As a matter of fact, if you had asked me to describe how I felt, I would have told you that life was good, I had a great marriage and an awesome family, and I had a wonderful childhood, and let me fix you too!

During this time, my husband was working several
miles away and was often gone three to five nights per
week. We rarely talked on the phone, and when we did
talk, it was superficial. We'd talk about the house and the
dogs, and I can remember him telling me that he was
attending events with a colleague from work. "She's just
a friend," he would tell me. I convinced myself this was
normal. In time I would come to find out that she was
not his first affair.

When we were together, our only connection was
through sex that was always initiated by my husband.
It felt mechanical. It was all about arousal and strength
and number of orgasms. I agreed to, participated in, and
endured this to keep him from getting angry. I convinced
myself that our sexual life was normal and healthy. Buried
in the tornado of thoughts, an occasional thought that
something was wrong would rise to the surface and just
as quickly, like a leaf floating in a whirlpool, it would be
sucked back down into the depths of my brain.

Prior to meeting my husband, I had several serious
boyfriends. I had ended the relationship with my first
serious boyfriend (the one everyone assumed I would
marry) because he started drinking more than I was
comfortable with. My father is an alcoholic, and at age
nineteen I had already made a decision that I would not
marry an alcoholic. I even made a point to look for someone who didn't drink much and who had a sense of
responsibility around alcohol.

I met my husband one year after I completed college.
He seemed nice enough and funny, but at the time I had
decided I was not dating for a while because of several
hurtful encounters. But one day, in a moment of weak-
ness, I agreed to have dinner with him. After dinner,
despite my request to go home, he took me to his house.
To make a long story short, I liked him, he asked me to

stay the night, I said yes but told him we would not be having sex, and he said that was fine with him. I trusted that this would be what happened. And of course I ignored myself when in the middle of the night he initiated sex. I gave in and started a pattern in our relationship that continued until we were well into recovery. For years I have acquiesced to his requests and ignored my needs, wants, and desires. I did this for the sake of keeping peace.

One of the things that attracted me to my husband was his creativity and knowledge about sex. At first it was exciting to be with someone who seemed to know so much and who suggested so many fun and different things to do sexually. But as our relationship continued to evolve, the fun and creative sex started to become more daring, more outrageous, and more frightening to me. I started to refuse. He would beg, cajole, and then get angry and I would give in. During sex he would want me to talk dirty to him, or look at pornography, or fantasize about sex with my female friends and later with male friends. The more I refused, the more he seemed to demand. He said he had needs and a good wife should meet them. I would feel bad and give in.

Early in our marriage he purchased pornographic stories so we could read them together. He took me to a nude beach; it seemed thrilling but also disgusting. I felt very uncomfortable, and again I chalked it up to me not being as worldly about sex as he. I found myself drinking to lose inhibitions to do sexual things to please my husband. During this time, my husband started using phone sex lines. When I demanded he stop (because it was too expensive), he told me he wouldn't need to do these things if I would meet his needs and do the things he asked. I felt guilty and degraded. I believed I was worthless for not meeting his needs, but at the same time it seemed wrong. During our marriage, I often suspected things weren't normal. I had such fear of speaking my piece and displeasing my husband. After all, I grew up in a home where my dad raged, yelled, kicked the dog, slammed doors, and threatened violence when he was displeased. Having often feared for my life due to sexual abuse by an older brother, I was easily shamed by men who were intimidating.

My friends frequently told me that my husband made sexualized comments to them. I shrugged it off and buried my feelings regarding any upset I had. History had proven that if I did say something or if I questioned him, he would call me a prude and get angry. He often suggested I was the one with the problem because of my childhood history of sex abuse.

Time passed and it was more of the same, with the phone sex escalating. We were moving around some. I thought changing where we lived would solve everything. What a fantasy. In time, there were more job problems and more money problems. About this time, his employer suggested we attend a workshop to figure out our lives so I signed us up to go. I needed to save his job so that we would have enough money to live. At this weekend workshop, we admitted to each other that we had both had an affair, we opened up, cleared our consciences, and apologized. I thought we were cured. We continued to attend the workshops and our lives seemed to be improving.

One morning during a common ritual—he was insisting on sex, I was saying no, he was telling me I don't meet his needs—he suddenly blurted out he was having another affair. I just cringed and screamed, "How could you? How could you tell me this while I am on my way to work?" He seemed contrite and remorseful. He apologized and said he thought he might be a sex addict. I remember telling him, "Yeah, right. Sounds like a great excuse." I went to work and we never talked of it again, at least not for a few years.

Over the next couple of years, when I saw flirtatious behavior, I simply ignored it. Then one night when we were in Las Vegas my husband asked me to join him at a sex club. I refused. He insisted, then he belittled, berated, and cajoled me. I finally gave in. I knew it was wrong, yet I could not say no. I didn't know how to say no and mean it. I was afraid of losing my marriage. L had made up my mind that when I got married, I was married for life. I thought I was stuck with nowhere else to go. I was afraid. I thought I couldn't support myself, despite the fact I had an awesome job with great benefits. I gave in and went to the sex club. There were many people there, some watching, some having sex. I was pressured into performing oral sex. Initially I refused, but as usual I wasn't strong enough to stand firm or walk away. I felt degraded and dirty. When we got back to the hotel he insisted on having sex. I was worn down, unable to say no anymore, and had sex just to get him to leave me alone. So here we were in full-blown sex addiction and, believe it or not, at the same time taking life-improvement workshops.

I was so afraid of being alone, so afraid of financial instability. Yet I was so alone. I felt like I was sitting at the bottom of a well, the walls slippery and slimy with no way out. I began to cry and it was as if I couldn't stop. My husband told me that he was leaving me for another woman. During a phone session with the life coach, I shared my story with her. I told her I thought my husband was a sex addict. I told her the story of watching *Oprah*. And this is how the chapter of recovery started. I began my work, and I don't know why, but when I told my husband what I believed to be true, that he is a sex addict, he began his work as well.

. . . .

While the addict is frequently engaged in compulsive behavior at the time he marries or forms a coupleship, his partner is often an object in his acting out. Jacque repeatedly engaged in sexual behaviors that denigrated her. Her low self-esteem and fears of abandonment set her up to rationalize her behavior and to be a participant. Jacque was also intimidated, cajoled, manipulated, and controlled by her partner's anger and rage. This is common during life with a sex addict. All of this was strongly fueled by the shame-based beliefs Jacque internalized about herself and is similar to Vanessa's lack of belief in her own worth and value.

· SARA ·

Twenty-four years ago, after two divorces, I married the man I thought was absolutely the most wonderful, successful, and admirable man one could hope for. He had me with his first hello. Looking back, I know today there were signs that Mr. Wonderful might have some problems: he gawked at attractive and sleazy-looking women; he drank to drunkenness on more than a few occasions; he went into rages when something didn't go the way he wished; and he had a sort of disconnectedness during sex. I was concerned enough prior to getting married that I went to a therapist and confronted my then fiancé about my fears. I was quickly told by both my husband and the therapist that I was projecting the behaviors I had experienced with my two previous husbands onto my fiancé, a very successful and upstanding man.

Having a history of being willing to trust others rather than myself, I unquestioningly went on with the wedding. On our honeymoon, my husband shared some of his sexual past that he had not previously shared. My heart went cold as he described encounters with prostitutes, friends, relatives, and so on. Knowing what I know now, I see it as a classic description of sex addiction. I was horrified, terrified, and literally frozen with the sinking feeling that

I had married someone weird. I freaked out.

We limped through our honeymoon and I made up my mind to put all his past behind us and forge ahead with a positive effort to make a good home for my three children, ages ten through sixteen. The years added up, filled with my husband's rages, drinking, flirting, and ogling women with abandon. We had countless arguments about his behavior and he would point to my theatrical behavior as just crazy. He was right: I was feeling crazy. I was terrified that I had made another bad marriage, that I was not desired, that I couldn't explain how hurt I was, and that he would never change.

We both spent countless hours in therapy, together and individually. The children had problems, and life was never easy or peaceful. After a crisis with one of our kids, my husband confessed to me that he had been unfaithful on several occasions. He was fired from each executive position he had. I had to leave graduate school and go back to work for financial reasons. My desperation grew and grew until I thought I must be clinically crazy. I was constantly threatening him. My anger and resentment built up to the point where I told myself, "Hell, if you can't beat them, then just join them!" I had a short revenge affair with my boss but quickly realized that was not what I wanted or who I was. It didn't help my hurt or anger. In fact it made my misery even worse, having dented in my self-respect.

One night after I had been diagnosed with early stage breast cancer, I discovered a book about sex addiction in the trunk of the car. When I questioned him, my husband said his therapist wanted him to read it, as he thought my husband was a sex addict. Well, I took the book straight into the living room of our house, sat down, and flew through every page. My first reaction was "Oh my God, I am not crazy after all. This is our life!" What followed was his agreement that this seemed to be what, in fact, we were living with. He confessed to having had sex with several massage prostitutes. I calmly told him we were finished. Before when he had confessed to affairs, I had told him if he ever did it again, we were through.

We separated and we both had therapists who insisted we not talk to each other. A couple times during my cancer radiation treatment I asked him to move back in, but he told me he wasn't sure he wanted to be with me anymore. In time we began to talk and I told him for us to get back together he had to go to a treatment program. He agreed, but he had conditions too. I had to agree to go to work on my part of the crazy relationship. My therapist had been working with me to see how my reactions, fears, and resentments, and my attempts at controlling the insane world around me, had created my own addiction. So we forged forward.

Ten years earlier my husband had quit drinking and began attending Alcoholics Anonymous (AA) meetings. I began attending Al-Anon meetings at that time. The teachings of Al-Anon are what I held on to with the initial disclosure around his sex addiction.

. . . .

Because of her experience with Al-Anon and the Twelve Steps, Sara is a woman with a solid understanding of addiction and family issues. But she didn't recognize the signs of sex addiction. Unfortunately that is not uncommon. Sexual acting out was tolerated without question in Sara's family. As she confronts the sex addiction in her marriage, she draws on her Al-Anon experience and believes in the process of recovery that comes with honesty. With that history, she moves forward with her life.

Through the ensuing months, there spilled out the rest of the confessions about money spent on one of my husband's victims, friends he had sex with, other sordid details that I had frankly conveniently forgotten. But I do remember the pain of how we struggled. I ranted. I got angrier and angrier. I can remember early in my husband's recovery when he was becoming honest with me and I thought, "I don't know that I can stand the pain." Between the breast cancer and the hurt of my husband's sexual acting out, it felt like I was sinking into a big black hole. It was at this time my therapist saved my life by saying, "You can either get revenge by continuing to yell and threaten; or get a divorce and feel better temporarily; or you can roll up your sleeves, get to work on yourself and your own problems, and feel better for the rest of your life." That simple piece of advice has given me my life. The work has been painful, exhausting, and sometimes embarrassing, but I have me, I have a life of which I am proud, and I have the integrity I always wanted.

We went to conferences, therapy, recovery meetings, therapeutic weekends, and on and on. I expected absolute immediate recovery on both our parts. It didn't happen. But what did happen was that I found me. I recognized my value, my beautiful imperfection. I got honest. I began to live what I have always wanted: an honest life. We were separated for nearly a year, and during this time I realized that since we had lived so long in the disease and we were both actively pursuing recovery, we might try doing that together. It has not all been uphill; it has been more like a roller coaster. It has not been easy. I lapse into hypervigilance when feeling insecure, and we struggle yet with our own sex life. In general we both want our marriage to be better, and we work on it both individually and together.

. . . .

As you have just read, after two divorces Sara thought she had met Mr. Wonderful, her soul mate. He was charming, fun, good-looking, and a great provider, and he embraced her children. With the information her husband shared with her on their honeymoon, she didn't know how to cope with what she perceived would be another failed relationship. Wanting to trust herself, she sought out counseling but was frequently told to give her husband the benefit of the doubt. During much of their marriage, her insides were screaming at the subtle and the blatant behaviors. As she says, "The worms were moving." Sara frequently appeared more out of control in her rage than her husband did in his acting out. Challenged with raising children who were struggling, and with learning the full truth about his behavior, she was also faced with a serious health problem. In my work with women, I have found that as they confront the issues of their fractured relationships, they are still faced with multiple challenges of life, such as caretaking of sick parents, losing their parents, losing children to illness, or health concerns of their own or their partners. People don't usually get to choose the best time to have major life issues present themselves.

• MAITE •

Twenty years ago, as a young adult, I came to the United States from South America. In my culture, it is perceived as normal and generally accepted that men will have mistresses and affairs. The men think those affairs make them look richer and more masculine. Women are never to complain, especially in public. In some way, as the wife, you are the honored one, the chosen one. You are the Madonna, the one he loves because he married you. That is supposed to be enough for any woman. But I wanted something different. Knowing that I was coming to America, and that in America women had voices and power and men had less pressure to be macho, I had my big wedding and got married. I thought my marriage would be perfect; there would be no infidelity. Three days after my wedding, my husband told me that he had gotten another woman pregnant and she was having the baby. Surprise, surprise—my marriage was a play of pretending, lots of lies and infidelities, lots of deceiving. Here I was in a new country. I didn't know anyone except his family. I didn't speak the language. We were living in his parents' house because our apartment was not ready yet. The worst part was I had no one to talk to. I had thought our marriage would be so blessed.

While growing up I learned I had to be perfect. That was the expectation from friends and family members. My father and mother were community leaders, very involved in politics, church, and education. I saw my father as a perfect dad, and he had high dreams of me helping humanity. My mother was the perfect educator and received multiple awards. There was a whole community watching and raising me. We were never to disagree; we were to believe and feel the way our parents or the church said or did. I was the most perfect child, accelerating through school, graduating high school as class valedictorian (of course), and rapidly moving through Catholic law school. Then to the surprise of my parents, I got married immediately after graduation.

My marriage would not be blessed as I had willed it to be. Over the years I would find out about things that were going on. Women would call my house and tell me things about my husband. Or someone at his work would pull me aside and tell me to open my eyes. There were hundreds of women. I would try to find out what I could before I would accuse him, and then I would be so self-righteous. I would find credit card slips from restaurants and hotels where he had no reason to be. I found receipts for women's presents that I did not receive. He bought perfume I did not wear. He had dinner vouchers for more than one other person. I became quite the investigator, quite the interrogator. I would check his luggage and plane tickets; a lot of his acting out took place when he was away from home on work-related trips. I would not talk to him for days; I would not sleep with him. When I would confront him I would give him an ultimatum. I would tell him, "I can have a better life. I am going back home." He would freeze; he would say nothing. I would move out of our bedroom for a few weeks, and then in time he would say he was sorry and act like he was ashamed. He would beg me to give him another chance. And time after time I would.

The worst part is that much of the time I knew the women he was seeing. Ninety-nine percent were women that knew me. I knew them in my committee work, my fund-raising work, or they were friends. I did not ever say anything to them. I was married in the early 1980s, and by the late 1980s I was seriously looking for answers as to what was wrong. I prayed for help in seeing the light.

I began to read books about women and oppression. I was looking at how class and gender impact women and men differently. I was reading about the role of money and how the more money a man has, the greater imbalance of the relationship in the marriage. I was reading that money was power, and the more power, the greater the abuse in marriages. I was beginning to see myself as a feminist and trying to understand my life from a feminist perspective. In that process, I began to see how he would use these women and then dispose of them like tissue paper. Then I began to see this was not about having an affair, this was something much bigger; something much sicker, worse than I could ever imagine. By now I was living my worst nightmare, and I was alone, disconnected, and powerless. I was angry at God, and in all of that I was pretending things were better and happier than they were.

When we got married I was a size two. I knew I was attractive, so why did he want someone else? Then as I got older, and after I had kids, I started to gain weight, and when I was in my mid-thirties, my body began to change. He would tell me he needed a younger woman. I knew he was with younger women then. I would do things like bleach my hair, exercise a lot, and go to the beauty parlor all of the time. I would dress sexy. I would do all of these things and nothing I did made a difference. This just made it worse for me, trying to please someone who I couldn't please.

Over the years, I went to as many as fifteen therapists. Sometimes I would get my husband to go. We were in therapy within the first two weeks of our marriage. But I was always seen as the one who simply wasn't happy here in the United States. He would say I was just not happy in America. I was told we had communication problems. Well, maybe my English was not so great, but my Spanish was just fine. I continued to ask for help, but I didn't get the help I needed.

His addiction was progressing. He was becoming more secretive with his behavior and hiding it within his workplace. There was eventually the threat of a lawsuit because it appeared he had nonconsensual sex with a coworker.

But let me remind you, I was still working very hard to be the perfect wife. We tried to keep our arguing very private so the kids did not see. But the kids were now teenagers and they would ask, "How can we be the perfect family when Daddy has two other kids and Mommy is not the mother?"

Then not too many years ago, my mother told me about my father's infidelities. I thought my father was very religious and would never do that. I felt so dumb because all of these years I thought I had perfect parents, and then I married someone who has affairs. I thought I should have known better. I beat myself up. So when my mother told me this, I understood that I was not dumb.

This is a part of my family history and I am repeating that history. Throughout my family, other women were a part of the men's lives.

Finally I told my husband I had had enough. I was leaving, I could not stand the emptiness in me, and I could no longer keep pretending and faking. Everyone thought we had this fairy-tale marriage, that we were the perfect couple. I knew it was not that way and never had been. I knew I loved him, but because I love myself I had to leave. I hadn't been true to myself for too many years. I was a beautiful package but there was nothing inside. I knew we loved each other, but something bigger was destroying our relationship.

I remember telling my children that I was not happy with their father and that I needed to breathe. I told them I needed to find out what was wrong with me. I blamed myself. My husband said he didn't know what was wrong with me either but now he knows I am going. I now have a name for what he has: sex addiction. I have read books about sex addiction. He said he will go see someone who knows about sex addiction, said he wants to stop his behavior but he doesn't know how; he wants help. Today we both go to recovery groups and we see a counselor who specializes in sex addiction. We have both changed.

. . . .

Maite presents a picture of how culture can support a man's sexual acting out and how that consequently makes it more difficult for her to trust and honor herself. This was a marriage where she knew early on about his affairs and even about his other babies. Irrespective of culture, it is not uncommon for a child to be born as a consequence of the acting-out behavior. Maite became aware of these other children when they were still babies, whereas in many situations the female partner may not find out for years. Many times the father secretly supports the child and is even involved in the parenting.

As is true of many women, Maite repeatedly sought professional help. Unfortunately, like others, she was often told that she was overreacting and bore unwarranted suspicions. It was when Maite was truly walking out the door on her marriage that her husband got honest about his behavior and sought the help he needed. That is what made it acceptable for her to stay.

In the following story, Jenny realizes very early on that her husband is sexual with other women. She trusts her own intuition but feels emotionally and financially trapped; she wants to try to make her marriage work. She quickly learns that to be able to stay without going crazy, she has to accept his rationalizations, thereby losing her sense of true self.

• JENNY •

The first time I found out my husband had been unfaithful I was eighteen years old, four months pregnant, and seven months into a marriage that I didn't really want to be in. So eighteen, married, pregnant, and deciding to give it my all, deciding to love him, believe in him, trust him, he comes home one night and I knew immediately that something was different with him. He was closed off a little, he was good at acting normal but I could sense the slightest change in him. I didn't push the issue until later that night when I just kept asking him what had gone on at work that day.

Finally, unable to persuade me that everything was fine, he started to tell me how much he loved me and how he was in love with me and that being in love with me was the most important thing, and that what he did at work didn't have any effect on that. As I listened it was like he was brainwashing me. Then he told me he had had sex with a coworker and how it was okay because she really wanted to do it for him; that it had nothing to do with love and that he loved me and it was just what men need now and then. He continued to drone on like a hypnotist, continuing to try to convince me that it was okay, that I should just accept it and know that it was just sex; that he loved me and that is what mattered; that I knew what he was like before I married him; and that I should just not let it bother me.

I remember taking our wedding picture down off the wall and falling to my knees and crying uncontrollably, grieving the loss of the perfect marriage that I had envisioned; a marriage that I let him talk me into and a pregnancy that I wasn't ready for. I was still a child with a childlike mentality, and he, being fourteen years older, had always been a father figure to me. I trusted him to be faithful and trustworthy. My fantasy was shattered.

In my childlike state, I had no ability to even conceive of leaving the marriage or telling him never to do this to me again; I didn't have the emotional resources to be able to do that. So my only psychological option was to believe him. To accept his reality, not mine. It was okay, he loved me; this is what men do. I had to believe a bunch of lies and make them my own in order to survive the situation that I found myself in. It was the only way I could psychologically survive. I told myself that he wouldn't do this again, especially because he saw how much it hurt me, and I knew he didn't want to hurt me because he said he loved me. So I rationalized that my brokenness and pain would stop him from ever being unfaithful to me again. He just kept minimizing it and telling me that I was over-reacting, that I didn't realize that this is what all men do and that I shouldn't be so upset by this. It really was no big deal, it was just sex! I guess the insinuations were that sex had nothing to do with love and that he loved me. As a very young woman, I found it mind-twisting.

· · · · · · · ·

For twenty more years, Jenny went in and out of acknowledging that her husband's addictive behavior was abusive. She was a master at her own deception. She frequently felt she had to engage in his sexual fantasies, even telling herself it was okay. Her life was on autopilot. She continued to relate to her husband as if she was the child, although she tapped into adult strengths in her parenting skills. She saw no way out of the situation, and that path did not show itself for many years until he sought help.

> My husband was acting out on all his addictions. Early on I begin to live a life of cover-up and compensation. And I became busier and busier and more and more distant from him. My marriage was as codependent as it could get: complete loss of self into the other. I had no idea of the trauma that I allowed myself to be subjected to by accepting my husband's infidelity and his excuses; I rationalized that the pornography was nothing because there was just so much sexuality spewing all over our relationship; I accepted his emotional and verbal abuse of me and the children; I accepted his emotional abandonment through drug abuse and his traumatizing through his fits of rage.
>
> Physically I worked with frenzy in everything I did. Emotionally and spiritually everything was mechanized. There was no emotional connection. Buried anger and exhaustion eventually sent me into such a depressed state of being that I was unable to function, even at the most minimal level. At that time, about sixteen years into our marriage, I went through two severe depressions and a nervous breakdown. These rendered me completely unable to do anything. My ability to hide behind accomplishment and being capable vanished. I became a mental midget. Even the simplest task of looking up a phone number would send me into fits of tears. Balancing a checkbook or even writing a check was no longer possible for me. I couldn't think, concentrate, or handle pressure or responsibility of any kind. My husband began to drink heavily, and rages were the norm. I had lost the ability to cope.

It was at this point that I turned to a power greater than myself. I asked Jesus into my heart and told him I couldn't do this alone. That started my spiritual healing. I prayed that Jesus would change my husband, change my circumstances, but it was not until I asked him to change me that things started to change. This is when I began to learn about codependency and co-sex addiction.

. . . .

Jenny began her journey by reaching out to her faith community and seeking guidance; Therese was directed to a counselor through her church; Vanessa and Jacque began their journeys forward at the height of crisis, Vanessa by contracting an STD during pregnancy and Jacque when watching her husband walk out the door to be with another woman. Maite's healing began at the time she was prepared to leave her marriage. Sara came across a book that her husband was reading as he began to come to terms with the fact that he had another addiction—sex. Whatever the impetus or crisis is that directs you to begin a healing journey, you have the potential of living your life differently.

Moving On to Your Journey

The deception and betrayal women experience takes many forms. Knowingly or unknowingly, you are touched by it daily. For some, it is pornography or fantasies with faceless names on the Internet with which you cannot compete. For others, it is the other women who may be one-night stands, a coworker, your best friend, escorts, or prostitutes. It may involve voyeurism, exhibitionism, or bisexual behavior. Often other addictions, depression, and rage issues all serve to complicate matters.

The pain for those in a relationship with someone acting out sexually is undeniable. You have been betrayed, deceived, and lied to. Your vows have been violated again and again. You have been ignored or manipulated emotionally and physically. You may have been asked to engage in sexual practices that you found repulsive and abusive. You may realize he has been or is currently in a long-term relationship that involves financial commitments and possibly even children. You may have been placed at risk of contracting sexually transmitted diseases. These offenses lead to a wide range of thoughts and feelings, from despair, anger, hurt, and desperation to wondering and pleading for answers.

To be in a deceptive relationship, whether you are conscious of it or not, frequently results in the following coaddictive traits:

> feeling crazy
> lying to yourself and to others
> not trusting yourself
> having emotional outbursts
> feeling anguished
> denying suspicions
> being emotionally numb
> walking on eggshells
> defending yourself with busyness or perfectionism
> being depressed
> burying your head in the sand; ignoring signs
> experiencing health problems
> changing yourself to please, accommodate, or pacify
> feeling inadequate
> being obsessive
> socially withdrawing
> having rageful thoughts and behavior
> acting out via food, alcohol, drugs, spending, or affairs

Your unhealthy behavior develops and reveals itself in a variety of ways. Chapter 2, "In the Face of Truth," will explore more fully the many behaviors and feelings characteristic of being in a relationship impacted by sexual compulsivity.

~~~~~~~~~~~~~~~~

There is hope. You've just met a few women who today are all joyfully living their lives differently as a consequence of changes they have made. Throughout this book, you will continue to hear from Jenny, Maite, Sara, Jacque, Vanessa, and Therese, as well as many other unnamed coaddicts who give voice to this book. While the unnamed women's stories are not followed throughout the book, their vignettes offer an added diversity to the experience.

Like the Women of the Lodge, you too can choose to identify and focus on behaviors that will free you from your pain. It does not mean that you must deny your intense feelings of anger and betrayal; rather, you will work through these feelings and even use them to build stronger relationships. Trust can often be rebuilt. But that begins with trusting yourself. Intimacy can be achieved emotionally, physically, and spiritually. That begins with your own healing. Whether or not your relationship is going to work out, understanding what has happened, and recognizing how you are impacted and how you have become a part of the addictive system can lead to life-changing transformation. It takes courage; it is painful. But the possibilities of living your life differently are worth the struggle. My hope is that you will allow yourself to begin this journey.

Reflective Thoughts and Questions

- Underline or highlight the parts of the women's stories with which you identify.

- Which coaddictive traits sound familiar to you?

- Is there any particular woman whose story sounds similar to yours? In what way?

- What feelings did you experience as you read this chapter? Relief? Sadness? Anger? Fear? Hope? Loneliness? Shame? Others?

- What was important for you to hear in this chapter?

Chapter Two

In the Face of Truth

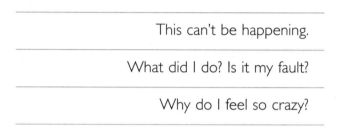

This can't be happening.

What did I do? Is it my fault?

Why do I feel so crazy?

After hearing time after time that you have quite an imagination, or that you are the one responsible for his unhappiness, or that it's your job to shut up and be grateful for what you have, or that you simply have trust issues, you learn to keep quiet. You keep fears and doubts to yourself while your self-esteem erodes away.

[Therese] Whenever I confronted my husband with my suspicions that he was interested in other women, he would always say that I was the one he loved. He said that while he found other women interesting to look at, I didn't need to worry. But I did worry. What if he decided to meet someone in one of those chat rooms that I knew about? From there my thinking was all a downhill spin inside my head: I'm not pretty enough, smart enough, or sexy enough.

[Coaddict] So many times my husband would say, "You are lucky to have me in your life. No other man is willing to take on a woman with four young children. You should just be more grateful and not so controlling all of the time." Then I'd tell myself I have trust issues with men and if I could just be more trusting, everything would really be okay. I try not to act so needy, so desperate, because I think that drives him away, but it is hard for me when I am so scared I will lose him.

[Jacque] Well, he basically told me it was about me. He had been telling me I was undersexed. That I just didn't know what a man needed. And I don't seem to enjoy having sex because when we have sex I always end up feeling used or even more alone than when we started. Then I notice other women noticing him, and he them, and I begin to compare myself to them. Maybe they are younger than me or have more money and can dress up better, but no matter—I basically always feel as if I am just not what he wants.

. . . .

Just as an alcoholic's partner frequently feels guilty for the behavior of the alcoholic—that if he or she was a better partner and could just do the right thing, the alcoholic wouldn't drink so much—partners of men who are acting out sexually nearly always believe that his behavior is a statement about themselves. They believe they must not be pretty enough, sexy enough, smart enough, thin enough, alluring enough, ample-breasted enough, or long-legged enough. The list is never ending. You are full of "shoulds:" *I should have taken more time for him. I should have been less focused on the kids or work. I should not have let my appearance go. I should have kept my weight down.* Again, it's a never-ending list.

You probably operate from the following belief: *I need to do or be something different and that will make him stop.* First and foremost you need to understand that you are not the cause of your partner's acting-out behavior. It isn't about you being different. He engages in his activity because of his own emotional wounding, which now manifests in a pathological relationship with a mood-altering behavior—in his case—sex. Chapter 3 will help you better understand the addictive nature of his behaviors. But because you are involved in an addictive dance with him—being preoccupied with him and disconnected from yourself—for now, let's keep the focus on you.

As lonely as your experience may feel, partners of sex addicts often have much in common with one another, beginning with rationalizing, minimizing, and denying.

Denial: Protecting the Illusion

Living with addiction is poignantly described by a young girl in an addictive family who said, "Denial is when you pretend things are different than how they really are." For years, partners of addicts, irrespective of the addiction, have pretended that things are different than how they really are. For both the addict and the coaddict, denial is at the core of addiction in action. When the addictive behavior is sex instead of alcohol or drugs, gambling, food, and so on, denial for the partner is often accelerated because of the greater degree of shame and implied messages about the person acting out and the coupleship. While addicts deny in order to satisfy their addiction, partners deny in an attempt to hang on to what is really an illusion, the fantasy that all is really okay. The fact is that life is out of control; the addiction is in the driver's seat. But deny you must when you can't see your way out. It is a form of self-protection.

> [Coaddict] It just can't be. It doesn't make sense. Our sex life is good, well I think so anyway. He loves me, he tells me so. I am just crazy not to trust him.

. . . .

To recognize denial is to think about what you minimize, discount, or rationalize. Also know that you minimize, discount, rationalize, deny, and pretend things are different than they really are because you want to trust your partner. You want to believe the relationship has a strong foundation. You want to be able to believe all is okay. That is absolutely understandable. Don't be critical of yourself. If you see the situation for what it really is and don't know what to do, it is natural to slide into a state of hopelessness and helplessness. The truth taps your greatest fear—that you are unloved and abandoned. You feel shame and humiliation. So as long as the addict denies or minimizes it, and particularly when you don't have proof, you can rationalize, deny, and pretend as well. The illusion of safety and security is an enticing fantasy. But in the process, you quit trusting yourself, your inner voice.

> [Coaddict] Whatever happened to me, I was made to feel I deserved it, I caused it. I learned not to make waves. I assumed I had no right to complain. So I just put my head in the sand, and whether or not it was denial or whatever I just wasn't going to deal with it. In my mind I had to make peace.

. . . .

Simply put, denial is dismissing your own intuition. It is blatantly over-looking what is right in front of you. Often there are clear indicators that you have a serious problem, but you may choose not to see it. You want to trust your partner. You want to give him the benefit of the doubt. After all, what does it mean if you find out you cannot? Does it mean divorce? More arguing? Disrupting the children's lives? A threat to your lifestyle? You are not desirable? Punishment from the church? While you are busy question-ing yourself, the addict stands strong in his denial and rationalization, pro-tecting his stash and continuing his addiction.

Denial doesn't mean not having a clue. It means you are dismissing the seriousness of the behavior, ignoring the consequences. You don't know what to believe, so out of fear you simply believe what makes you feel safest. Denial stems from a yearning to believe that all will be fine or that all will return to how it was before this acting-out behavior reared its ugly head. The addict lies to you, and now you lie to yourself. Confused by self-deception, you do not take action and you spend your energy reacting or stamping out fires. Denial is the oxygen feeding the fire.

> [Coaddict] I actually found out because he told me. He thought I was going to find out anyway. He apologized, begged me to forgive him, and pleaded with me not to leave, saying it was just this one time and it wouldn't happen again. He told me he had already told his boss he couldn't go on road trips anymore, that he had to be closer

to home. So I thought this time maybe this cloud had a silver lining for us. But in time I was aware he would get off the computer abruptly when I came in. He was late coming home from work, or was at a ball game with clients. It wasn't clear, but I just had this feeling. He kept telling me he loved me and we were still having good sex. I made sure of that, I initiated it. I would buy sexy clothing that I knew he liked. I thought that meant something, like I was the only one. He often told me what a good mother I was and I know that meant a lot to him, as his mother left him when he was young. Somehow I thought that was so important to him that he wouldn't do anything more to hurt me. I just wanted to trust him, to believe him. So I ignored and dismissed all of my fears and my inner voice. I trusted him when I should have trusted myself.

[Sara] Time would pass, months, a few years, and I just wanted to believe his words so I turned the other way and got busy. I dove into my job and the kids. Having a family takes time. I remember telling myself he was there for the kids, at their events. But looking back now, that wasn't true. I often had this strange feeling. It was like this little voice in my head, and then I would tell myself more loudly, "He is a good guy. I am lucky to have him. I don't have any reason to not trust him." By then he had owned up to two affairs. Because he cried and asked for forgiveness, I guess I thought that earned him my trust.

Then he got fired for sexual harassment. He told me it wasn't fair, that the woman had actually harassed him, meaning she seduced him. We were having financial problems and I didn't understand why, and now he had no job; we just sort of let the financial stress and the need for him to get a job become our focus. It would be another year before I would know I was just seeing the

tip of the iceberg. I so wanted to believe his lies. When I get honest, I realize how frightened I am to be alone. I equate it to not being loved, being unlovable. It is like this failure of a marriage just confirms all I have ever believed about myself: I don't deserve to be loved.

. . . .

I encourage you not to chastise yourself for your denial but to learn from it. Denial is meant to be a protective defense. It is a natural response to hurt and loss. Unfortunately it only perpetuates your situation and your pain in the long run.

I worked with a woman whose husband had numerous affairs, had frequented many prostitutes, and ultimately passed on a sexually transmitted disease (STD) that rendered her infertile. Yet she made repeated excuses for him and each time took him back into her heart. While she didn't deny the acting out, she was denying the compulsive nature of the behavior. She was denying the impact it had on the intimacy in their relationship; she was denying the continual eroding of her esteem and values. Such a dynamic becomes more complex than denial and may actually include symptoms of Stockholm Syndrome, which is a condition sometimes seen in abducted hostage situations where the hostage takes on the values and beliefs of the one who holds him or her captive.

The term Stockholm Syndrome was coined in 1973 when two bank robbers held four people hostage for 131 hours in Stockholm, Sweden. The hostages were strapped with dynamite and held in a bank vault until they were finally rescued. Even though they were threatened and abused, and they feared for their lives for more than five days, in their media interviews it was clear that they supported their captors and actually feared the law enforcement personnel who came to their rescue. One woman later became engaged to one of the criminals, and another developed a legal defense fund to aid in their criminal defense. Clearly the hostages bonded with their captors. Such emotional bonding is also seen in controlling and abusive relationships.

The following four dynamics lead to this extreme form of bonding:

1. The presence of a perceived threat to one's physical or psychological survival and the belief that the abuser would carry out the threat.

2. The presence of a perceived small kindness from the abuser to the victim.

3. Isolation from perspectives other than those of the abuser.

4. The perceived inability to escape the situation.

While the majority of women involved with men who act out sexually are not experiencing Stockholm Syndrome, many will identify with an attachment and loyalty that is symptomatic of such bonding and defies their own well-being.

Fear and Manipulation

The fear of what you think you might need to do if you were confronted with the truth is so immobilizing that it reinforces the need to stay in denial. Denial induces numbness; it is a lot like frostbite. People who get frostbite are often unaware of the damage that is occurring because they simply cannot feel the burn. Now couple your need for denial with the fact that sex addicts are masters of misdirection. They perform sleight-of-hand tricks that create illusions, distort events, and make crises disappear. They can quickly tap into your vulnerability and charm you or shame you right out of your distrust.

[Addict] I told myself that what she doesn't know won't hurt her. I work away from home, I work hard, and no one thanks me for it. I was lonely; I deserved some fun. When she would accuse me rightfully of my many affairs or my phone sex, I would tell her she had guy friends at work, so why can't I have a friendship with a colleague who happens to be a woman? I took on a lawyer mentality. It was easy for me to line up evidence, like I was trying a case. I had proof that I wasn't doing what in fact I was. I would stick to my guns. She didn't need me to line up a lot of evidence because she didn't want to believe it. I knew she was looking to be talked out of her perceptions. My lies, sprinkled with reassurances, gave her something to hold on to, a little life preserver. I know it sounds sick now, but then I was justifying my own behavior. I wasn't thinking about her, or us. My addiction was in control.

[Addict] I was always on the offensive. Even before I walked into the house, I would start to intimidate her. I would call and quickly begin to ask her if she had gotten certain things done that day that I knew she couldn't have. Then I would act exasperated and without saying it I would let her know how disappointed I was. Other times when we would be out publicly I would start to accuse her of flirting or maybe having an affair. The whole time I had affairs going all the time. If she even began to question me I would turn the conversation to things such as telling her how she reminded me of my ex. I didn't like this part of me, but I didn't like any of me. I was just protecting myself, and my stash—the other women.

· · · · · · · · ·

An addict in recovery is very capable of recognizing and admitting to his manipulations. His manipulations may include being charming, bullying, threatening, and playing the victim. Often a combination of these manipulations is used.

[Addict] My partner never wanted to believe what she suspected or was told by others. I knew that. As much as she was upset, I took advantage of the relief I saw in her when I denied it. And that is what I would do: I denied, denied, and denied. If she pushed, and sometimes she did, I would finally just throw my arms up and ask her in a threatening tone, "What do you want? Do you want to leave? Do you want a divorce?" Mostly I used this angry tone to intimidate her, and she would readily back down. I could go on the defense in a second. She would start accusing me and within seconds I would say, "Why don't you just leave?" And that was always followed by name-calling. Oh, I was also real good at trying to make her think there was something wrong with her to be so mistrusting. I would act like I was this victim of her paranoia, that she was the one who was crazy.

· · · · · · · · ·

This conduct is beyond hurtful. It's cruel, abusive, and traumatizing. It is also a natural aspect of addictive behavior, a manipulative attempt by the addict to take the focus off him.

Denying, Minimizing, and Rationalizing

Other examples of denial, besides the ones shared by the women at the beginning of this chapter, include statements such as these:

- The pornography doesn't really bother me, it's only pictures.
- If I were more attractive he would not be doing this.
- He can't help it if other women throw themselves at him.
- Work must be his problem; if he would just change jobs then things would be different.
- If we move he will stop this behavior.

Your denial is supported by extensive rationalization. Examples of rationalization include these statements:

- Men will be men.
- He is an honest person; he would not lie to me.
- The lipstick on his collar got there when a coworker asked him to dance. He didn't want to be rude and say no.
- He's not really staring at women; he's just interested in watching people.
- He's not flirting, that's just his nature; he's a very friendly guy.
- We took vows before God. He would not break his vows.
- He is such a religious man. He takes his faith seriously.
- It doesn't hurt to look at pictures (porn). At least he is not having an affair.

○ It's easier for him to be friends with women. It doesn't mean he is having an affair.

○ His business calls him away—after all, he does it so the kids and I can have a good lifestyle.

○ His business takes priority over me and the kids, but I understand. It's just while he is building his career.

○ It's important for him to go to business functions without me. I'm not comfortable there, and I have to take care of the kids anyway.

○ I must have gotten this STD from a toilet seat. He told me I couldn't have gotten it from him.

○ Just because they have lunch together doesn't mean they are having an affair. He has to do business with her.

○ He told me the long-distance calls were not his. The phone company must have made a mistake.

○ It's okay if he gives her a Christmas gift—she does work for him.

○ Those Internet spammers are infiltrating our email with porn sites.

○ The police are exaggerating his behavior.

○ I bet the babysitter called these telephone sex numbers when she was here.

○ This is the way he grew up.

○ He's such a good dad.

○ It's not his fault that I can't fulfill him sexually.

○ I am the one he comes home to.

Does any of this sound familiar?

When rationalizations become weak, the tendency to minimize comes next. That only strengthens the denial. Minimizations common to those in relationships with sex addicts include statements like these:

○ It's not that bad.

○ I'm the only one who really understands him.

○ He needs me—now more than ever.

○ It's just a phase.

- It's not his fault that whore went after him; he didn't have a chance.
- He's so great in all other areas—it's just this one area.
- I'm not that interested in sex anyway.
- It could be worse. At least he is not addicted to _____ (something other than sex, such as alcohol, drugs, or gambling).
- It doesn't matter if I don't know everything he does.

How often have you had these thoughts?

Think about the beliefs and fears that bolster your rationalizations and minimizations. Partners of addicts share common beliefs and fears. Some of them are:

- I can't live without him.
- I might end up alone, and if I am alone that proves I am not worthy.
- No one else will ever love me.
- I don't deserve better.
- He's the father of my children, and they need their father.
- All men are like this.
- If we separated, I would have to give up some aspects of my lifestyle for lack of money.
- My family might find out and I'd feel humiliated.
- The kids might find out and I won't know how to handle it.
- I might have to give up my home.
- I've never balanced a checkbook, paid bills, or paid attention to our retirement, and I am not capable.
- If others found out about his sexual behavior they would think I'm not a good sexual partner, because if I were, he would not stray.
- If he is a sex addict, then all the good times in the past were a lie.

Does any of this sound familiar?

At this point in your reading, it's easy to start to berate yourself, to feel like a fool. If you are beating yourself up, stop. Denying, minimizing, and rationalizing are the most natural responses to living with someone acting out an addictive disorder. Of course you want to protect yourself. You want to believe it's not the problem it is. You want to give him the benefit of the doubt. It's so painful to get to the truth when the reality is only he can change his behavior; you can't do it for him. But you can honor yourself by challenging your own addictive behavior—your denial. This begins with identifying what you know or suspect and seeking out literature to learn more about codependency, sexual betrayal, and sexual addiction. You don't have to believe your partner's behaviors are an addiction, but be open to understanding what the addiction may look like. Pay attention to his behavior, not his words. Be willing to seek out a clinician trained in working with sexual betrayals and addiction.

Preoccupation

Many cosas live their lives in response to their partner's behavior. You have this insatiable need to know what your partner is doing, thinking, and feeling so you will know what you are supposed to do, think, or feel. You have suspicions, a sense, a knowing. You wonder; you question. You want to know, but at the same time you don't want to know. You want validation, or you want invalidation. Preoccupation is a major codependent attribute.

> [Therese] I don't know how I raised my kids. I was forever distracted. I was always wondering what he was doing, what I could do to be more attractive to him. What was I doing wrong, or what else would he find wrong with me?

> [Jacque] I would be nice to him when he would come home late, when he would smell of another woman, and when he would blatantly lie to me and I knew it. And then I would go to bed and think of everything I wanted to say to him. I wondered what these other women looked like, what they did together, and what they said to each other. I cannot tell you how many sleepless nights I had.

[Maite] I was like a detective checking his calendar, his cell phone account, and his trip schedules for work. I asked pointed questions of his coworkers. I would set traps for him, not trusting him to act responsibly. And all of the time I certainly felt I had this right.

[Coaddict] I would drive by where I had heard they met, or drive by her house and look at her to figure out what it was that was so special about her. Even when I had kids, I would load them in the car and go on my searches. I did this with more than one woman and in more than one town as we made several moves across the country. I snooped in his briefcase, his desk, and his wallet. It was my whole life. And yet I never confronted him.

·   ·   ·   ·   ·   ·   ·   ·   ·

Hypervigilance becomes a way of life. You vigilantly watch his behavior and try to attach meaning to it. "He came home early, that means . . ." "He's acting all loving, and that means . . ." "He is being nice to the kids, that means . . ." "He's angry, that means . . ." "He's quiet, that means . . ." You may be consumed with what you think he is feeling and thinking. You pride yourself in being able to read his innermost thoughts and feelings. No wonder you are tired, have no time left for yourself, and are losing yourself in the process. You are trying to live inside his body, mind, and heart.

Control

Preoccupation with the addict's problems frequently leads to controlling behavior on your part. Controlling behavior is the manipulation of people, places, and things. It is an attempt to bring stability to chaos and to bring safety to that which is dangerous. Controlling behavior is also a defense against shame. When you are controlling, you don't feel a sense of inadequacy. Instead you feel empowered. Controlling behavior imparts a sense of power at a time in your life when you are overwhelmed with fear and helplessness. It is a false, hollow power that, at a time of desperation, seems like a quick fix.

You may have learned controlling behavior during your growing-up years when you felt vulnerable; it was a survival mechanism. You then quickly reengage in that behavior whenever you and the things important to you, such as your relationship with your partner, are threatened. When you attempt to control the addict by throwing out his stash of magazines, videos, and sex toys, you act like the partner of an alcoholic who pours booze down the drain. It is not an effective means of controlling the addiction, but you buy into the delusion with the grandiose sense that you have the power to control the addict's behavior.

Examples of controlling behavior are:

o throwing out the stash

I would find his porn and throw it away. Obviously he knew, but we never talked about it. Maybe that was my way of telling him I knew and therefore believed he would stop.

o canceling plans

There were times I'd cancel plans and I would stay home thinking that would make it harder for him to make excuses to go out. Or I thought if I was home he wouldn't get on the Internet.

o the silent treatment

That was my favorite way of punishing him. "I'll show you—I'll just ignore you." He probably liked it, for all I know.

o relocating

We moved from one city after another, telling our family it was always for my job or his, as if it were a promotion for us. I was always capitulating to his promises that he would never do it again. We would start over, but nothing ever changed.

o lying

I'd lie to him by telling him no one called when I knew that his girlfriend had. I would also lie to him and tell him he had to stay home to be with the kids, and then I would stay at work late on the nights when I was pretty sure they had plans to meet.

○ making threats

> *I threatened to tell the kids, tell his parents, tell his boss; to divorce him; to go to her house; and to have my own affairs. My threats were endless.*

○ sexual manipulations, such as flirting with others or threatening to be sexual with others to create jealousy in the addict; acting or dressing sexy to gain or maintain his attention; or being sexual with the addict to prevent the addict from being sexual with others

> *I pretended I was into certain types of sexual acts that I hated just to try to keep him at home. There were many times I would respond to his sexual advances when I didn't want to, or would even initiate sex when I didn't feel sexual, because I thought that if I was sexual enough with him he wouldn't find this need to stray. And looking back, we had a lot of sex, but he had as much if not more with other women. So the truth is he had two stashes: me and the other women.*

Controlling behavior is about survivorship. While it is ultimately ineffective and harmful, don't be judgmental about yourself. Be empathetic to how you got here—from fear, desperation, and shame. Your actions are understandable and natural, but they are also the behavioral ingredients of enabling. Enabling is any behavior that supports the addict's delusional thinking that his acting out is not the problem and aids him in avoiding responsibility for his behavior.

Controlling and enabling behaviors rest on the assumption that you, the coaddict, have power over the addict. In his book *Contrary to Love,* Patrick Carnes offers an apt analogy: in a traditional African method for trapping monkeys, fruit is placed in small wooden boxes with narrow slats on the sides. The monkeys are able to reach in and grab the fruit but they are unable to pull the fruit out through the slats. Because the monkeys refuse to let go of the fruit, the tribesman can easily capture the monkeys. The monkeys have, in essence, trapped themselves by holding on too tight.[1] This is a metaphor for your coaddict plight. You won't let go of control, and so you become imprisoned within the addictive system; you mistake control for security.

Image Management

Projecting to the world that you and your family are well and happy reinforces your delusion that everything must be okay. Coaddicts frequently learn to live in fantasy, inventing a false reality that is less painful than the truth. You become adept at living with a high tolerance for inappropriate behavior to the extent that you don't even recognize the inappropriateness any longer. You chronically give your partner the benefit of the doubt; you give away your own reality. You lose yourself in this process, living a life of internal chaos, emotional isolation, and pain marked by control and numbness.

> [Coaddict] I was busy with the kids and my part-time work. We had all of the family toys: a nice home, a nice neighborhood, and vacations once or twice a year. I always had a smile on for the world and even when I was alone I stayed preoccupied with any and everything, truly ignoring the subtle signs. By the time my perfect life was shattered, there had been multiple women, a child he was financially supporting, and job changes that all occurred as a result of his behavior. I just wanted my perfect life where I don't think, don't talk, don't hear, and don't see.

. . . .

Perfectionism becomes a part of many women's image management. It often stems from internalized shame, operating from the belief that a woman has to be the best to get her partner's or society's approval—or even simply to not be rejected. The belief is this: "If I do more, if I am all things right, everything will be okay." At some point you learned to push yourself to excel, to be the best. But that means that there is no room for mistakes or vulnerability. Anything less than one hundred and fifty percent becomes unacceptable. It would mean failure, and there is too much at stake to risk failure. In your mind, not only is your relationship at stake, but also the possible impact on your children, your livelihood, and ultimately your esteem.

> [Coaddict] How could I not act like everything is okay? How could I say to people that my life and my marriage were a farce, a lie? They probably knew, but what did that say about me? I'm a fool? To allow myself to realize I was

no different than his previous two wives when I had been
so smitten. I was sure he would be different with me. I
liked our lifestyle, our friends. I loved him and believed
he loved me. So I just kept up the pretense, the image,
because to do anything differently would make me question what this meant about me.

. . . .

Controlling people, places, and things is a part of image management.
This external type of control, coupled with a form of internal control
where you don't show your feelings or own your needs, is also a part of image
management and perfectionism—a cocktail of codependent traits.

For some women, image management is about having a perfectly sculpted
body. Many cosas submit to liposuction, cosmetic surgery, and breast aug-
mentation in an attempt to contain the addict's behavior.

> [Coaddict] When I found out about his first affair, I delib-
> erately dieted and decided to have my breasts enlarged. I
> thought it would please him, but it didn't stop his acting
> out. I ended up feeling like my body parts were just
> another part of his addiction.

> [Coaddict] For years he acted out, then one day he left
> me for good. I was devastated. I went out and had lipo-
> suction, Botox, and my breasts lifted. It was as if I wanted
> to be one of the women he was choosing, yet in reality
> they didn't look a whole lot different than me. Now I
> was simply left with a false me.

. . . .

Having cosmetic surgery is a personal choice, but it is a decision that best
comes from a strong sense of self and not from trying to control, sustain, or
contain a relationship.

Many women become compulsive about being attractive to their partner. After years and years of being in competition with other women (even

if only in fantasy via pornography) and believing you are in constant comparison to other women, the sense of attack on your desirability as a sexual partner wounds your spirit. Adding to this, addicts often lose interest in their partners sexually, as their sexual behavior is not about intimacy. Some women finally give up and become the exact opposite of the firm, gorgeous, made-up woman they were trying to be for their partner. It is not that uncommon for coaddicts to give up on how they look and feel sexually after striving for perfection.

> [Coaddict] **In time, I looked the way his rejection made me feel, totally unlovely. It is ironic that pornography and cybersex created the exact opposite in real life of what they must have promised him in his fantasy life.**

. . . .

Distorted Anger

You have the right to be angry; you have reasons to be angry. Anger exists along a continuum, from avoidance to feeling frustrated to blatant rage. Because you are reading this book, you are most likely at one of the ends of the continuum: you are either steely in your outrage with ironclad control or you are fully out of control, or perhaps you are completely anger avoidant. You may have moved all over the continuum multiple times. Unfortunately, by now that anger is often both distorted and fueled by a myriad of other feelings and negative thoughts.

Rage

"Hell hath no fury like a woman scorned."[2] In the movie *Something to Talk About,* Julia Roberts plays a character who shows up at the local PTA meeting, stands up, and shouts, "Is there anyone here who hasn't slept with my husband?" In the fury of rage you may do things that you never would have imagined yourself doing.

> [Sara] **I was hell on wheels and Mt. Vesuvius at the same time. Not a pretty picture. I was ready to string the other women up high. I was most angry when I knew the women, from work or our neighborhood. My husband**

saw a lot of prostitutes, but I wasn't so angry with them, just him. I guess I thought that is what prostitutes are supposed to do. It is not what a coworker or your neighbor is supposed to do. I would rant and rave at my husband, and he would just stand there most of the time. I think maybe he felt he deserved it. But all it did was offer me a very brief respite and no answers because I had no path, no direction to heal. And my ranting certainly didn't change his behavior.

I would also tell people how awful he was. I once made him bring a coworker to our house so I could yell and rant and rave at her. Another time I went to a motel just to catch him in the act. I was screaming. Oh, I had the anger part down. I was like a spewing volcano, and looking back now I was screaming three generations of women's voices and three generations of anger for betrayal and abandonment—betrayal as the result of substance abuse, sex addiction, suicide, and being untrustworthy.

· · · · · · · · ·

For some cosas, rage is homicidal. Stories of murders and threats are common news. Remember Lisa Nowack, the astronaut, who drove nine hundred miles with a diaper on intending to confront, kidnap, and possibly kill the lover of her lover? Another woman, Betty Broderick from San Diego, shot and killed her ex-husband Daniel, a prominent attorney, and the longtime mistress who had become his wife after a bitter four-year divorce and custody battle. Clara Harris, a dentist from Texas, ran down and killed her cheating husband in a hotel parking lot after confronting him with his lover.

Many other women do not make the headlines, but their rage is just as destructive. Women have killed or attempted to kill their partners, attempted to throw their partner out of a moving car on the freeway, poisoned their partner's drink or food, sabotaged a partner's parachute, and hired others to commit murder. Sometimes women have burned down their house or removed their partner's belongings and set them on fire. Many betrayed women are empathetic to Lorena Bobbit's behavior and have threatened or followed through with cutting off their partner's penis.

Only a minority of betrayed women actually act out their fury violently. More prevalent are homicidal thoughts and moments of fantasy that plot revenge. When you are in a rage, there is a temporary suspension of believing your behavior is wrong. This gives you the perception that what you are doing is defending yourself.

While some people see rage as the behavior of acting out intense and deep anger, I perceive rage as a holding tank, not just for anger, but for the embarrassment, the humiliations, the fears, and the sadness. Of course you are feeling all of those feelings. There is no doubt you have many reasons to be angry at him: his betrayal of your trust, his disregard for your relationship, the impact of his behaviors on the family and on your health, and the ineffectiveness of loyalty you have shown him in the face of the betrayals. You may be thinking you have wasted a lot of years of your life with him. Or perhaps you are feeling doubly betrayed because of all the years you knew about his behaviors but stayed with him, only to have him walk out once the kids were raised, or after you put him through school, or after you took care of his sick parents. Maybe your rage comes from feeling trapped, perhaps because you're financially dependent on him, or maybe he's your ticket to a green card that allows you to stay in the country, or you don't know how you'll raise your kids by yourself. The intensity of your feelings is understandable. The key to greater health is finding the settings in which to express them.

Betrayal hurts. It hurts more deeply than anything you have ever known. But the act of rage will only hurt you in the long run. It's healthier to find something constructive to do with that rage: pound pillows or rip newspapers, scream from the top of a mountain, or write a venomous letter you don't mail. But don't act out your rage toward anyone, including yourself. You deserve better than to act on it and then endure the consequences.

Sideways Anger

Often anger becomes sideways or passive-aggressive. Sideways anger occurs when you act it out and then deny it, or you act out in revenge and end up hurting yourself more than him. Your expressions of anger toward the addict can range from threats, screaming, and blaming to giving him the cold shoulder. You may deflect it toward others, often the innocent. In the long run it doesn't make the difference you are hoping for and only creates further chaos.

Listen to the following coaddicts describe their experiences with sideways anger:

- *When I thought he was with a woman, I would get her phone number and call her number incessantly and then hang up.*
- *I had an affair myself to show him.*
- *I verbally raged at my kids for things that had nothing to do with them.*
- *I spent thousands of dollars shopping when I believed he was lying to me.*
- *I keyed his car (damaging property).*
- *I binged on food.*
- *I emailed everyone we knew after I discovered emails that told me he was sleeping with a friend. I wanted revenge. I wanted him to be shamed and humiliated. I wanted people to be angry with him and see him as a bad person. In the moment I felt glorious and empowered. But it made no difference other than to scare people away from me in my anger.*
- *I would set traps for him in various chat rooms. Sometimes I would surprise him in some humiliating form, but other times I just kept quiet and stored the information to use it as ammunition down the road.*

It's so easy to direct blatant or sideways anger toward a third party. You'd rather not hold your partner accountable. It is almost as if the addict is the victim of the situation, victimized by the very person he acts out with. Getting angry with the addict can be threatening to you when you are fearful of being abandoned. It may be construed as pushing him away.

[Coaddict] I spent years being angry with the other women. My husband was a doctor, and in my mind the nurses were always throwing themselves at him. It seemed that every time I became aware of another woman—and they have been in our lives all of our forty years together— I was into another pregnancy or had my own health problem. The timing was such that I thought I needed him, and that meant being angry with someone other than him. Besides, if I got angry with him, maybe that would push him more toward them.

[Sara] Most of the time my anger was with my husband unless I knew the other woman. Then it was as if I thought she had assaulted him and he had no part in it. I would switch my emotional alliances back and forth between my husband and the woman, seeing one as the victim of the other.

. . . .

Anger Avoidance

Some cosas say they just don't feel angry; instead they feel defeated or numb. They may acknowledge that they should feel angry but aren't. For many women, avoidance is a learned response to stress over time; a response that is often acquired in childhood and/or as the consequence of long-term hurtful adult relationships. It is often a part of low-grade chronic depression (dysthymia) or major depression. You may have learned that by responding to a bad situation with judicious anger you didn't change the predicament; you only felt helpless. When anger doesn't restore your sense of control over the environment you eventually begin to feel apathetic; you come to believe that nothing good will ever come of it, so why expend the energy to just feel more battered?

You may be using the distraction of busyness to help stuff your anger. Busyness is often demonstrated through housework, shuffling kids to activities and appointments, shopping, or work. Some women act out their busyness by getting overly involved in the community. It could mean that you spend hours at the health club or on the computer. By themselves none of these behaviors are bad, and in fact they are often esteemed. But for the cosa, involvement that is excessive, that is done in a way to avoid the issues in your relationship and family, merely serves as an unhealthy diversion.

[Coaddict] I became like a spinning top. I had myself so busy with kids, work, parents—anything to avoid the reality. I didn't know what to do. I didn't want to lose him. So I

**just kept my mouth shut and dug my head into my work,
my career.**

. . . .

Rage and sideways anger can provide fleeting moments of revenge or
personal satisfaction. However, in the end they, or the acts of anger avoidance, only lessen your self-respect, dignity, and self-esteem. The potential
fallout and consequences can be devastating.

Chronic Grief and Loss

Loss of what you have hoped and worked for in intimacy, loss of the way
you know yourself and your partner, loss regarding the way you think
about people and the world you live in, and/or loss of a relationship—
whatever it is that is gone or has now changed in your life will generate all
of the basic stages in the grief process.[3] Initial shock, disbelief, denial,
anger, guilt and bargaining, despair, loneliness, and acceptance are natural
responses to any loss. Losing a loved one to addiction has the potential of
keeping you stuck in the process of grief because the addict has not died;
he is still present and his acting out continues. Living with addiction and
reacting to addiction causes you to live in a chronic state of loss. You feel
the loss, go in and out of denial, experience anger and guilt, attempt to bargain, feel despair, and at times are lifted by hope. Partners may live for years
caught up in the cycle of chronic grief and all of its many feelings. Your
losses are ongoing and repetitive with denial entering and leaving the picture. Not having the truth validated, discounting your own perceptions or
having them dismissed by others, and needing to minimize feelings all lead
to a distorted and unmanageable internal life. It's enough to make you feel
crazy.

In the throes of living with addiction, you may spend more time processing one aspect of grief than another. It's only natural that you stay in
the stage that is familiar or safe. If anger is a haven because you feel empowered by it, you might go there and get stuck. If you are anger avoidant and
you have taken on a lot of guilt in your life, you may readily go there. Guilt
and bargaining frequently work together, causing you to make statements

like "If I _____, he will _____." *If I pay more sexual attention to him, he will not stray. If I am the perfect wife, he will never leave me.* You may refuse to accept reality, become angry and blaming, and keep trying to bargain with the addict. *I'll move anywhere you want. We can change churches. I will change my job. I will do whatever will make you happier so you will stop this behavior.* You may get stuck in sorrow, feeling the pain, hurt, and sadness, but you don't find a way out of it. In defeat, you succumb to depression. To compound the tragedy, you may engage in actions that are self-degrading, self-destructive, or that profoundly violate your own values.

While you are stuck in your grief, you go through a wide range of feelings about the addict as you increasingly suspect or become aware of the behavior. Feelings fluctuate wildly, from intense rage to profound sadness, fear, embarrassment, shame, and guilt. You may keep these feelings tightly controlled and to yourself, or they may leak everywhere. You may be out grocery shopping and when someone bumps into your cart you react as if the person has just stolen your child. A casual conversation with an acquaintance who simply asks you how you are, not knowing what is happening in your life, sends you into inconsolable grief and you end up spilling your guts.

So what do you do to cope with your grief? It is overwhelming when you feel at fault and you are emotionally isolated. Your responses probably run the gamut.

At times of great fear, angst, and shame, women employ a variety of disconnection strategies: they move toward, move against, or move away.

- In moving *toward* you seek to appease and please, you become Ms. Perfect, Ms. Accommodator.

- In moving *against* you act aggressively to garner power. You can do this with rageful or spiteful behavior. You may engage in your own acting out via self-destructive behaviors, such as using drugs, having affairs, or spending money.

- In moving *away* you withdraw, hide, silence yourself, and keep secrets. You numb out or slip into depression and anxiety. Overeating, anorexic behavior, and the use of alcohol or other drugs (particularly sedatives or depressants) also aid in withdrawing and hiding.

Most people relate to using all three or a combination of strategies. None of these movements help; they keep you stuck. They are all self-defeating.

Which of these do you implement?

[*Coaddict*] **In the early years of my marriage I bent over backward to be the accommodating wife. I suspected he was with other women, yet I felt trapped financially. I was scared to leave, scared to be on my own. I was scared the kids would blame me because they wouldn't understand why I wanted to leave. In time I started to secretly drink and then use pills. I felt so defeated. I just wanted to disappear but couldn't. I got so preoccupied with my suspicions, and yet felt so defeated, so I sent threatening letters to the women I suspected he was with and damaged the possessions he seemed so fond of, such as his musical instruments and his car.**

. . . .

In addition to your codependency, it is not uncommon for you to have your own addictions. Many female partners raised in a substance-abusing, physically or sexually violent, or otherwise restrictive authoritative family feed their negative esteem and internal emptiness with alcohol, pills, and other substances. Food is a particularly strong anesthetizer for women. Anorexia and bulimia with themes of control and image management are pervasive and common for cosas. Frequently cosas identify with compulsive spending and gambling. It is also possible that any sexual acting out on your part may be addictive. These addictions could be a part of any or all of the strategies of disconnection. While it may be your partner's behavior that led you to read this book, this is also the time for your own self-exploration.

In a healing journey you will learn how to stand tall in the face of truth without the need to move toward, against, or away. Standing tall means finding the voice to speak your truth, knowing and honoring your needs and feelings, and having boundaries that offer both containment and protection. This takes work on your part, but as you are reading this book, it is

possible, particularly with the support of other women who have made this
journey before you.

The Body Knows

One of the consequences of not acknowledging your feelings is the real
possibility of health problems. Your autoimmune system can become
severely compromised when you are undergoing emotional stress.

> [Coaddict] After a few months in recovery, I was able to
> see how much I rationalized my feelings away and ration-
> alized my trust in my husband. But by this time I was in a
> chronic state of physical pain. I had been going to doctors
> for the past couple of years and had a host of different
> tests. I was just given many different diagnoses and med-
> ical suggestions. Then I got into recovery and realized
> I hadn't seen a doctor in over two months, then three
> months, and then four months. Today I don't run from
> conflict. Today I know when I am angry. Today I don't
> keep that stupid smile on my face like all is fine with the
> world when I really feel as if my world is crumbling.
> Today I have no mysterious physical pains.

. . . .

Whether you know for sure that you partner is acting out sexually or
not, you are living with stress. You are dealing with both acute stress and a
more subtle chronic state of stress. Living with the fears of what it may
mean to your marriage and your family if you acknowledge the sex addiction, and living with the suspicion that something is off in your marriage
but not knowing exactly what, are both anxiety-provoking. This stress is
traumatic to your body. While you may normalize, minimize, and rationalize something in your mind, the physical body knows something is wrong.
When it's in jeopardy, be it physical or psychological jeopardy, the body
mobilizes its defenses. Stress can trigger the body's response to perceived
threat or danger. This reaction, known as the *fight or flight response,* generates
the release of certain hormones such as adrenaline and cortisol that speed

the heart rate, slow digestion, shunt blood flow to major muscle groups, and change various other autonomic nervous functions, giving the body a burst of energy and strength. Originally named for its ability to enable us to physically fight or run away when faced with danger, this response is now activated in situations where neither response is appropriate, like during a stressful day at work or at home. When the perceived threat is gone, our bodily systems and chemistry are designed to return to normal function via the relaxation response, but in a state of chronic stress, this adjustment often doesn't happen enough, causing damage to the body. When a machine is operated at maximum speed, the sustained high speed pushes the mechanisms past their limits or begins to burn out the elements. Our bodies and minds will react the same way. When pushed past their limits, they begin to break down. Pretty soon things start to fall apart. In this process, as a consequence of our stress, the autoimmune capacity is lower, rendering us more vulnerable to illness.

The Impact of Stress

Critical factors that affect the impact of stress are twofold: how far your system is taxed and for how long. Some stressors may occur only once or a few times but their impact is so great that trauma takes hold. Rape, an accident, or an assault may fit this form of trauma. Other trauma experiences may be less acute, but they happen every day and the hurt accumulates. In a coupleship, little acts of degradation, manipulation, secrecy, and shame on a daily basis take their toll. The body knows.

Many cognitive conditions are caused or exacerbated by stress. They include:

poor memory	seeing only the negative
indecisiveness	anxious or racing thoughts
inability to concentrate	constant worrying
trouble thinking clearly	loss of objectivity
poor judgment	dread

Common illnesses and physical symptoms associated with stress are:

headaches or backaches	diarrhea or constipation
nausea, dizziness, fatigue	insomnia
weight gain or loss	skin breakouts (hives, eczema)

frequent colds or flu

shortness of breath

high blood pressure

chronic back pain

sleep disturbance

sweats

anxiety disorder

heart disease

tooth and gum disease

asthma

grinding teeth (TMJ)

chest pain

rapid heart rate

ulcers

hair loss

depression

diabetes

hyperthyroidism

rheumatoid arthritis

[Maite] Today when I have sleep problems, or when a headache begins, or when my back begins to hurt, I know it can be something organic, but knowing what I know about me, I use it as a warning that I may be in over my head with stress. Usually these things happen when I am neglecting myself, not taking time for myself, eating poorly, or have not done any exercise in months. Clearly I am ignoring my feelings. I see it as a symptom that I am not doing what I need.

[Coaddict] At the height of the insanity I'd experience as many as seven facial tics in rapid succession. They began as small twitches near my eyes; then they expanded to include more twitches in my cheeks and around my mouth. This phenomenon continued for years, abating and increasing with tension and stress. I felt I must look like a contortionist. After I separated from my husband and began living alone, all such symptoms disappeared. In the past years, when under stress, I have been aware of some less intense twitching. When I became quite stressed while witnessing my daughter during her divorce proceedings, ending a very abusive marriage to an alcoholic, I noticed my face twitching again. I think I was thrown into a memory pool and began swimming in my own situation again. For now, I am tic free and hope to keep stress at a manageable level.

[Coaddict] I don't know what caused my fibromyalgia, but now that I'm in recovery I no longer experience the physical pain or incredible fatigue that I once did. I can now do all kinds of things that I wasn't able to do previously. I can get up, get dressed, and go out; I can drive again, and I'm not depressed. Is my being in recovery helping to diminish the pain of my fibromyalgia? Is one connected to the other? I don't know, but I'm not going to give up my recovery to find out. I believe I am in remission because I now have a voice and no longer accept being bullied, and I no longer doubt myself. It's like my body was forsaken by my heart and soul and once I began to honor me, my body began coming back to health.

· · · · · · · · ·

When faced with chronic stress and an overactivated autonomic nervous system, people begin to experience physical symptoms. The first symptoms are relatively mild, like chronic headaches and increased susceptibility to colds. With more exposure to chronic stress, however, more serious health problems may develop. Stress has the ability to worsen many diseases that may be caused by other factors.

Stress and Serious Illness

Today medical researchers certainly recognize the role stress plays as a contributor to cancers. It's believed by many medical professionals that stress weakens the immune system, significantly reducing the body's number of T cells, which are responsible for defending against malignant cancer cells. The T cells in the immune system are the body's only real means of defending itself against cancer cells, and they can only be created during the body's relaxation cycle.

Two Women of the Lodge have been challenged by cancer. They both believe their recovery from their coaddiction decreased their stress and heightened their physical well-being.

[Vanessa] As my husband and I began recovery, I was diagnosed with aggressive ovarian cancer. When presented with a scenario like this, the medical community is anxious to label it as genetic. I'm sure genes do play a role in it, but I also strongly believe that my family's inheritance of cancer has been related to the fact that we all operated from the ingrained belief that emotional suppression equaled survival. We bottled and stuffed anything that wasn't happy. You can't keep pushing every negative feeling and event into dark places in your soul and not expect them to have an impact. I never learned to deal with painful situations in a healthy way, so I believe my body was storing those memories at a cellular level, which would later manifest as cancer.

There is no question in my mind that much more than genes contributed to my cancer. I had suffered severe emotional abuse from a very young age. Keeping secrets set the framework for emotional suppression and abuse to become the foundation of my psyche. I held myself and those around me to perfectionist, unrealistic standards. I led an incredibly stressful lifestyle. I was a work addict and had very intense, high-pressure jobs and always pushed myself to higher levels of achievement. I was dealing with the ongoing and progressive infidelity of my husband, and my own raging codependent behaviors, and I was doing so much for others that I was putting basic self-care at the bottom of the list.

I also believe that much more than chemotherapy contributed to healing from my cancer. When I was diagnosed, the cancer had already moved into my liver. The prognosis was grim. I defied the odds and am now deemed a medical anomaly—or miracle, depending on the circle. I believe this was achieved through approaching my healing on many levels. I worked with every medical modality—traditional oncology, Ayurvedic, Chinese alternative, holistic, and naturopathic—and I changed my diet and fitness.

I engaged in the deepest therapy available to address the many suppressed areas of my life. I had strong mentorship and support groups. An amazing network of people rallied around me and gave me the strength to do all this incredibly hard work while fighting for my life. Rigorous purging of the old traumas, rethinking accountability, and owning my own issues and negative messages were key elements. This multi-layered work continues to occur, though less intensively, on an ongoing basis. I believe it was all integral to my healing and ultimately focused me on authenticity and self-love.

The combination of all these things saved my life and gave me the strength to make healthier choices. My perspective on most everything has changed, and now I try to live from a place of making the most of every day.

[Sara] I know that my concern, anger, stress, and living with addictive behaviors were the enemies of my immune system. My survival instincts were strong too. I asked for an MRI for some reason, and it found the cancer cells years before they would have been discovered by mammography or other standard diagnostic tests. This instinctive stand for my own life and health was a true paradigm shift for me. I turned forward and began the process of setting boundaries around the respect I had for my life and my value. It works both ways. While I believe my lifestyle compromised my immune system, my willingness to hear my inner voice and trust myself got me to a diagnosis and treatment at an early stage. Then embracing life and health drove my desire for recovery—to live life in truth—my truth with integrity. It's been ten years now, and I've never been healthier in mind, body, and spirit.

· · · · · · · · ·

Clearly chronic stress has a strong impact on the immune system, particularly one that is already compromised. Learning how to take care of yourself in recovery will help you to relieve stress.

~~~~~~~~~~~~~~~~

To live in denial, in a state of preoccupation, defending against the pain, is to live underneath the shadow of addiction. You lose sight of your true self when you act out in emotional pain. The good news is that there is a path out of the pain; you can live your life differently.

Reflective Thoughts and Questions

- Give three examples of your denial process.
- Name three rationalizations and minimizations you most identify with.
- Have you been preoccupied by the addict's behavior?
- In what ways have you attempted to control the addict's behavior?
- Describe your anger. Have you felt or acted out in fury or rage? Is your anger a sideways anger? How have you expressed it?
- Has maintaining an image been important to you? If so, describe how you've been presenting yourself and what it's been covering up.
- Would you describe yourself as perfectionistic? If so, describe your perfectionistic thoughts and behaviors, and then identify what you think fuels this behavior.
- Where do you see yourself in the grief process?
- How do you identify with the disconnection strategies of moving toward, moving against, or moving away?
- Are you aware of any behaviors other than coaddiction that could be an addiction for you? Identify and explain your thoughts and concerns. Are you willing to seek help to assess this?
- In what ways has your body been speaking to you?
- What was important for you to hear in this chapter?

Chapter Three

His Behavior Is Not About You

Why is he doing this?

Why won't he just stop?

First and foremost, you need to know that his behavior is not about you. As hurtful as his behavior is, he isn't doing this deliberately to hurt you or to punish you. Regardless of what he may say, he is not doing this because of anything you have done or not done, the way you look or don't look. It is not willfulness on his part. He has reached a stage where he cannot stop acting out sexually without help.

However you describe what it is you are living with, it is very important to see the addictive aspect of your partner's behavior. Historically, the term *addiction* was first identified as the out-of-control use of alcohol and other drugs. Today, we recognize that many behaviors—such as gambling, eating, and engaging in sex—can spin out of control and become addictive.

Just as alcoholism has existed over the centuries, using sex in a compulsive, addictive manner has also been occurring for many generations. The Italian-born libertine Giacomo Casanova was such a famous womanizer that, a full two centuries after his death, his name remains synonymous with the art of seduction. Benjamin Franklin is believed to have abandoned his devoted wife, Deborah, and become a lecher in London and France. In his book *The Autobiography of Benjamin Franklin,* Mr. Franklin confessed that as a young man, his "hard-to-govern'd passion of youth" led him into intrigues with women.[1] It is said he went to women hungrily, secretly, and briefly. Wilt Chamberlain, famous professional basketball player, devoted an entire chapter of his autobiography to his sexual exploits. He said that if he had to count his sexual encounters, he would be closing in on 20,000 women. "Yes, that's correct, twenty thousand different ladies," he wrote. "At my age, that equals out to having sex with 1.2 women a day, every day since I was fifteen years old."[2] Elvis Presley and his entourage became renowned for their womanizing and wild parties. Historically, this kind of behavior by men has been normalized by our society and in many cultures continues to be accepted. The media continues to expose sexual secrets and escapades of well-known politicians and celebrities who are engaged in compulsive sexual exploits outside of their committed relationships.

Whether or not your partner's behavior is ultimately diagnosed as addictive, you and he both deserve the opportunity to seek professional help. You can still find a path for yourself as you understand your own role in this partnership and a path out of your angst and despair.

The Addiction

Sexually addictive behavior is an equal opportunity addiction that spans all boundaries: economic, political, gender, sexual orientation, intellectual, religious, racial, and ethnic. Sex addicts come from all walks of life: they are factory workers, salespeople, truck drivers, janitors, policemen, accountants, physicians, politicians, executives, and clergy members. Most people who act out sexually during their adult years were abused sexually, physically, or emotionally during their childhood. The majority grew up in families where addiction already flourished. Many grapple with other addictions in addition to their sexual compulsivity.

Addiction is not about a particular behavior but its overall context. Just as there is a distinction between the social drinker and the alcoholic, there is a distinction between the person who has one affair and the person who repeatedly has affairs even when a job or marriage may be at stake. Not everyone who has affairs, participates in unsafe sex, or keeps sexual secrets is a sex addict. Not everyone who views pornography, engages in anonymous sex, visits prostitutes, or performs acts of bondage/dominance or sadomasochism is a sex addict. The type of sexual activity one prefers, the choice of sexual partners, or where one goes to have sex does not determine sex addiction. When a person deviates from the established sexual norms it does not make him a bad person, nor does it mean he is addicted.

The elements that define sexual addiction are the compulsive nature of the experience, the repetition of the behavior despite its negative consequences, the need for more and more to achieve the same effect, and the bad feelings that it engenders. The escalation in the amount of sexual activity or intensity of the experience occurs because the current level no longer provides the fix it once did. An addict has a persistent pursuit of self-destructive or high-risk sexual behavior, wherein cherished aspects of one's life are potentially sacrificed.

> [Addict] At times I would tell myself this is it, no more. But that never lasted for long. I would again find myself acting out. I didn't see it as acting out. I was just still doing what I had been doing, be it an affair, pornography, or a massage parlor. I would totally forget that I had a moment of thinking I shouldn't be doing this. The truth is, most of the time I just didn't see it as something I needed to stop. I was so caught up in just me or my next conquest. It was like I felt I was entitled to this life. If I were to think about it, I just totally separated it from my relationship with my wife. Today I know that is hard to grasp, but that is what I was thinking during the behavior. My behavior had nothing to do with my marriage, nothing to do with my wife. It was about me. I would have been doing this no matter who I was married to.

· · · · · · · ·

An accepted definition of alcoholism or drug addiction is "a pathological relationship with a mood-altering chemical." The addict's relationship with the substance of choice becomes more important to him or her than family, friends, health, or work, and it progresses to the point where consumption and/or use is necessary to feel normal. In order to feel adequate, the addict comes to depend on a change in neurochemistry and the accompanying mood-altering experience; it becomes central to his or her life. The vow to stop the behaviors gets lost against the power of the addiction. All of that is equally true for the sex addict.

The Behaviors

As an alcoholic may drink both rum and beer, sexually compulsive people often engage in a combination of behaviors. The behaviors can range from compulsive masturbation and pornography to one-night affairs and long-term relationships. He may be engaging with prostitutes (escorts), massage parlor workers, telephone sex operators, and/or making indecent phone calls. Some sex addicts are drawn to voyeurism, exhibitionism, or engaging sexually with someone of the same gender, even when one is not gay.

Today we see a sharp escalation of cybersex—sex via the Internet. An estimated 70 percent of sex addicts report having problematic online sexual behavior. People who are acting out sexually find the Internet exacerbates their problem. Even if someone has not previously been acting out, Internet access to pornography and cybersex often incites escalating and provocative behavior. It also contributes to acting out in real life. Online sexual behavior was described by Al Cooper, clinical psychologist and one of the pioneering researchers on sexual addiction from Stanford University, as the "crack cocaine of sex addiction"[3] because of its accessibility and affordability. Just pushing a button gives a person access to his secret world. He doesn't have to go to adult bookstores, put himself at physical risk, or cruise the streets. Anytime, day or night, in the comfort of his home or workplace, his fix is available with devastating consequences just as harmful as real-time sex addiction.

Just as the majority of alcoholics are not homeless, most sex addicts do not fit the erroneous stereotype of criminal offenders who satisfy their needs by forcing themselves on helpless victims. This is not to say that there are not victims in sexual addiction. In reality, all addictive sexual behavior is victimizing; the addict and his partner are both hurt in the process. The behaviors of a sex addict are often emotionally hurtful and disrespectful of others, but only a few are considered crimes, and those differ in the degree of personal violence involved. Certainly, child molesters and rapists inflict deep emotional wounds, but many people who commit sex crimes, specifically child molesters and rapists, are not compulsive. They are sociopaths engaged in acts of aggression. Sexually addictive behavior does not necessarily indicate criminal behavior; likewise, committing sexual crimes does not necessarily indicate sex addiction.

Research in the field of addiction over the past several years supports the belief that different addictions tap into the same brain chemistry.[4] Today we recognize there are three different types of addiction: 1) arousal, 2) satiation, and 3) fantasy. Whatever the substance or behavior, it can manifest in any one of these types.

Arousal-type addictions are also thought of as intensity addictions; the sex addict is hooked on the rush that occurs with risky sexual activities—the combination of fear and danger. The danger can be physical danger or a social danger, such as being caught in the act. Satiation-type addictions are seen in behaviors that medicate personal pain and anxiety. Fantasy-type addictions involve imagined sexual experiences.

Many sex addicts mix and match their sexually addictive behaviors as well as other addictive disorders. One can move from fantasy and escape to arousal and back to escape. Take, for example, a man who masturbates while fantasizing he is having sex with a woman he sees on the Internet. Then at greater risk to himself, he moves on to meeting this woman in person and after having a clandestine meeting of rough sex he returns home to a night of drinking to oblivion.

Addicts live an all-or-nothing kind of life, not knowing how to moderate themselves. They know two ways: full-out high speed or full-on brakes. Intensity addicts who are more apt to engage in high-risk dangerous situations commonly engage in satiation fixes to calm down and soothe their heightened energy, enabling them to be able to resume normal activities.

> [Addict] **My father raged and was abusive. By age eleven I found what my father had—power in raging. It protected me from my fears, my sense of unworthiness. Then I discovered masturbation and it calmed me. It was a solace. Rage gave me the high, the power, and masturbation was my anesthetic. They worked in tandem for years.**

. . . .

Because a sex addict is a person who never learned to tolerate his painful feelings, he seeks escape from these feelings. Sexual activity and sexual fantasy alter brain chemistry in the same way by producing profound feelings of pleasure. Sex addicts are altering their brain chemistry, and therewith their mood, all the time. They use sex as a drug to produce a high. As his disease progresses, the sex addict cares less and less who his sexual partner is. If he can't find a partner, masturbation will give him a quick fix. His chief pursuit is the high.

The Science of Addiction

While a nonaddicted individual can quickly see how the addict's behavior causes problems or has the potential to do so, the addicted person continues the behaviors despite the risks. He either doesn't recognize the impact his behavior is having on his committed relationship, or he is willing to risk the relationship. He may lose jobs, put himself (as well as his loved ones) at high risk for sexually transmitted diseases, and be willing to risk lawsuits or experience bankruptcy, all the while downplaying these possibilities.

> [Addict] I think back about my behavior. There was so much deception, lying, working the room. There was no turning it on or off. I really thought it was okay. I was clueless to the damage. I rationalized my first divorce not being about my behavior but that she just wanted different things. Today I am stunned at my own thinking, or lack of thinking, back then.

> [Addict] I didn't know how to stop. It sounds so strange, but until I got help I didn't realize that it was truly an addiction for me. I was incapable of stopping on my own. I needed help. Left to my own thinking, I thought I had my life in control. The twisted thinking here is that I thought I had all of my lies covered and that meant all was okay.

· · · · · · · · ·

The science of addiction indicates that the inability to recognize the impact of behavior on others or the willingness to risk what is significant in one's life appears to be connected to brain chemistry. How many times have you said or wanted to say to your partner, "What are you thinking?"

The answer is: he is not thinking.

When people use substances or engage in escape behaviors, the brain releases neurotransmitters, such as adrenaline and dopamine, that trigger the brain's pleasure/reward center; or it may release serotonin, which lessens anxiety and depression. With repetitive engagement, the triggers in the brain's reward center override the cognitive, rational thinking part of the brain. Brain scans show there are reduced levels of activation in the pre-frontal cortex, where rational thought should be able to override impulsive behavior. But under the influence, it doesn't. In essence, the addiction is a hijacked brain.

Dr. Martin Paulus, a professor of psychiatry at the University of California San Diego, reinforces that addiction is not about substances or behaviors, but in fact "is about disrupting the processing of pleasure; the balance point is shifted so you keep creating more and more urges, and you keep wanting more and more."[5]

Science also tells us that stress alters the way we think. Parts of the brain that help us problem solve shut down at times of stress, fueling impulsive behavior. When this behavior becomes excessive, the brain interprets the feelings as positive and cannot recognize the long-term consequences, telling us "this is good; we should do it again."

The good news in looking at the science of addiction is to know that the brain has plasticity to it. That means the practices people learn in treatment and in recovery affect brain function. An addict can learn skills to calm the emotionally reactive area of the brain, avoid triggers that activate the emotional area, and enhance the decision-making area where he can rationally think through his decisions, rather than responding impulsively and from such a strong emotional basis.

The Addictive Cycle

Being addicted means that at some point a person loses the ability to choose whether or not he is going to be sexual. He is unable to say no to his impulses and cravings. Be it alcohol, gambling, or sex, the addicted person either doesn't see it or denies the problems that his compulsive activity is continuously producing in his life, maintaining his denial with rationalizations. Sex addicts are preoccupied with and compulsive about their sexuality. They engage in distorted thinking, rationalizing, and defending and justifying their behavior while blaming others for the problems that result. Like alcoholics and drug addicts, sex addicts progress through stages in which they retreat further and further from the reality of friends, family, and work, and potentially destroy those important relationships, sabotage careers, and risk significant health issues and violent death.

Sex addicts describe their euphoria with sex similarly to that described by drug addicts with drug use. This may be an effect of endorphins and other endogenous brain chemicals that are excited during sexual behaviors, creating a drug-induced state. The mood-altering experience is not just the sexual act itself; it can be produced by sexual fantasy and rituals as well.

Patrick Carnes, Ph.D., a pioneer in the sex addiction field, delineated key components of the addictive cycle as it relates to sexual compulsivity.[6] Obsession and preoccupation are the thinking disorder aspects of addiction. People can become obsessive about any activity that generates a positive mood for them, whether it is the self-nurturing feeling of eating, the excitement of gambling, or the arousal of seduction. Addicts find that just thinking about a sexual act leads to a preoccupation that in itself produces pleasurable and exciting sensations, creating a positive mood in order to avoid a negative one. It can be employed at any time of the day in any situation. Often sex addicts seem as though they are not present even when they are physically there. Their mental arousal makes them less and less in tune with the emotional stresses that triggered the fantasy and creates a pressing desire to act out their thoughts. The fantasy, the anticipation, the planning, and the risk taking are as important as the sexual act itself. For some addicts, the thinking about, planning of, and anticipation of the behavior is the most pleasurable part of their addictive cycle. As the addict moves into fantasy, his neurochemistry begins to unleash the chemicals that an actual sexual encounter would prompt. Spurred to action by sexual fantasies, the addict begins to prepare for sexually acting out.

> [Addict] My actual sexual indiscretion was only minutes, but the planning and anticipating took hours. I couldn't even remember things about my job or what was happening at home. I was mentally consumed with the fantasy or was covering my bases and finessing my lies.

Engaging in pre-sexual rituals intensifies the powerful emotional and neurochemical high and drives the addictive cycle forward. Rituals are as varied in number and complexity as there are sex addicts. Some rituals may take minutes, others hours. Some sex addicts will travel great distances to obtain pornography and won't act out until they return home. Some will make elaborate travel plans in order to connect with partners from around the country or the world. The ritual might include changing into erotic clothing, listening to specific music, cruising by car in a favorite neighborhood, or going online. For some, the ritual involves the use of drugs or alcohol. Just like fantasies in the preoccupation stage, rituals produce excitement. Perhaps the excitement comes from anticipating going to a massage parlor that practices techniques that the addict hasn't experienced before. Maybe the excitement is produced by the amount of risk involved in a certain activity. Danger and intrigue are exciting to the addict and summon the release of adrenaline, which is in itself addictive. Through the preoccupation and ritual stages, the addict's brain has literally created a chemical cocktail that is as addictive as any drug. Any addictive behavior can be dangerously pursued and therefore is exciting, giving addicts a rush.

Once addicts have reached their ritual stage, it is almost inevitable that they will go on to the acting-out stage. Moments, hours, or even days into their fantasies and rituals, sex addicts arrive at the full-blown expression of their sexual behavior. Compulsive masturbation with pornography, exhibitionism, voyeurism, hiring of prostitutes, paying for sexual massages, and visiting adult bookstores and sex clubs are intensely stimulating.

Once he has acted out, he may or may not look back with regret, fear, or anxiety about what he has been doing sexually or otherwise. He may suffer direct unwanted consequences as a result of his sexual conduct, which makes him feel even worse. Since addicts act out in part to compensate for their limited emotional coping skills, their sexual behavior and its consequences often make them feel worse about themselves over time, which in turn causes an escalation of the frequency and intensity of their behaviors. They lose faith in themselves and turn more frequently to sex to try to feel better. The depression, shame, and anxiety generated by their sexual acting out can bring addicts back to the very need for emotional control that initiated the addiction cycle at the outset. Each addict has his own particular response to his behavior and his unique way of gearing up for the next time. Think of a merry-go-round in motion; it is difficult to get off.

All addiction is characterized as progressive with diminishing returns, meaning there is a need for more of the chemical or more of the compulsive activity to get the same level of satisfaction. Over time, alcoholics require more and more alcohol in order to feel good. Likewise, the sex addict will find himself taking more and greater risks in order to feel the same level of excitement. Early in his addiction, an addict establishes rules that allow him to believe he has control over his behavior. While the addiction serves its purpose to anesthetize an inner shame, to offer a false esteem, or even to produce feelings of power or control, the addict is certainly not delusional in his thinking all the time. There are times when he is aware of his dishonesty, ashamed of his lies, and feels guilty for the pain he is causing his partner. It is then he tells himself he won't do it again, or he puts restrictions on himself. He often promises himself he will do things differently next time, and then he feels twice as bad when he cannot keep his promises. As the alcoholic tries to control his behavior by saying to himself he will only drink after a certain hour, or only on weekends, or only a certain liquor, people who are sexually addicted impose their own restrictions (as seen in the examples below) and soon break their own rules:

- I will only engage with prostitutes when I am on business out of town, never in my own city.
- I will only have affairs with single women.
- I will only have affairs with women that my wife would not know.
- I will only get on the computer for cybersex after hours at work.

Eventually, the addict comes to break all of his own rules as he takes more and more risks. He starts to have affairs with women in his town, then a neighbor, and then a woman at his church. He starts to visit massage parlors in his own city and starts his day at work by downloading pornography on the Net.

When he continues his risky behavior despite negative consequences and he requires more and more to obtain the same effect, then addiction has set in, no matter what the specific behavior. The behavior will continue to progress and it will ultimately destroy the addict's life unless the cycle is disrupted with a new start in recovery.

Unlike complete abstinence that defines alcohol and drug recovery, sex addiction recovery does not require total abstinence from sex. In this way it is similar to recovery from compulsive overeating. Sexuality is a part of one's natural human state, as is the need to fuel one's body with food. People in recovery from eating disorders, specifically compulsive overeating, avoid eating certain foods. They learn to eat for the nutritional value of the food rather than eating out of boredom or to anesthetize anger or pain or other feelings. Ultimately they develop a whole new relationship with the role of food in their life. In recovery, the sex addict also develops a whole new relationship with the role sex plays in his life. There will be certain behaviors he will no longer engage in. The act of sex will be for the experience, for the sharing of sexual pleasure, and for relational connection rather than out of his emotional reactivity and woundedness or for the sake of garnering power and control. He'll learn how to identify and voice his needs and feelings and to honor those of others, creating greater emotional and sexual intimacy. The recovering sex addict will develop boundaries that are based on respect for self and others. Whether the addiction is food, gambling, substances, or sex, all addicts in recovery learn how to identify their triggers and how to avoid them or not react in self-defeating ways. While all addicts need to develop greater emotional and relational skills to create healthier ways of getting their personal and interpersonal needs met, recovery for the sex addict is about learning how to get those needs met in a nonsexual way and addressing the issues that created barriers to healthy intimacy.

Why Am I Not Enough?

It is my hope that in better understanding the addictive nature of sexual compulsivity you will be able to answer the age-old question: *Why am I not enough?* Wives and partners often wonder why sex with them, and only them, is not sufficient for the sex addict. It's important to know that when the addict is in the throes of his addiction, he doesn't have sex with you to forge a connection and develop intimacy. He's doing it with you to keep up his pretenses, to reinforce your falsely held and unspoken belief that if he has sex with you then he isn't seeking it outside of your coupleship. Or you may simply be an element of his stash and part of his addictive cycle. In the act of his addiction—in the immediate moment—he may feel complete, whole, good. But that feeling disappears once the activity is over, and he will go out and seek that feeling, as fleeting as it is, again and again.

> [Addict] I like having sex with my partner. She partici-
> pates willingly and I find her attractive. I know she tries
> hard to please me. So why isn't that enough for me? All
> I can say is that my addiction isn't just about sex. There is
> this self-hate part of me that I try so hard to never show
> my wife. But when that self-hate gets triggered, and it is
> always there waiting to be triggered, that is when I act out.
> I have sex with women I don't know so I don't worry
> about displeasing them, nor do I have to be respectful to
> their needs. I also engage in totally different sexual acts
> that I would never ask my wife to engage in. My twisted
> thoughts about power, pain, and anger all come into
> play during my acting out. I am just into me, me, me,
> totally me.

· · · · · · · · ·

The addict's feelings of shame, fear, and inadequacies are a bottomless pit. His behavior is an endless vicious cycle that has nothing to do with you.

Multiple Addictions

Addicted people often have histories of abuse, and the more profoundly abused they have been, the more likely they will have multiple addictive disorders. Some people have several addictions operating simultaneously, while others trade off addictions, giving up one only to get lost in another. It is common that when one addiction is addressed, other addictive behaviors that do not get addressed gain strength. Many women have partners in recovery from one addiction only to ultimately be confronted by sex addiction.

> [Addict] I got help for my alcoholism and I quit drinking
> because it was messing up everything. But I didn't give up
> all of my womanizing and affairs for another twenty years.
> I didn't see the sex messing up things. My marriage was

struggling, but I just thought that was a problem between the two of us and had nothing to do with this secret world I had going on.

[Addict] I used sex just as I used alcohol: to ignore pain, to block out my feelings. It separated me from a lot of loneliness, confusion, anger, guilt, and shame. I know I look like I have my act together to the outside world, but for my whole life I have felt lonely, starting as a kid. I was never confident of myself. I was confused about why I did a lot of the things I did, and I felt guilty and ashamed. I sort of lived in two worlds: what I felt inside and what the world would see. They were two very different things. But I got good at buying into the outside image and ignoring that inner world. Well, that is exactly what alcohol and then sex did for me. They allowed me to disconnect from that inner world and believe my own lies about myself. I told myself that my behavior wasn't different from other men's behavior and that my behavior didn't really hurt anyone else because they didn't know about it.

· · · · · · · ·

Addicts will often seek help for the addiction that is most visible to others, the one they have the least shame about, or the one that is the most disruptive to their lives. Addictions such as substance abuse, for example, are usually much more disruptive on a daily basis and are often more visible to others than a sex addiction. It is also common for someone addicted to alcohol, drugs, or gambling to initially be willing to get help but continue to hold on to sexual secrets. Sometimes, while receiving help for one compulsive behavior, an addict is acting out in another addictive disorder because he believes he can handle it, or thinks once he no longer uses drugs or drinks it will no longer be a problem. The denial and rationalizations about the hidden behavior go unrecognized. He does not fully understand that addiction takes on a life of its own. Unfortunately, many who get help for their identified addiction do not undergo any additional assessment for other problems. It's possible for his sexual acting out to continue for years before a crisis compels him to address his long-standing sexual compulsivity.

> [Addict] **After ten years of being clean and sober from alcoholism, I knew I needed help again. I was not drinking or using. I was still going to a Twelve Step program, but I was sexually acting out and being dishonest about our family money. Knowing it was catching up with me, and that my wife was very suspicious, I went to a treatment program. I had been to treatment ten years before, but I didn't get honest about anything but the alcohol. This time I told them I was in trouble for these other things.**
>
> **The first time in treatment I thought that because my sexual acting out was always associated with my drinking that I just wouldn't do it if I didn't drink. And I also knew that if I exposed my sexual acting-out behaviors, they would want me to tell my wife, and I didn't want to do that. For two years I did okay, mostly because I just deliberately kept myself away from women as much as possible. But slowly I got myself back into my old behaviors. I was crazy in a sense because I knew what I was doing and knew I wasn't being honest with my recovery friends, my sponsor, or my wife. I was increasingly out of control. Shortly after my tenth sober anniversary I got help for my sexual acting out because I also knew I was close to drinking again.**

· · · · · · · ·

Addictions exist in layers. Some are more deeply embedded than others. Sometimes two addictions are ritualized together such as sex and alcohol, or sex and other drugs (a form of speed such as cocaine or crystal methamphetamine is the most common). For example, an addict's ritual could be using crystal meth or cocaine as a part of his pattern of sexual acting out.

Combining speed with sex is a way that addicts try to find an even greater high. After acting out, an addict will often use alcohol or marijuana to afford a greater sense of calmness in coming down from the previous high. Typically, this means that a person does not engage with one addictive behavior without engaging with the other.

Work, rage, drugs, alcohol, sex, spending, gambling—it doesn't matter what the behavior or substance is, if it has the ability to (falsely) empower, to medicate or soothe, to help you avoid, and/or to move you from a feeling of "less than" to "better," then it can be addictive. A man in recovery from his many addictions told me, "I was an addiction binger and trader."

> [Addict] I started a paper route when I was just a kid and found that work was a source of pride and solace. It got me out of the house and distracted me from all my fears. The money I made gave me independence. I became quite the entrepreneur and soon had other kids working for me. Reading was another source of solace and a way for me to disconnect from the pain and confusion of my life. I was really very angry with my father during that time, and my paper route and withdrawing into reading and numbers (I loved overseeing my bank account) gave me a sense of well-being and confidence that ultimately fueled a strong work and gambling addiction. Then I began to drink, and it too gave me a sense of well-being. Adding sex to that made it become one big, powerful cocktail.

. . . .

Problems and behaviors that are often overlooked include raging behaviors, compulsive spending, and work obsession. Work obsession and distorted thinking about money are culturally supported, and rageful behavior is often hidden and a last vestige of recovery.

> [Addict] Anger, alcohol, marijuana, work, and sex—all were my validation. They also became my form of power. After I got sober, my sexual behavior went underground and my anger became sporadic, but my work addiction

flared. I was on a see-saw, professing recovery. Finally I decided to do some therapy around my childhood. It was then that I was confronted by a clinician about my sexual behavior. This led to my anger problems and work addiction being addressed in my recovery.

. . . .

Another prevalent combination of addictive behaviors is violence, drugs/alcohol, and sex. The violence component nearly always has its roots in a childhood that included parents or caregivers who were alcoholic, physically violent, and/or sexually abusive. In some cases, the child received affection only after being abused or after a family fight. Thus, for that person, violence and affection (sex) are paired. It may be that as a young boy the addict listened to his parents arguing and heard the physical abuse as his father literally threw his mother around the bedroom. In his powerlessness as a young child, he found comfort in masturbation. Today he cannot get an erection unless he fantasizes about something of a violent nature while listening to music with violent lyrics. When addictions are ritualized, they feed each other and intensify the addictive cycle.

To keep from merely switching addictions and to support a healthy recovery, the addict must identify and address all his addictions as well as the internal source of his pain. Today, addiction specialists recognize that multiple addictions are interactive; they present as a package. If you cut off or treat just one branch of a diseased tree, it does not necessarily heal or get to the root of the problem. Whether there are dual or multiple addictions, each addiction is a primary issue, and each needs to be addressed simultaneously.

Even though not all sex addicts are addicted to alcohol and drugs, all reputable sexual addiction treatment programs strongly advise abstinence from alcohol and any so-called recreational drug use since any use is a disinhibiter. These substances weaken a person's judgment to the point that one cannot remain committed to healthy boundaries, which are a part of recovery from sex addiction. They can strongly influence a relapse into addictive thinking, which sets up the addictive behavior.

Any process or behavior that interferes with the ability to be honest deserves attention. Whether it is an addiction or otherwise, self-defeating behavior doesn't support healing and recovery.

Depression and Anxiety

It is very common for addicts of all types to experience underlying depression and anxiety as a consequence of both biology and traumatic family histories. In addition to a generalized anxiety disorder, post-traumatic stress disorder (a subset of an anxiety disorder) often underlies the addiction. These co-occurring mental health disorders may be substance-related but very often are their own primary issue. Like multiple addictions, depression and anxiety often go unrecognized for many years. It is not uncommon for a sex addict to seek treatment for substance abuse, then ultimately for his sex addiction, and then without a substance or behavior to give him false esteem or to medicate, his underlying depression and anxiety become much more apparent. While we all know the typical symptoms of depression are apathy, lethargy, and feeling blue, it is not uncommon, particularly for men, for depression to be expressed as blatant hostility and unmanageable anger and rage. The symptoms of undiagnosed disorders such as depression and anxiety can be masked and managed through patterns of addictive and compulsive behavior.

[Addict] I am not the kind of guy who thinks of himself as depressed, but in my recovery from sex addiction I was still acting out with explosive anger and really rageful behavior. My size, words, and loudness are intimidating, and I used them. A therapist suggested antidepressants, and I had learned to be open to suggestions from those I respected. To be honest, I was shocked by the recommendation, but now it is apparent that alcohol and sex just covered up this depression. My anger was always close by, always ready to protect me. So depression was just more and more apparent without my other fixes. Today I still have some inappropriate anger, but that is not so related to depression as just a lifetime of being quick to use anger, and it's my first defense. But treating my depression has made a world of difference that I never would have identified as an issue for me. After all, big men are not supposed to be depressed.

. . . .

Addictive behavior—whether it's satiation, arousal, or fantasy—can be a cover to depression. In our society, it is far more acceptable for a man to get treatment for an addiction than to be diagnosed with and treated for depression. It is considered unmanly to be depressed. In our culture, girls and women are socialized to internalize pain; they blame themselves and draw distress into themselves. Boys and men are socialized to externalize pain and are more likely to discharge distress through action. A man is running from the pain and emptiness he has felt for years, engaging compulsively in work, financial goals, and sex. Money, prowess, and prestige become the drugs that sustain him and take the place of authentic relationships. He has trouble being intimate with others because he can't be intimate with himself. His sexual acting out is an attempt to escape the sense of unworthiness and emotional impoverishment that has haunted him throughout much of his life. To relieve the threat of depression, the addictive substance or process in this case works to transform the emotional state from feelings of worthlessness to feelings of extraordinary worth.

As Terrence Real says in *I Don't Want To Talk About It,* "the depressed man frequently buries himself in work, wraps his internal discomfort in anger, and numbs his discontent with alcohol, other drugs, and sex. As a society we have more respect for the walking wounded, those who persist, deny their pain and difficulties."[7] Men readily engage in satiating and fantasy behavior, and at the same time they are pushed toward arousal-type behaviors. They are expected to engage in risk taking but are to avoid being vulnerable or owning or showing those feelings. Pain is something they are to rise above. As a consequence, an addict's untreated depression sabotages his recovery.

> [Addict] I went to AA because my wife threatened to leave me due to my drinking. She knew about some of my sexual acting out but thought it only happened because of my drinking. The truth was I drank more in response to the shame I felt about my acting out. But who really knew that? So I went to AA to save my marriage. I was also tired of all the drinking and I couldn't seem to stop. But when I went to AA, I left half of me outside the door. Then in time, with recovery from alcoholism, I found food to be the solace that alcohol once

was to hide my sexual shame. So I had this odd fight going on of esteem-building in AA, yet I had this secretive sex life. Finally my growing esteem took me to Overeaters Anonymous (OA). Now where were my fixes? I couldn't hide from myself, and my sexual acting out was leaking everywhere. My dishonesty was challenged by the principles of the Twelve Step programs. That was when I finally got help for my sex addiction, and soon after I was in full-blown depression.

• • • • • • • •

Current research confirms that a vulnerability to depression is genetically inherited. Any person, given the right mix of chromosomes, will have a susceptibility to this disease. Major depression and bipolar disorder are the two forms of depression most likely linked to biology—a genetic history. Bipolar disorder is characterized not only by depressive symptoms, but by a switching between what are referred to as the poles of manic and depressive episodes. These episodes can vary in duration and intensity, depending on the person. Bipolar disorder has a specific link to sex addiction because one of the symptoms of bipolar disorder can be hypersexuality. Hypersexuality is the increased need, even pressure, for sexual gratification driven in part by the physical activation, heightened sensory and sexual interest, and risk taking that are often symptoms of mania for a person with bipolar disorder.

With the exception of bipolar disorder, in the majority of cases, biological vulnerability alone is not enough to bring about depression. Usually a combination of genetic susceptibility and psychological injury produces depression. Such psychological injury—especially physical or sexual abuse or being raised in extremely impaired family systems—is often seen in men who act out sexually. Many times the dominating source of impairment in his family was an addiction that created loss and modeled addictive behavior as a solution to pain or a source of power.

It is also possible the addict may experience dysthymia (low-grade, chronic depression) due to the shame he feels as he confronts his behavior and the sense of emptiness or hollowness that often accompanies the initial absence of his acting out. When diagnosed appropriately, depression of all types can be treated quite effectively with medication and/or psychotherapy.

As with multiple addictions, a strong diagnostic work-up in a treatment process is advisable to identify or rule out mental health issues that could interfere with and/or sabotage the recovery process. The most common issues are depression, anxiety, and post-traumatic stress symptoms, most often due to childhood abuse. This may seem overwhelming, but neither you nor your partner needs to carve the path of treatment, as a qualified sex addiction therapist will do this. With a desire and willingness to change, recovery is possible.

~~~~~~~~~~~~~~~~~

If you see a repetitive pattern to your partner's behavior, and if he continues his behaviors in spite of adverse consequences to himself, to you, and to his family, it is most likely this behavior needs to be addressed with a specific addiction focus and not just seen as a painful lapse in relationship fidelity or an innate perversion. There are emotional reasons for this acting out that ultimately lead to repetition and compulsivity, the inability to willfully control himself. Of course, these explanations don't excuse his behavior; what they do is contribute to understanding. It is also important to know that there is a path for treatment and healing.

Reflective Thoughts and Questions

• What did you learn in this chapter that helps you understand your partner's behavior?

• In what way does understanding the addictive nature of his behavior aid you in your recovery?

• Are you concerned about your partner having other addictions? Explain why.

• Are you concerned that he may have depression, anxiety, and/or other mental health issues? Explain why.

• What was important for you to hear in this chapter?

Chapter Four

You Didn't Get Here by Accident

Why does this feel so familiar?

What did I do to deserve this?

I$t's true. You didn't get here by accident; it is not coincidental that you are in a relationship with an addict. It probably feels familiar to you. Yet you don't deserve to be treated with disrespect.

How exactly did you get here, then, if not by accident? Influenced by both culture and family, your coaddictive behavior was well learned long before your partner came into your life. As much as the socialization and empowerment of women in Western industrialized culture has changed, women are still more apt to defer to men by giving them the benefit of the doubt, taking on false guilt, believing they need a man to be okay, and prioritizing his needs over their own. Women are taught to acquiesce, be polite, and refrain from showing anger. They often feel inadequate about their sexuality or have a distorted and shame-based body image.

Yet this socialization of women, by itself, is not the strongest factor in your coupling with a sex addict. Far more influential is your family history. While you may have not thought of your childhood as being significant to what is happening now, and while there are no perfect parents or perfect families, looking at family history and dynamics will be significant in your healing. It's critical to examine the beliefs you developed about yourself and others, the ways you learned to experience connection and/or protect yourself, and the behaviors that helped you to garner esteem.

The behaviors and belief systems of both coaddicts and sex addicts are strongly influenced by individual childhood experiences. For the cosa and the addict, it is common that one or both parents were addicts themselves, alcoholics or sex addicts in particular. It may not have been called *addiction,* but coaddicts and addicts often say their father was a womanizer, or their mother had lots of affairs or drank a lot, and so on. There may have been a history of extreme parental rigidity, strict all-or-nothing parental codes. Messages about sex were shaming or distorted, creating confusion for their children.

In essence, both the coaddict and addict were raised in very similar family systems in which they experienced a range of emotional and physical abandonment.

Abandonment

Physical abandonment means that a person's basic physical needs are not attended to consistently. A child looks to his parent for food, shelter, clothing, and appropriate supervision. Any time a child experiences physical and/or sexual abuse, that is physical abandonment. If you were not afforded the protection, the safety, and the security you needed to thrive, you experienced abandonment.

Emotional abandonment exists somewhere on the continuum of experience ranging from total acceptance to absolute rejection. When you feel that you have to hide major aspects of your being in order to be accepted or to protect yourself, this is abandonment. When you believe it is not physically or psychologically safe to make a mistake, to have your own needs, to have accomplishments, or to freely express the range of feelings that are part of the human experience, this is abandonment. If boundaries were lacking, permissive, too rigid, or otherwise seriously distorted, if you were expected to live out another person's dreams or to engage in peer-like relationships with those in the parental role, or if your parents' expectations were not age-appropriate, then you have experienced abandonment.

Physical or emotional abandonment is hurtful, painful, and traumatic to a child's development. Depending on the severity of abandonment, it can be disruptive to healthy self-esteem, your sense of worth and value, emotional maturity, and social and relational skills. In psychological terms this is regarded as *arrested development.* As a result of abandonment, what you see is that coaddicts and addicts can act out in similar, and at the same time very different, ways.

The Coaddict: Trauma Repetition

Kate has much in common with the other women sharing their stories in this book. She was raised in an alcoholic and violent family. She is divorced from two different alcoholic men, and is now married to an active sex addict. Her husband has had multiple relationships with other women and now he is flagrantly acting out in a manner that she cannot totally deny. She knows he visits pornographic bookstores, and on a recent visit he brought their four-year-old son with him. Yet she still has the ability to rationalize: *He is stressed by our two young children. He wouldn't do this if he wasn't on drugs.* She deliberately does not ask questions. If she doesn't ask, then it is as if she doesn't have to know. She doesn't ask for help because, as she says, "I just need him to stop." She doesn't assert any limits because her fear is that he will leave her. In ultimate desperation she finds herself left alone in a hotel room with a baby just a few weeks old and a four-year-old, no car, no food, and no money while he goes to get more drugs and meet up with a girlfriend; and she just wants him back.

Kate didn't get to this place overnight. Her childhood history was her training ground long before she entered any of her three addictive relationships. As with most partners of addicts, dysfunction ruled her original family. As a child, she learned to:

overlook (deny, rationalize, minimize) behavior that hurt her deeply

appear cheerful when she is hurting

make excuses for the hurtful behavior

avoid conflict to minimize further anger

tolerate inappropriate and hurtful behavior

prioritize the needs of others over her own needs

take care of others

fault herself for her family's problems

discount her own perceptions, giving others the benefit of the doubt

believe she has no options available

not ask for help

accommodate

Kate was reared to be the perfect candidate for partnering with an addict. A natural consequence of being raised in a shame-based family, very often an abusive or addictive family, is that the child grows up to be an ideal partner for an addict, one whose codependent traits enable him to act out his addiction with little disruption.

> [Addict] I look back now and know that my wife was the perfect partner for me to be able to have this other life. She always wanted to believe me. I controlled her with anger. She had been raised by a raging father, and then her stepfather sexually abused her. All I had to do was raise my voice and ask, "How can you doubt me after all I do for you? You should be grateful." I'd see the shift in her eyes and she would crumble. Then I'd switch to telling her everything was okay, telling her I really loved her, and acting like I forgave her for her suspicions.

. . . .

As each of Kate's husbands' addictions escalated, her fears of abandonment and rejection also escalated, driving her coaddictive behaviors. She became more compulsive in her busyness, which wasn't hard with two young children and a part-time job. If she kept busy enough, she didn't have to feel or see. If she was good enough, no one could find fault with her, nor would this husband ever want to leave her. The busier she got, the more depressed and anxious she became. Her esteem eroded; her neediness surged. Each marriage ended with her husband leaving. Their addictions became so severe they could not shoulder any responsibility. The divorces simply reinforced Kate's feeling that she was flawed in some fundamental way.

While the names change, the stories of repetitively partnering with an addict are common and span generations. What Kate and other coaddicts experience is referred to as *trauma repetition*. Although Kate repeated it many times in her own life, others simply repeat it generationally. Trauma repetition means you create behaviors and situations similar to those you experienced earlier in life. You are reliving a story out of your painful history. When you find yourself in the same situation with the same type of person over and over again, you seldom link the behavior to your original betrayal and trauma. Reenactment is living in the irreconcilable past. You may have been raised with addiction in your household and may even have that knowledge, but that doesn't necessarily keep you from marrying addictive and/or abusive men. Replaying your past trauma is often repeating what you know, the familiar, or what you believe you deserve. It may be an attempt to change the outcome of an old family script. Patrick Carnes, in *The Betrayal Bond,* summarizes trauma repetition as characterized "by 1) doing something self-destructive over and over again, usually something that took place in childhood and started with a trauma; 2) reliving a 'story' from the past, 3) engaging in abusive relationships repeatedly, 4) repeating painful experiences, including specific behaviors, scenes, persons and feelings."[1] Ultimately, it is as futile as attempting to survive the sinking *Titanic* by repeatedly changing your seat as the ship is going down.

Sara also has a history of repetitively changing alcoholic and/or sex-addicted partners, repeating her generational family patterns. Yet by recognizing her trauma repetition, by claiming her inner voice and embracing acts of recovery, she let go of her role of family savior and moved on with the business of changing her life.

[*Sara*] **My life has been riddled with the horror of addiction. My father committed suicide when I was only a year old. My mother had just left him due to his "womanizing" (that's what they called it back then). Today we know it as sex addiction. My Irish family was filled with alcoholics and sex addicts. I stayed with my aunts until my mother remarried when I was five. I began believing early that if I could just keep the peace, protect my cousins, stop the depression, everyone would be happy, and then I would be safe. This illusion of control grew throughout my life, and I would repeat my family's history over and over. My idea of an attractive man was my uncle, a hard-drinking, raging, handsome woman-chaser. Over the years I realized I didn't have a chance. I was attracted to the image burned into my little psyche long ago. Over and over, unconsciously, I would try to solve the problem, fix history, and create a new ending. In a way, I realized that I used sex addicts in much the same way they used me to re-create our family history. I just added a new twist: change the ending by** just being better, explaining the hurt effectively, and magically transforming the outcome for us and our families. What grandiosity!

. . . .

Like other Women of the Lodge, the following coaddict readily identifies with the analogy of changing seats on the *Titanic* as it is sinking. She found that by recognizing a need to "fill herself up from the inside with greater esteem and skills" that there was a lifeboat available to her.

[Coaddict] My boyfriend and I broke up after a few years of his acting out. He was never willing to get help. I spent those years trying to be the person I thought he needed or wanted me to be. I did a lot of things that I regret today. When I left, I simply wanted out—I was running. Then I ran right into another one of him. He looked different on the outside, but within a few months I found out I was just one of his harem. Funny how things happen, but I was seeing things in magazines, on talk shows, and on other television shows about women who repeat their relationships time after time with different guys. I know I had heard this before, but somehow I heard it differently. I guess I was ready. So I threw myself into lots of self-help reading. You would have thought the authors knew me firsthand. It helped me not feel so stupid. I knew I wasn't alone. I have a lot of girlfriends like me. But I thought all this time it was the guys who were bad and we were just stupid. Well, I am not stupid. I have made mistakes but I have come to realize I didn't know how to do it differently, and I had a lot I could work on that would lead me in a different path. So I set about learning how to trust myself. Figuring out what made me feel good in life. I developed my own interests so I wasn't just attaching myself to someone else. To do this I had to be willing to not date. That actually was a relief. And then one day I realized I wasn't going to hang on

to my resentments, I didn't need them; my life wasn't
about these guys, it was about me. Funny how once I
took the focus off them, suddenly I knew in my heart
they weren't bad guys. They maybe did or didn't love me
along the way, but they didn't know how to love me or
how to do it in a healthy way. I found forgiveness for me
and for them. But that doesn't mean I have to live with
or marry them.

. . . .

Perhaps you have entered into a relationship with someone who has the
same addiction as your parent, but because you were so young when your
parent was in the early stages of addiction you have no distinct recall of it.
People often don't realize that there are early, middle, and late stages to
addictive disorders. Because of this, women often don't see the similarities
between a partner's addiction and a parent's addiction because they were in
different stages. Or maybe, like many women, you are so focused on making
sure you don't end up with a partner like your alcoholic or drug-addicted
father, that you are ever-vigilant to look for someone who appears to drink
responsibly or who doesn't drink or use drugs at all, that you end up ignoring the signs of other addictive behavior.

[Coaddict] My father was a raging alcoholic. No one in my
family ever spoke up to him; we lived in fear of speaking
up, and yet when he handed out favors, I was his favorite.
I was hungry for his attention, hungry for his approval.
And it was the setup for a perfect match for the sex
addict, really any kind of addict. But I was so busy making sure it was not someone who looked out of control,
like my father with his drinking and rage, so I was looking for the "class president" and in doing so, not realizing
I was simply a magnet for another kind of addiction. I was
the perfect match for the high-achieving, professionally
visible sex addict. For over thirty-four years I was obsessed
with my husband's behavior. My whole existence was in
attempting to know the details of where he was, when,

and with whom. In that time I managed to raise three children, and today my middle daughter is repeating my marriage exactly. I shouldn't be surprised at this, as I had repeated my mother's marriage, with a slight variation, and as I look at my family history, I see that she repeated her mother's marriage.

. . . .

This repetition has long been recognized as expressed in the following quote: "The gods visit the sins of the fathers upon the children."[2]

[Vanessa] Much of my recovery work has taken me back to my childhood. I have had to repeatedly work through the core belief that I am not good enough. I was the reason my parents got married; they had to—a sad beginning for an unwanted baby entering a loveless marriage. To compound the situation, I was supposed to be a boy to take over the family business. I carried an anti-female stigma with me most of my life. Even my gender wasn't good enough. Both of my parents were work addicts. My dad was rarely home, leaving before I woke up and home long after I went to bed. When he was home, either he was raging and belittling my sister and me or eerily quiet. My mother seemed to have little time for nurturing. On the outside we were a typical religious family and strictly admonished to ensure the world believed that. Clearly we operated with the theme: Don't talk. Don't talk about any problems or feelings you might have. If you can't say anything nice, don't say it at all. Do what you're told. And most important, never talk outside of home. We didn't air our dirty laundry, whatever it was. Combine that with the idea that we were only to show good feelings, which of course meant to suppress anything that wasn't a happy face. Don't feel. My sister and I were highly disciplined, smiling, perfect little girls. I took that discipline into my adult life and became a party girl/work addict. And who

would I choose for a partner? Not a rager, not a worka-
holic, but another type of addict.

. . . .

Perhaps you are aware of your partner's behavior but have impoverished
expectations due to low self-esteem wherein you don't expect more out of
life. You see yourself as a survivor; you believe you can tolerate and handle
things.

> [Coaddict] I've had two husbands who left me after years
> of my putting up with both of them having multiple affairs,
> from one-night stands to longstanding girlfriends. It never
> dawned on me to leave or that I could confront them or
> ask for anything different. I felt so poorly about myself. I
> allowed myself to be degraded and belittled, all the while
> projecting this false bravado of being tough. I acted like a
> victim-martyr, and all it did was fuel my depression.

. . . .

Dysfunction in families occurs along a continuum. You do not have to
be raised with addiction to partner with addiction as an adult. Abuse, addiction, and mental illness are blatant sources of dysfunction; their common
denominator is loss—loss of nurturing and safety. Within other types of
families, loss certainly exists but is more subtle, such as in families where the
parenting and relational styles are rigid or too permissive. Families that are
highly enmeshed, and those with severe relational disconnection, also fuel
codependent behaviors. Many women strongly believe they were raised in
healthy families, but as they are confronted with their coaddiction, they
come to recognize how aspects of their growing-up years may be impact-
ing their coping strategies today. This is not about blame but about recognizing generational influences that will help you focus on your recovery
needs.

> [Coaddict] My being so powerless in my marriage came
> from a long history of being powerless. I was raised with
> two older brothers and I was the baby. I had a very

emotionally neglectful home. It looked good on the outside, and my parents looked loving, available, and responsible. However, in actuality, they were emotionally absent
and emotionally neglectful. They never taught me about
the outside world. I was sheltered from reality, very naive
and sexually shamed. What I mean by this is that it was
immature or shameful to have normal romantic longing.
As an adolescent, I remember them making fun of my
friends who had crushes on boys or who had posters
of male actors, athletes, or music stars on their walls at
home. Or if a couple was being affectionate in public
they would say something like, "Look at those two, they
ought to be ashamed of themselves!" or "Don't they
know better?" or "They must have been raised in a barn."
The implication was that no civilized, educated person had
romantic or sexual longings. I never saw affection or any
sexual energy between my parents. The only thing they
would show was a bird peck kiss on the lips as my dad
would leave for work. I remember thinking it looked
strained and like neither one of them really enjoyed it,
but it was the thing to do. So I learned from this that sex
was bad and that it was only to have children. I learned to
be ashamed of and afraid of my own longings for intimacy
and sexuality. I felt like I was always on stage with my
parents, and I learned to act like I was on stage with
everyone that I knew.

. . . .

Prior to her marriage, this coaddict had already internalized an overwhelming sense of helplessness, a sense of defeat. She had also learned the
art of *image management*—how not to be real or authentic but to be "on
stage" and in character. The negative messages she inherited about sex and
sexuality set her up for confusion and self-doubt about healthy sexuality
and poor sexual esteem in her marriage. Coupled with her overall low self-
esteem, she was easily exploited by her sexually compulsive husband.

Therese, like the previous coaddict, was raised in a family who failed to acknowledge her sexuality or curiosity. As a coaddict, she internalized sexual shame because she didn't learn healthy expressions of sexuality or acknowledgment of it. "It was shameful to have romantic longings. Affection was perceived as disgusting." Image was also very important in her household, which meant she had no opportunity to learn how to deal with conflict, times of fear, and uncertainty.

> [Therese] My friends thought my family was the best and always wanted to be at my house. Our house was safe and full of good feelings; only good feelings. What a distortion of reality. Anything that was contrary to good feelings only had a short life before it was ousted or pushed underground, never to be acknowledged again. There was total dismissal of the struggles a girl could have as a teenager and I couldn't be anything but fine or great. Anything else just didn't go with the image.
>
> When my husband first acted out, I felt like I couldn't tell anyone. Who would I tell? I was so ashamed. I couldn't risk breaking the image that everyone had of me and our marriage. I was so emotionally isolated that I didn't tell my closest and only girlfriend. I kept it buried inside of me. I felt like my husband's need for pornography and other women implied that I was not good enough for him. To compensate and cope with my growing feelings of unworthiness, I lost track of myself and became what anyone else wanted. I began to drown in my worry, fear, and shame.

· · · · · · · ·

Like many cosas, Therese grew up in a family that taught her that only good feelings were acceptable. She got the message that she was to defer to others and give them the benefit of the doubt over herself—that other people's needs were more important than hers. In her family she did not learn conflict resolution skills, therefore had little modeling for healthy communication, and because the focus was on image or outcome, she didn't learn about being intimate and chose a partner with similar traits.

For the sake of not being alone, you have accepted or found ways to deny the painful reality of being in an active-addicted relationship. You have allowed yourself to be in this relationship because to be alone taps into your feeling of abandonment, which translates into the pain that comes with the belief that you are not worthy, not of value. Whatever the influences, this is the time not to be judgmental but to empathize with yourself. There are reasons you got where you are. Typically you get to this place from an original family script. Without recovery from childhood wounding, you don't have the relational skills or internalized beliefs to make different choices. Today there is a path from which you can let go of your self-defeating thoughts and behaviors. You can actualize a stronger sense of self based on esteem. But it means you have to act, not react.

Sexual Messages

Both coaddicts and addicts frequently received unhealthy messages about sexuality when they were children. It is very common for one or the other of them to have experienced sexual abuse. Some experienced overt, blatant incest or molestation. It is from this experience that children can come to believe that sex is what you do to be lovable or to gain attention, or it's the only way they know to experience power or control and avoid victimization. The abuse can also fuel conflicting feelings, ranging from guilt and shame to fear and excitement about sexuality.

The sexual abuse may have been more covert or subtle. Some children were never touched inappropriately themselves, but they may have witnessed adult sexual activities, or were subjected to repeated comments about their bodies or their sexual development, or were exposed to pornography. Home may have been a highly charged sexual atmosphere with sexually explicit jokes, sexualized clothing, or frequent sexual innuendos. A sexually restricted family where children are taught that sex is bad, dirty, or disgusting is unhealthy as well. These children don't know what healthy sexuality is. Families where sexual boundaries are distorted or nonexistent are a breeding ground for people who will eventually act out sexually and those who will partner with them. In these situations, children are abandoned and violated, and they learn how to deny pain.

[Coaddict] I was sexually abused by my stepfather for several years. I didn't tell anyone. By the time I was a teenager, I was proud of my ability to get any guy into bed. I just wanted their attention, and I felt that was the way to get it. To me it meant being noticed, not discarded. In time it became my source of power. I got this warped sense of esteem from my promiscuity. I have had to grapple with my own sexual compulsivity as I have had to grapple with my co-sex addiction. Because I have had so much shame around my own previous behavior, it has been hard for me to think I was worthy of asking for more in a relationship. But I am learning I deserve more than abuse and addiction in my life.

[Jacque] I was abused by my older brother for several years when I was only a small child. He would come into my bedroom late at night and literally threaten my life, sometimes with a gun, if I didn't do what he wanted. I was a sex toy for him. By late adolescence, I felt so degraded and worthless I set out to prove I was of value. I'd go to bars, flirt, drink, and see how many guys I could attract. It was a vicious cycle because in the moment I would feel invincible yet it ultimately only eroded what little esteem I had. In many ways, by participating in my husband's sexual fantasies I was repeating my cycle of thinking it made me desirable to him, yet feeling humiliated for myself. I was now an adult allowing myself to be victimized. I have struggled a lot with signs of post-traumatic stress, particularly with an inability to manage my emotions. My fear and anxiety only fueled greater victimization because I was too frightened to set boundaries and didn't think I was worthy of having them. I'd often use alcohol to numb myself. My recovery as a sexual abuse survivor actually began prior to my knowing that I was dealing with sex addiction.

[Jenny] I know now that I had been objectified as a child by my dad. There was no overt sexual abuse by him but there was covert sexualization just by the feelings that I got when I would wear a dress. I didn't like those feelings so I continued to want to be a boy. By being a tomboy I could get my dad's attention and affection, but as a "pretty girl" I felt that he was uncomfortable with me. At about age twelve I discovered some pornography in my parents' bedroom. I remember feeling afraid and somehow dirty. I think of my family life as abusive from the standpoint that it was sexually neglectful. No one ever talked about sex, and it was taboo. The only education I even got about my own body and reproductive system was at school in the sixth grade, and I was so ashamed during the class that I couldn't really listen or learn. Everything about my body—sexual feelings, romantic desires, and even menstruation—was shameful and had to be denied at any cost. I believe these things are a part of my history that set me up to tolerate my partner's sexual acting out and to be abused sexually by him.

. . . .

When the only way you are validated by a significant other who is supposed to love you is through sex, you can develop a twisted belief that sex is love. It can set you up for your own sexual acting out and/or be the reason that you are attracted to a man who acts out sexually, allowing you to be exploited by him. Jacque, who was sexually abused by her brother for four to six years while growing up, resumed her role as a sexual victim in her adult life. She agreed to participate in some of her husband's addictive behavior such as performing sexually at a club. She struggled with honoring herself and her desire not to participate, but she craved validation from her husband. Many cosas feel ashamed about what they have willingly engaged in sexually to placate a partner. Women such as Jenny struggle with any sense of what feels good to them sexually, as sex is not okay—it is simply an act they engage in, hoping for love.

To grow up with addiction and/or sexual abuse means you learned to distrust your own perceptions. As children share their thoughts with adults, they are frequently discounted and so they spend their entire lives doubting the truth of their own experiences and pretending they were never hurt. They stop trusting their own intuition or their own version of reality. That is as damaging as the violation itself and certainly is coaddiction in the making.

When both addiction and sex abuse occur during childhood, dysfunctional beliefs and needed defenses—such as not talking about your feelings, not trusting others, not asking for help, and so on—are doubly reinforced. For example, if you are raised in a situation where there is either addiction or abuse, you will have difficulty trusting others. But if you are raised in a situation where both occur, you will have even greater difficulty trusting others, as there is a synergistic effect. One plus one does not equal two; now it equals three. Those raised in households with either addiction or abuse will have a high tolerance for inappropriate behavior. Those raised in households with both addiction and abuse will have an even higher tolerance for inappropriate and hurtful behavior. Clearly it is hurtful to be raised with addiction and/or abuse; when they coexist, the negative consequences reinforce each other.

Covert sexual abuse such as drunken nudity, sexual name calling, or the lack of appropriate sexual information during childhood can cause sexual shame during adulthood. Overt sexual abuse such as molestation is a much stronger betrayal and violation and a far greater emotional, physical, and spiritual injustice. A cosa with this experience is more likely to 1) dissociate (separating emotions from thoughts as if existing outside her physical being and controlling her actions by remote control); 2) regard sex as a form of control and power; 3) equate sex with love; 4) view sexuality as the primary source of his or her identity.

As the addict often has underlying and co-occurring problems of depression and anxiety, partners often enter the relationship with undiagnosed major depression or dysthymia (low-grade, chronic depression), anxiety, and/or post-traumatic stress disorder. The likelihood that you entered your relationship with these issues is high if you were raised in a shame-based, addictive, and/or verbally, physically, or sexually abusive family system. If you entered your relationship with depression, low self-esteem, self-defeating thoughts, and/or shame-based defenses, it creates an environment in which the addict is safe to maintain his secret double life without being caught or held accountable.

Your first efforts in understanding your coaddiction and addiction begin with exploring the dynamics in the family in which you were raised. For many, the roots of addiction may in fact span generations. It is essential to look back at your early life and identify the critical experiences that shaped you. This is the beginning of the road to your healing. Consider these questions:

- What words would you use to describe your family when you were growing up?
- What messages did you get about having needs? How has that been hurtful or helpful to you?
- Was it okay for you to express your opinions?
- What messages were you given about being female? How has that been hurtful or helpful to you?
- What messages did you receive about being sexual? How has that been hurtful or helpful to you?
- How have those messages influenced your present-day situation?
- How would you describe the use of alcohol or other drugs in your family?
- Are you aware of any family history of physical or sexual abuse?
- What addictive or abusive behaviors are you aware of generationally?
- How do you think your family dynamic has contributed to your being in a relationship with an addict?

The Addict: Reenacting the Wound

As recovering sex addicts review their histories, many recognize they come from strongly impaired family systems, families impacted by various addictive disorders and forms of mental illnesses. Situations of physical and sexual violence are extremely common. Often these boys had emotionally unavailable fathers and highly enmeshed relationships with their mothers. With their dysfunctional histories, these are very emotionally wounded boys who learn to project to the world one persona but act out another.

Just as the coaddict often identifies with trauma repetition, so too does the addict. But the addict also perpetuates the affront to him. This means that in addition to reliving a story from the past, continuing to engage in self-destructive behaviors over and over, and repeating painful experiences, addicts often do to others what they experienced as an early life trauma. Maureen Canning, author of *Lust, Anger, Love,* writes, "All sexual acting out is motivated by feelings of shame and manifested in acts and feelings of anger."[3] They are men (and women) who have become the perpetrators of their own pain and of the pain of others.

> [Addict] **By the time I was thirteen I was so angry I wanted to scream, but I had no way to do that. What do you do with that anger when you're just a kid? I was angry about life in general—too many divorces by my parents, too many moves, total neglect by my father, and rage from my stepfather. My mom loved me but she was too caught up in her life to know how to cope with my problems at school or my depression. My first way to "scream" was by skipping school, and then I found porn on the Internet. My hormones were starting to rage, sex became the answer to my pain and anger, and I was on my way.**

· · · · · · · ·

In the movie *Prince of Tides,* the character played by Nick Nolte says, "I don't know when my parents began their war against each other, but I know the only prisoners they took were their children. When we needed to escape we developed a ritual, we found a silent soothing world, a world of no pain." For many, this is what addiction is about: a silent soothing world, a world of no pain. A world of disconnection—kindled by fear and shame, often rooted in trauma.

> [Addict] **At age eleven I had a hole in my gut that was so big only alcohol and drugs would fill it up. It would become my answer—my solution—and I would get blithering numb. Then I found masturbation and pornography,**

and they took me to another realm. For a moment all I knew was my escape from feeling unwanted and unloved. Now I needed no one. I had me.

[Addict] Masturbation was a form of escape and solace when I was just a young boy. I'd often take myself to an open lot down the alley from our house and spend my time alone, fantasizing and masturbating. It was actually in that lot where I found my first pornography. The sexual pleasure of pornography and masturbating made a powerful tie when I was anxious, stressed, and scared. My mother was very domineering and volatile. She disciplined in anger, physically, with belts. Dad took the path of least resistance. He left us kids to take the explosion. He was very demanding, though, with high expectations. He pushed us hard in sports and academics. Because we were physically small, he pushed us even harder to be the best. I'd use masturbation to wake up in the morning, as an eye opener. It got me up and moving. It was a way for me to calm myself and to go to sleep when I was anxious. As I got older I'd also use sex as a reward. I would tell myself I was entitled, that my behavior didn't hurt anyone else. Pretty crazy thinking, but it had become a predominant source of reward, way to relax, and a boost of esteem. It quickly became my answer to fear. I was just this overgrown, scared, terrified little boy inside.

. . . .

Strongly influenced by his childhood history, an addict uses his sexuality to meet different needs. Pleasurable feelings of sexuality were perhaps the only relief he ever knew during childhood. Sex was his escape, a mood-altering experience. As he grew up, sex continued to be a means of coping with stress. Early on, the addict learned to use fantasy and arousal to stabilize his mood temporarily or to avoid anxiety. Later, as he discovered sexual pleasure, fantasy served an even more powerful and distracting role, and the addict began to lose himself in it in a way that characterizes sexual acting out. When an addict begins to feel something painful, he uses sex as a way to medicate that pain. Even fantasizing without personal physical contact can be soothing to a sex addict.

When stressed by any difficult situation (whether it is work, family, money, or loneliness), addicts turn to using an external substance or engaging in an addictive behavior to distract them from what feels like an uncontrollable internal experience. Uncomfortable with and most often afraid of their feelings, they tend to be emotionally reactive. Simply put, addicts use sex, food, gambling, alcohol, drugs, spending, and other stimulating or numbing combinations in an attempt to feel better and gain control over their feelings.

Addicts, frightened of the depth and intensity of feelings they have been suppressing for years, will go to any length to avoid vulnerability. They engage in distorted thinking, which is termed *cognitive distortion*. Examples of distorted thinking are seeing things from an all-or-nothing perspective, difficulty perceiving options or choices, catastrophizing (seeing only the worst of outcomes), operating from shoulds, and creating unrealistic expectations that only set themselves and others up for failure. The nature of distorted thinking creates further stress and painful feelings. To deal with this, addicts use the intense, familiar feelings provoked by sexual fantasy and sexual behavior to feel in control of deeper emotions, to feel power when they are feeling vulnerable, and to feel desirable when they are feeling needful. Many of their behaviors take advantage of somebody else's vulnerability or victimizing through intrusion or the use of power.

Escape, mood alteration, and validation are not the only reasons certain behaviors become addictive. Sometimes behaviors are used as a reward. Sex addicts do not usually have a healthy sense of how to reward themselves. Whether it comes from a core belief in their unworthiness or their entitlement, they have a belief system that others will not take care of them and they must do everything for themselves. That builds up resentments. Their resentments can be expressed in a sense of entitlement: *I deserve*. Whether it follows surviving stressful events, performing well, or doing a good job, sex addicts may believe that they deserve to be rewarded, and sex is the manner in which they can do that for themselves.

[Addict] I was so full of resentments and I took them into all of my relationships. I had been beat up a lot by my father and watched him beat my mom. Nothing I ever did was okay. By my mid-twenties I was into full-blown sex addiction with chronic masturbation, pornography, and escorts. As I'd get a new girlfriend I'd try not to do those things. I always hinted that those things were a part of my past, never sharing the whole picture. I think I did that so that I could say I didn't lie when she eventually found out what I was doing. As much as it's possible for me to get outside of always thinking about just myself, I'd say I'm in love with my present girlfriend. But it's been only a few months and I'm already rationalizing that I deserve my fix. Those lifelong resentments only stay down so long, and I find that they sprout up like weeds in the cracks of a sidewalk. I use her like a balm, but no salve will take care of my anger. As painful as my life is, losing one loving woman after another because of my infidelities, it's too overwhelming for me to address my trauma history. So again I juggle hiding my secret life, and I can hear myself rationalizing how it is that I'm entitled and deserving of doing what I want when I want without having to think of anyone else.

· · · · · · · ·

Shared Codependency

How is it that some of these children act out sexually when they grow up and others don't? How is it that some become addicts and others become coaddicts? Many factors influence the way children develop. The most apparent is the socialization process that directs males more toward *acting-out* behaviors such as rage, substance abuse, and behavioral addictions (intensity and arousal behaviors), and females toward *acting-in* behaviors such as being nice, being tolerant, and not questioning others. When they feel overwhelmed, girls tend to respond by acting in through depression, anxiety, eating disorders, or sedating-type addictions, such as alcoholism or prescription pain pills. Men are much more apt to be culturally influenced to find a (false) sense of empowerment and esteem in their sexual prowess. Women are socialized to be timid and reserved in their sexual feelings and thoughts. Certainly this stereotyping is not always accurate; many women sexually act out in highly compulsive and self-defeating ways. And there are many men in coupleship with women sex addicts. But generally speaking, our culture has done much to influence who and how someone *acts out* or *acts in*. Many times people display both types of behavior. As you are considering whether any of your behaviors could also be addictive, know that addicts most often have significant underlying codependency traits. Addiction and coaddiction are fueled by similar histories; they frequently coexist.

Codependency traits common to both the coaddict and addict include:

>   need for outside approval
>   fear of rejection and abandonment
>   inability to identify and ask for what you need
>   fear of conflict
>   feelings of inadequacy
>   inability to identify and express a wide range of feelings
>   shame-bound defenses, such as controlling, procrastination, victimhood,
>   and so on
>   fear of specific feelings
>   adherence to rigidly ascribed roles learned in impaired family

[Addict] I was so afraid of conflict. I was the peacekeeper type of guy. Peace at all costs—peace at work, peace with my wife—and I always felt inadequate, like I was never good enough. But I had my secrets. I would pay for women to do whatever I wanted. A lot of the time I had no expectations from them, I just wanted their attention. I wasn't scared, and it was easier for me to perform sexually because they were strangers; they didn't need anything from me.

. . . .

A household in which family members internalize their shame-based beliefs frequently trains a child to seek the approval of others, an approval he cannot give himself. Because of this the child becomes dependent on the positive response and praise of others to feel good about who he is. Both addicts and coaddicts seek what is called *outer esteem,* which is esteem through others. They have not learned to internalize self-worth and value so they are in a perpetual state of looking for affirmation and validation. While women tend to seek outer esteem through their people pleasing, image management, and relationships, the sex addict comes to believe the only way to feel approval is through sexual activity. How much sex he scores, how many secrets he can get away with, how large his pornography collection is, how great he looks, and how much attention he can solicit— all are delusional ways to temporarily fill the emotional void.

The following story illustrates more fully the duality of codependency and addiction for a sex addict.

[Addict] By the time I was a teenager I was really angry, quietly angry. No matter what I did, the message I got from my father was that I wasn't good enough, and my mom was like a ghost: emotionally and mentally nonexistent. My father would rage at us kids and Mom would have this look on her face as if it was just something interesting. I would get violent spankings from my father. I was an impressionable kid who, like most kids, just wanted to be loved.

Today I am quite sure my father had affairs. People have told me they saw him with other women. And one person told me that when we were kids she saw an article about him being arrested for something of a sexual nature. My dad was abandoned young and had to go to work to support himself. He had a strong work ethic, and that was a positive trait I got from him. Mostly I feared him and our relationship was very poor due to his outbursts of temper, being unpredictable, and periodically drinking too much. My mom was so codependent; she never knew what she wanted and would never directly make a statement. She was emotionally disconnected but she was my confidant, as I was hers.

We had our share of family secrets too. I didn't even know my paternal grandfather was alive until I was an adult and found out he had been locked away in a state mental institution for years due to wet brain, being a town drunk.

My primary belief of thinking I was not good enough fueled my addictions, but I was also strongly influenced by a neighbor girl. When she was about twelve and I was nine or ten, she wanted to be sexual with me, but I was physically too young and couldn't. She was emotionally dominating, demanding, and intimidating, both sexually and physically. Looking back, I suspect she was being sexually abused because her knowledge of sex was too sophisticated for her age. Because of her, I didn't engage sexually with girls until I was older. I was always scared of them.

In college I was still scared of women and I let them be the pursuers. After a few sexual experiences, I found that the conquest gave me a sense of power and acceptance. But I had such a distorted perception about what women wanted or needed. My mother certainly didn't give me any positive direction, and my father only spoke of women in negative terms: "You marry the good girls and have sex with the bad girls."

. . . .

From a young age this sex addict had a strong foundation for sexual addiction and codependency. Sex allowed him to ignore his pain; it provided a high and temporarily allowed him to feel important and valued. It was difficult for him to give it up because it had become his coping strategy. Sex kept him from drowning emotionally, and it was a quick fix.

He experienced emotional abandonment from a very frightened boundary-less, codependent mother and an abusive father who acted out with alcohol and sex. Secrecy and addiction were multi-generational issues in his family. The way he describes his mother as codependent is the same way that he describes himself. He learned to not ask for what he wanted or needed and became conflict avoidant. He constantly sought outside approval with a strong need to look good. While treated for sex addiction, his codependency had to be addressed, as it would be a significant relapse trigger.

Compartmentalizing

The highly developed defense of compartmentalizing, used by both addicts and their partners, is strongly influenced by childhood history. In our humanness we all compartmentalize, that is we set aside feelings and thoughts about one moment while we are engaged in another. For example, if you have an argument with your teenage daughter prior to going to work, you may feel upset and think about it while you commute to your job. But when you walk through the door of your office, you mentally put it aside because you have work issues to attend to. We all do that and need to do it. But people who are raised with fear and shame practice the art of compartmentalizing more frequently, and its use is fueled from a place of greater need, often stemming from fear. It begins as a necessary defense but it becomes a skill that is practiced day in and day out, week in and week out, month after month, year after year. You can easily become masterful in the ability to live in two different worlds, or compartments, simultaneously.

Compartmentalizing starts at a young age. For example, you may listen to your parents argue night after night, but when you go to school the next day you act as if everything is fine; or you listen to your father molest your sister but you pretend it is not happening. Perhaps your mother told you how worthless you are, or you wonder why your father doesn't come home. How can you possibly talk to someone about these things? It's too painful. No one knows what your internal personal life is like, or your thoughts or feelings. You learn the dysfunctional family rules: don't talk, don't feel, don't ask. While everyone compartmentalizes to some degree, it becomes a large part of emotional survivorship when you are raised in an

environment of chronic loss, fear, and chaos. This ability to compartmentalize can set up many men to lead highly secretive, compartmentalized
lives. It is a learned skill that enables this particular addiction.

> [Addict] I was very skilled at living in two worlds, or
> even three—home, work, and my outside world of sex.
> They were different compartments of my life that were
> never to meet. I was masterful at lying and simply couldn't
> allow myself to think about my work colleagues or wife
> finding out about my secret life. Since I was a kid I've
> been skilled at living in different worlds; I lived with
> terror at home, so I'd escape into my sexual fantasies,
> and then find relief at school. So it came easy. As I said,
> I was skilled.

> [Addict] Each day as I left my family home and went
> into the day, it was as if I crossed an invisible line. I didn't
> think twice about how what I was doing would affect my
> family life. I truly didn't think about it.

. . . .

Such thinking on the part of the addict may be difficult to understand.
His inability to empathize with your situation is a testament to the darkness and pervasiveness of addiction. It is also just as possible that as the
addict has compartmentalized unsparingly, so have you.

> [Jacque] As a young girl, I learned how to compartmen-
> talize, keeping my sex abuse in a box, separate from the
> rest of my world. I'd tell myself this can't be happening
> to me, or this doesn't really matter, or it doesn't bother
> me. That's exactly what I would do around my husband's
> addiction. As a child, I found that school was a wonderful
> source of validation. As an adult, I've found that validation
> through work. Throwing myself into school and/or work
> helped me to stay separate from the pain and confusion in
> my life.

[Therese] I am so compartmentalized! Having kids helps—
they keep me so busy. I dive into the Mom role. I think
in some ways compartmentalizing has kept me from going
crazy, but in the long run it allowed me to ignore what
was happening in my marriage. Because I had no direction as to what to do about my situation, facing reality
was too much. So like recipes clipped from a magazine, I
filed the truth away as if I planned to get back to it later.

. . . .

As a coaddict, you project to the world one image while internally living
another, a well-developed habit you use to bury your head in the sand and
pretend that everything is fine while the house burns down around you.
While we all compartmentalize in the course of a day, this severe and
chronic form of compartmentalizing supports you in the denial process.

~~~~~~~~~~~~~~~~

Just as the addict in recovery needs to address the addictive nature of his
behavior and learn how to get his needs met without being intrusive or
exploitive of another person, both the coaddict and the addict need to
examine how their belief systems, their emotional defenses, and their
childhood wounding contribute to this relationship. As you do that, your
relationship has the opportunity to be one of choice rather than a relationship of script, repetition, or traumatic bonding. In this process you
both learn how to develop empathy and compassion toward self and others.
You learn how to develop healthy boundaries, greater emotional literacy,
and the ability to handle your feelings without the need to engage in self-
defeating behaviors.

Whether or not you have a lifelong commitment or are attracting the
same man over and over, recognizing your pattern of how you choose a
partner and contribute to the dance is critical to your ability to make
healthy relationship decisions for yourself.

Reflective Thoughts and Questions

- Underline or highlight the parts of the stories with which you identify.

- In what ways did you experience abandonment in your childhood?

- To what degree have you engaged in trauma repetition? Explain.

- In what ways has abandonment influenced your behavior in your relationship(s)?

- What sexual messages did you hear growing up? Completing the following sentences may help.

   Sex means . . .

   I have the right to . . . (regarding sex)

   I don't have the right to . . . (regarding sex)

- What do you know about your partner's family history that may have contributed to his sexual acting out?

- What was important for you to hear in this chapter?

Chapter Five

Learning the News

What should I do? Do I want to know everything?

How can I show my face to those who may know?

How can I ever trust again?

Women learn about their partners' sexual acting out in a variety of ways. Perhaps you heard about your partner's behavior from a coworker, a friend, a neighbor, or a family member. It's possible someone told you inadvertently and didn't even realize what they said. Or perhaps the person knew full well what he or she was saying and did it out of respect for you. It could be that someone shared the information out of vindictiveness. You may have read about your partner's activities in the newspaper or seen him on television. Perhaps the police came to your door to take him away. His angry lover may have called and left a message or sent you a letter and/or pictures. It is possible you happened upon your partner with his lover. You may have inadvertently found Internet sex sites he bookmarked on the computer. Maybe he went to a treatment program for his addiction to gambling or drugs or alcohol and you suddenly found yourself sitting in a counselor's office, surprised to be learning about his sexual acting out. It's possible your child told you about something he or she saw. Sometimes women visit their doctor and learn they have a sexually transmitted disease. This news, whatever the setting or form of delivery, can be a bombshell. It can also be no more than a validation of what you've been suspecting.

[Coaddict] **The first time I learned he was acting out I had gone to his office after work with my baby in my** arms just to see him. I had no idea I would find him in a compromised position with someone at work. I was numb. They laughed at me. I stayed with him several more years and had two more kids. He would never admit openly to what he was doing but I found the evidence: the hotel slips, the letters. At the time I didn't think of it as an addiction, only betrayal.

[Coaddict] My husband had been in some intensive psychotherapy, and after one of his therapy retreats he came home an emotional mess and disclosed he was a sex addict. He told me it was a one-time ongoing affair with someone out of state. He told me it was over, and that was all that was said. Well, I had a history of sex abuse as a child and to use the word "sex addict" was so scary. Sex addict, sex abuser, sexual molester—were they all one and the same? I didn't know what to think, so I focused on what he said about this affair being over and I thought, "Good, it's over with," and locked it up in some mental container in my head to not think about it. But what I did not know for a long time was he was acting out more and more.

[Coaddict] Because I was suspicious, I went searching for proof and found his journal, which was the darkest day of my life. I read about affairs that had been going on for years, for one night, one hour, several months, and multiple affairs at the same time. I thought I would die. I actually thought about suicide. I was overwhelmed and wanted a divorce. He went to treatment. I didn't hear any additional information. I really got it all in his journal so there was nothing more to add. As hard as it is to know—and I did need to know, to get to where we are today—that was not the way to find out. I wish it had been a structured therapeutic disclosure.

. . . .

When you first hear the news, you may only take in a piece of the whole picture. It's likely that even if you are aware of the severity of the acting out, you may not view it as an addiction from which one recovers, but more like something that men just do. You may believe if the man feels guilty enough, he will just stop. Your response may be one of shame, guilt, fear, and rage, and very often you have no safe environment to express these feelings or even begin to understand the ramifications of what is occurring. Even with the very real threat of leaving the relationship or getting a divorce, unless the addict is in a treatment/recovery program for sex addiction, you are probably not hearing the full extent of his behavior. Therefore, neither you nor he is seeing its addictive nature. Now is the time to get professional help. Whether or not your partner is willing to seek help, you need more information about sexual compulsivity, co-sex addiction, and recovery. There are many organizations listed on pages 237–240 where you can find guidance and help.

While some women are genuinely unaware of their mate's behavior at the time they hear the news, most suspect or are somewhat aware of the acting out. And many, when they do find out, say they would prefer not knowing. In the long run, it is my professional bias that you will benefit more from knowing about his behavior than not. Addiction professionals have long recognized that addiction and coaddiction flourish in isolation and secrecy. It is a therapeutic tenet that secrets not only interfere with recovery, they preclude the possibility of recovery and they will fuel relapse. As difficult as it is for him to disclose the extent of his behavior and for you to hear it, it is a vital aspect of the recovery process both for you individually and for your relationship.

The value of knowing the truth about his addiction is that it reinforces trust in your own perceptions and allows you to deal honestly with the relationship. Knowing the truth gives the relationship the potential for an honest foundation. You deserve to have the information to make objective choices about whether or not you want to continue in the relationship and/or go through the journey of potential recovery with him.

Disclosure

At the time of initial awareness, in the heat of rage or the pain of shame, you may demand to know everything. Whether you are at home, in a car, in a motel room, or in a public place, it doesn't matter to you—you want to know and you want to know now.

[Coaddict] My boyfriend disclosed all right—I discovered him all over the Internet. That was my experience with disclosure.

[Coaddict] Well, I thought my husband disclosed, meaning he told me about the pornography. But later he told me about the chat rooms and then he told me about the woman at work. I have been disclosed to a lot.

[Coaddict] My husband did this disclosure and we didn't have any facilitation. I was so angry I think I scared him, and because I insisted, he told me lots of details. I kept screaming that if he wanted me to stay he had to tell me everything, so unfortunately I got everything, including her clothes size and color of hair and eyes. I wanted to know exactly which Internet sites he was on. I wanted to know what they did when they had dates, where they had gone, etc. So what did I do with that? I made him take me to the places he took her. For whatever reason, he mostly acted out with redheads, and so being a brunette I quickly colored my hair red. I had him buy me the exact presents he bought the other women. Well, none of this did anything for me or him. It just kept me wound up and him crazy.

. . . .

These women certainly "got the news," but that's not what I'm talking about here. The word *disclosure* is a therapeutic term that describes a structured conversation mediated by a professional counselor who provides both physical and emotional safety, wherein the addict shares (discloses) the extent of his sexual acting-out behavior. While it is emotionally painful, when it's done in a manner that offers support to both of you, it has the potential to lessen the craziness you have been experiencing and provide much-needed validation to your suspicions.

While the need for disclosure is a debated topic, my belief is that you need to know only the generalities—not the specifics—of the acting-out behavior. Some partners insist on all the details down to the color of a lover's clothing. The Women of the Lodge refer to that as *pain shopping*. You seek the details, but the consequence of your behavior is that you become more obsessed and have more to ruminate about. Essentially you are taking the detailed information and recycling it. Traumatized by knowing his every behavior, you re-traumatize yourself. Unfortunately, being privy to minute details only tends to help you stay obsessed and reactive, resulting in more pain and anxiety.

Some women don't want to know anything about what happened. They just want to hear that the behavior has stopped. To assume the behavior has stopped because it has been exposed is denial. Seeing only one piece of the picture maintains your denial about the seriousness and extent of the problem. Ignorance is not bliss.

When you know the bigger picture it may seem like your relationship is in even more trouble than you previously thought. Yet addiction thrives in secrecy. Truth is the only way intimacy is ever truly achieved. There is no doubt that this is a time of intense feelings and great uncertainty, but disclosure levels the playing field. Since you are no longer in the dark, you are in a better position to know how to go forward and make informed decisions.

I strongly recommend that you and your partner work through the disclosure with a counselor experienced in sex addiction, and that you have identified a support system and informed them when the disclosure will take place. Family and friends may not necessarily be the best support. It is very difficult for them to remain objective. They may be so incensed that they fuel your feelings and you do not get heard or have your needs met. Your best support may be a peer group of others in recovery from coaddiction or experienced counselors.

[*Therese*] I suspected when my husband asked me to see the therapist with him that he would be telling me things I didn't know whether I really wanted to hear. Yet I also knew that I could no longer put my head in the sand and pretend. The pretending had to stop. Just being ready to try to move on wherever we went in our relationship made it easier for me to hear. Oh, I hated him in the moment. I couldn't look at him, though I hung on to every word. I did ask a couple of questions. It was important for me to know if any of our family knew of this and to know the last time he was on the Internet. I heard him talk about what he was going to do to stop this behavior, but what impacted me was how much more serious this was than I had guessed.

[*Coaddict*] I'd already heard a lot about my partner's behavior before his formal disclosure, but it was helpful for me to hear it in a more level way. It wasn't so emotional now. I knew we were having this conversation because we were trying to keep our marriage and I am hopeful that we will, but I'm aware he and I both have a lot of work to do.

·　·　·　·　·　·　·　·

Suggested generalities to be shared in disclosure are:

1. In what type(s) of behavior was he engaged? (for example, extramarital affairs, prostitution, pornography, voyeurism, masturbation, fetishes, and so on)

2. How long has he been acting out?

3. Is there a possibility that either of you is at risk of sexually transmitted diseases? Will his acting-out behavior affect your health?

4. Have the family finances been impacted? How has the money been acquired, and how much has been spent to engage in the behavior?

5. Are there any legal issues, such as the possibility of other children or legally binding arrangements with others? (owning property with a mistress, outstanding warrants, pending court action, and so on)

6. Did he engage in any behaviors with friends, family members, or other individuals known to you?

Most sex addiction experts believe disclosure is beneficial to the addict, the partner, and the coupleship. Truth telling is an important component in restoring trust. In an extended follow-up study of 164 recovering sex addicts and partners, 96 percent of spouses and partners and 93 percent of addicts reported that making a full disclosure benefited mutual recovery.[1]

For the coaddict, this type of disclosure has the potential to:

○ allow for an adult-to-adult relationship on an equal basis

○ empower her with the truth

○ give her the ability to make informed choices based on the truth

○ allow her to embrace recovery

For the addict, it:

○ reinforces accountability in his recovery

○ reinforces honesty with others and self

○ facilitates the letting go of his shame

For both, it begins the opportunity to:

○ break the addictive system

○ heal the relationship

[Addict] I was pushed into telling my partner by my counselor in treatment. I went to treatment only because I knew this time she would really leave me. I didn't really get what it meant to be an addict. When questioned in treatment, I was honest about what I had been doing. But I didn't want to tell her because I knew she would be mad and I would disappoint her. I knew deep down she was the best person ever in my life. I knew she loved me when I couldn't and hadn't been able to love myself. I didn't want her to see the terrible person I was. But I put my trust in those counselors, and today I believe it was important to put the information into the light—it is what allowed us to move forward.

[Addict] I'm sitting in front of the woman I married and she can't look at me. She seems so fragile, and I tell her all of these things about myself. I felt worse than an animal that lives underground. I felt I didn't deserve her. I so didn't want her to leave me but knew she might. I had to do this for us to have a chance.

. . . .

For you to be empowered, you need to decide how much you want to know and to convey that to the counselor and to your partner. But remember that the counselor is most apt to adhere to the philosophy that recommends disclosing major elements without the details.

The Dribbling Effect

A one-time full disclosure of the major elements is strongly advised but many women get the news from their partners dribbled out over time. You think you have been told the whole story, and then with time more and more information gradually reveals itself.

[Coaddict] As we sat in a therapist's office and he told me what had been going on throughout our entire marriage, I kept asking him if that was all, had he told me everything. He swore that was it. He was crying, asking me not to leave. I told myself somehow I would cope with this. Somehow we could find a way to go forward now that I knew. But then over the next two years I would find out more. He was no longer acting out but he hadn't told me a lot of the real story at the supposed time of disclosure. I would find out more because I found pictures when I was in his office. I found out more when I was reviewing some retirement accounts. I found out more when he told me one day he had something else he needed to tell me. It was about his once being involved with a woman I knew who was moving back to our community. Each time I got more information, it was a setback for me. I honestly believe that as painful as it would have been, it would have been better for me to know everything all at once. He would tell me he had told me all, and then more kept coming. It made it hard to believe there wasn't yet more to come.

· · · · · · · · ·

If your partner is not in a self-help program or involved in counseling that focuses on his sexual behavior, it is very likely you are not getting the whole truth. Even when he is working with a counselor and encouraged to be as honest as possible, he may not be prepared to be totally honest. Although his intention to be honest is honorable, it is incredibly difficult for him to share the full truth. This may sound strange to you after he has engaged in such hurtful behavior for as long as he has, but he is most likely ashamed and certainly scared of the impact your knowing may have on the relationship and on you.

It's also possible that at the time an addict is making a formal disclosure he may not fully remember some of his past behaviors. He has been very skilled in compartmentalizing his behaviors and has learned to detach from them often within hours, if not minutes, after engaging. So when months and often years pass, some behaviors may be quite distant from his consciousness. Additionally, to be able to live with the shame he carries, he has learned how to push aside specific memories and details.

As those memories are triggered (by a conversation, by being in a specific place, or while watching a movie, for example), he is then confronted with how he is going to reveal this information to you. Either he shares it and risks you believing he has deliberately been deceiving you, or he says nothing and you inadvertently discover the information.

No doubt, this dribbling disclosure is debilitating to building trust. But if you and he are engaged in recovery practices, you can get through this excruciating phase. I strongly suggest that you take any new information that has dribbled out after disclosure to a counselor to facilitate healthy discussion and accountability.

After Disclosure

Hearing the news is painful and your response may vary from relief that finally your perceptions and your senses are validated to humiliation, shame, rage, disbelief, and back again. This emotional roller coaster can stay like that for days and even weeks. You may be asking, "What now? Just because he's finally honest doesn't make everything okay." It's not okay—it hurts, and it hurts deeply.

The first few days and weeks after disclosure will be very overwhelming depending on your level of surprise and the extent of the behavior shared. After taking in the information, remember that you do have choices, and it is important that you ascertain what you need as far as contact and distance are concerned. For the moment, make no major decisions other than those that involve your safety. Most partners need time apart from the addict. It may be an hour, a few hours, one night, a few days, or even longer. You may choose to sleep separately for a while or not even stay in the same house. It is natural to not want to be sexual or physically intimate with someone you are very upset with and cannot trust. While the addict may perceive this as punishing behavior, it is more about honoring the pain you feel. It is about establishing your boundaries. You may feel confused about boundaries and ultimatums. You aren't setting boundaries to punish him, you set them to honor and protect yourself, to help you feel safe and confident so that you can heal. If you are not already working with a therapist, this is the time for you to reach out to a professional and/or self-help peer group meetings for support. It is your opportunity to seek your "Lodge." (See the resources listed on pages 237–240 to get started.)

Whether the disclosure came as a surprise or was professionally mediated— or perhaps it was both—there is a lot to do as a consequence of hearing the news. Your life is already busy with work, school, raising children, and other activities. You now may have reason to review financial records or seek legal advice. To use a Twelve Step phrase: Keep it simple. Do one thing at a time.

Slow down, take a deep breath, ask for guidance, and do the next indicated step. Then breathe again, ask for guidance, and move forward again—one thing at a time.

Getting Tested for STDs

As difficult as it might be to do it, it is important for you to get tested for sexually transmitted diseases, including HIV. Even if you believe your partner had no physical contact with another person (because he was engaged in voyeurism, exhibitionism, or pornography), this step is essential. It's a healthy precaution, as you may not yet know the full extent of the acting out, and it may be more than he is telling you. Your doctor visit is another dark moment in the process of living with sexual compulsivity. Most partners say that being tested is humiliating, and for many it evokes incredible anger. Nevertheless, your responsibility to yourself is a priority. This is a positive step in your self-care, your healing.

> [Coaddict] Here I am looking at this questionnaire in the doctor's office. Do *I* use IV drugs? Do *I* have multiple sex partners? Do *I* practice unsafe sex? Do *I* engage in unusual sex? Then I see the "Other" box in which I get to write, "My husband of twelve years has sex with prostitutes and then comes home to me." I want to scream. I want to die. I want to tear his eyes out. And instead I hold my head up and act like this is an everyday occurrence. Funny, maybe it has been.

> [Coaddict] I'm sitting in my doctor's office and she asks me if I'm okay, as obviously I don't look okay. My face is bloated and my eyes are red from crying and I tell her I need to be tested for STDs because my husband is a sex addict and I'm really not sure I know who he has been with. I then burst into sobs and she simply takes my hands in hers and waits until I'm done crying. Then, without any judgment but with great compassion, she tells me we will find out what we need to know.

· · · · · · · ·

Codependency and denial of the consequences can prevent or stall you from being tested because you want to give your partner the benefit of the doubt. You might be thinking, *My partner would not engage in something that would cause me to develop a chronic or even fatal health problem. And if he did, of course he would tell me.* But being tested is necessary and will relieve or confirm any thoughts about possible exposure.

> [Coaddict] My first exposure to an STD was pretty significant, as it threatened the welfare of our unborn child. I was having herpes outbreaks during my pregnancy and we had a serious talk about a caesarean section to deliver the baby safely. I had never had herpes until after I had been with my husband for a few years. I told myself it couldn't be from him, but I also knew I had not been exposed to anyone else.

> [Coaddict] When I became aware of the extent of his acting out, I don't know if I felt more anger about anything other than the fact that he would thoughtlessly risk my health and even my life with unsafe sex. How could he do that to anyone, especially me, his wife? Today I get that he just didn't think about that, and that it is a part of the addiction. In spite of being terrified, I did not go get tested because I had a life insurance physical exam coming up and knew there would be some blood work that would verify if I had HIV or another sexually transmitted disease. Even after the exam, as scared as I was awaiting the results, I was so ashamed I couldn't talk to anyone about it.

> [Coaddict] I discovered during my husband's disclosure that his way of reassuring himself that he was safe was by donating blood, because part of the blood donation screening process is testing for HIV. How could he be so careless with his and my safety? To stoop to those bizarre levels of justification and denial around what he was doing to us was incomprehensible to me.

. . . .

Again, being tested is an act of self-care. You don't have to explain your circumstances to anybody, not the nurse, not the doctor. Just tell the physician you have a need to be checked for all STDs, including HIV.

Being Sexual After Disclosure

How can you be sexual with a man who has betrayed you? If you are *not* sexual with him, are you giving him justification to act out again? If you *are* sexual with him, are you crazy to even want to be with him? These are normal and expected questions at this stage. There is a lot of emotional intensity attached to these concerns.

First, you are not giving him justification to act out if you do not want to be sexual right now. If he is serious about wanting a healthy relationship with you, he will honor this boundary. Remember, addicts use whatever they can to justify their behavior. It is not your responsibility to control him. If you find yourself wanting to be sexual after hearing the disclosure, and that surprises you, know that for some women this desire to be sexual is a form of validation that they are still desirable. For him, sex is the answer to most things, and his desire for sex with you may be to garner assurance that you still love him and won't leave him. The consuming desire to be sexual by either of you in the face of crisis, often referred to as the *honeymoon effect,* is an attempt to reaffirm that all will be okay. Unfortunately it only offers a temporary and false sense of security, an illusion of safety. This doesn't mean that the relationship isn't going to work. It is a combination of time with active recovery practices that has the potential to sustain the relationship.

Answering the following questions as honestly as you can will help you recognize your motives and help you decide whether or not you are ready to be sexual with your partner. Ask yourself:

- Do I want to be sexual out of fear he will go elsewhere if I am not?
- Do I think I will be able to control his behavior if I am sexual with him?
- Do I believe having sex reaffirms he still loves me?
- Do I withhold sex as a way of punishing him?

- Do I not want to be sexual because I don't feel the intimacy sex would imply?

To aid in this initial decision, it is helpful to know nearly all sex addiction specialists recommend an initial ninety-day period of no sexual behavior in early recovery. The purpose of this abstinence contract, which is really a verbal agreement, is to help the addict learn how to better articulate his feelings and thoughts without using sex as a medicator or fix. It is essential for him to learn new skills for getting his emotional and relational needs met. This ninety-day sabbatical recommendation also affords you time to begin your healing. The intent of such a contract is not to punish either the addict or you. While some cosas say the sex between them and their partner is still good, this is not a time-out that focuses on the physicality of sex but a break from the physical act to rebuild trust, emotional intimacy, and safety in your relationship.

When being sexual with your partner is an option for you, it is critical that you approach it from a place of strength. Know what feels good to you sexually. Have the ability to communicate this in a healthy manner. Set the unfinished business between the two of you aside during this time. Know your boundaries and trust they will be respected.

Should I Stay or Should I Leave?

Many women have threatened to leave a relationship if their suspicions are validated or the behavior reoccurs; some do leave, while others, in spite of their threats, do not. If family and friends know of your situation, they may encourage you either to leave or to disregard his behavior and stay. Regardless of past threats, to leave or stay is a decision that you want to make from a position of inner strength, not because of emotional reactivity (a time of emotional overload interfering with the ability to think through the situation clearly). If you are just beginning your own recovery, you don't have to make such a major decision right now. When you feel as if your head and heart are spinning, make as few life-changing decisions as you can. It is easy to believe that the problem is totally him and that leaving him or getting a divorce is the quick, simple solution: *If he was just out of my life, it would be such a relief.* But quitting the relationship out of spite causes more problems in the long run. I'm not saying you should stay in the relationship. I'm simply saying if you take some time, things will become more clear. When you immerse yourself in finding your voice and your strengths and can objectively assess how seriously your partner is engaging in his recovery practices, you will have clarity.

> [Maite] I was going to leave, and that was when he chose to address his behaviors—so I was no longer the crazy one. As long as I see him in therapy, hear him be honest and capable of listening, I choose to stay. I'm becoming a different person, as is he, and therefore our relationship is different. It is certainly more respectful, more genuinely intimate. Irrespective of what he does, I know I have to find myself and pursue my avenues of healing.

> [Coaddict] It's odd because I knew of some of my husband's behavior and suspected even more. But it wasn't until a counselor guided us in a disclosure process that I insisted upon some level of separation. I asked that at least for a few nights he stay with a friend or at least outside of the house. I couldn't make a decision past just a few days. After those few days, it felt okay for him to come back home. We have two young children and we both thought that they needed to see him. So for the next few weeks, I simply asked that he sleep in a different room. We managed to have dinner together with the kids. Our conversation at home was very superficial. Our much-needed serious conversations were with a counselor. I was also quickly directed to a women's group where I did a lot of talking that I needed to do. But I also heard a lot of things that I needed to hear. While I was still incredibly hurt, angry, and unsure, we gradually resumed sleeping in the same bed. What I came to realize is that I didn't want to "throw the baby out with the bath water." I believe there is hope.

. . . .

When women leave in spite, they take their confusion, righteous anger, blame, and pain with them, contaminating all aspects of their lives. It impacts how they feel about themselves, how they relate to others, and their parenting skills. It increases the likelihood of not completing the grief process or addressing any family of origin dynamics. As much as you vow and can't believe you'd ever repeat this experience, not addressing these issues sets you up for trauma repetition.

> [Coaddict] After three years of my husband having countless affairs and berating me sexually, I left him for another man. What I didn't know was that this new guy already had a girlfriend at the time. So sure enough, it was happening again. But I was determined to make this relationship work, thinking that somehow I was just a failure at relationships. After a couple of years, he left me. I took a break from relationships for a while. Feeling better about myself, I then met another man and after a year of dating we married. Within days of my wedding I was a raving coaddict, totally searching for "the other woman." I nearly drove this husband away. He was the one who told me I should go address my issues. He called them mine—not my previous husband's problems. I was clearly taking my fears of abandonment, my anger, and my pain from my previous relationship and dumping them into my new relationship.

. . . .

Making the Decision

In the long run, the decision to stay or leave often involves incremental steps to garner a stronger foundation to make that decision.

> [Sara] Over the years, in spite of my suspicions and even some knowledge, I stayed in the marriage because I craved safety more than anything. But when we had a real name for it, when he and I both recognized it was sex addiction,

by then there was so much muddy water under the
bridge that the additional knowledge was too much. I
needed a time-out. I pretty much knew that right away.
I couldn't contain my anger in his presence, and I had
so much to deal with—my breast cancer in particular. A
separation was suddenly a very clear and viable option.
But he was motivated and getting the kind of help he had
needed for years. I didn't know for sure what I wanted.
The time-out gave me clarity and I could go forward.
After nearly a year of separation, we both arrived at the
same decision: since we had been together in the addiction, we wanted to try being together in recovery.

· · · · · · · · ·

Sara is acknowledging that she and her husband didn't have the opportunity to know what was possible in their relationship in a healthy way
because for years he was trapped in his addiction and she in her codependency. This was a profound moment in her life as well, as she was battling
cancer. She knew herself well enough to know that her judgment about
any decisions she would need to make regarding her physical care and her
marriage was severely impaired by the depth of her anger. The anger was
so great that she wanted the physical separation; she wanted time with herself so she wasn't in a state of reactivity. She needed to gain clarity.

After months of separation she was now experiencing her husband differently. Even more important to her, she was experiencing herself differently
and she wanted to see if there was potential for them as a couple. She
understood that there were no assurances about her husband's behavior, but
she saw a commitment on his part to be in therapy and attend workshops
and Twelve Step meetings for his sex addiction. She also experienced him
differently in his communication. She didn't see or feel any of the old
behavior. This gave her hope. But, more important, she was learning a lot
about herself in her own therapy process. She realized she had a self-
destructive pattern with men and that it was not about her choosing a different man but about being different herself. She was finding her voice in her
ability to know what she wanted and needed; she was learning to own that

verbally. She was learning about boundaries. She was learning to focus on herself more and to act from a place of self-care instead of self-protection.

Therapeutic Separation

The process Sara has described is a *therapeutic separation*. It is not unusual to want some degree of separation to sort out your thoughts and feelings. Best facilitated by a therapist or counselor, together you and your partner agree to a separation for a specific amount of time. Then you will come back together to renegotiate the terms of the relationship at the end of that time. Significant to this process is that each of you has a specific plan about what you will be addressing during this separation period. For example, you commit to work with a therapist on childhood issues once a week, you agree to read specific books related to codependency, he agrees to go to a treatment program, or he agrees to end certain relationships. You will also make decisions as to what type and amount of contact you will have during this time and what specific financial and parenting responsibilities are maintained.

The following couple decided to take a therapeutic separation very soon after the initial disclosure. Being together was simply not an option for them.

> [Coaddict] By the time my husband went to treatment for his sex addiction, I wanted a divorce. Nonetheless I agreed to participate in the therapy process they had for family members. Our relationship was so antagonistic and acrimonious that we both agreed to an immediate separation. I really thought we would divorce. But I followed the therapist's advice and made no legal decisions. I used this time to focus on myself and try to figure out what I wanted and more of who I was. I had so much anger long before this marriage. I was such a control freak. I liked our separation; I found a freedom. It felt better than being together. While we thought it would be a three-month separation, it was actually a year. We both attended Twelve Step programs, and both of us did a lot of therapy. It took a lot of discussion for me to have ownership of

myself and some independence of him. After a year we
got back together, but I still wasn't convinced it would
work. Well, here we are twelve years later. I never would
have imagined we would be the people we are today. We
committed ourselves individually to our respective therapy
processes and by doing so came together as a family.

· · · · · · · ·

The next example of therapeutic separation is less acrimonious. This
couple believes therapeutic separation allowed them to learn more of what
they needed individually, separately from each other, to allow them a
healthier relationship down the road.

[Coaddict] My husband and I have been in recovery for
many years, he regarding pornography and myself for
codependency. During this time he has had a few relapses.
In our seventh year of recovery his acting out escalated.
He was going to massage parlors and having physical contact. I requested that he sleep in a separate bedroom for a
few nights. I was angry, scared, and confused, and I didn't
feel I could honor him or myself by sharing the same
bed. Due to his relapse behavior, our counselor recom-
mended shifting the dynamics in our coupleship with
a ninety-day therapeutic separation. The first thirty days,
outside of counseling, we would have no contact unless
there was a physical emergency. The next thirty days
would be renegotiated. Immediately I felt scared as to
what this meant for our marriage. We had been married
for twenty-six years; he is my best friend. Yet I understood
that something had to change. I didn't want to keep living
a life of his acting out. I cried a lot during the first few
weeks. The accumulation of fear, sadness, and not knowing
where our marriage was headed worried me. But clearly
both of us found the separation helpful. He is confronting
some major underlying issues that with my presence were
being glossed over, particularly owning his anger. I also see

how enmeshed we were, to the point of being unhealthy. In just a short period of time I see how, as individuals and as a couple, we will be healthier and have a greater possibility of recovery.

[Jacque] We had a therapeutic separation a couple years after we began recovery. He had a slip in his sexual sobriety and it was my sponsor who suggested to me that a time-out may be what I need to do for me. The separation coincided with his decision to seek treatment for his loss and trauma issues, which were triggering relapse. One of the things I worked on most for myself during this time was what life would be like if I chose to divorce. While I did not make the decision to divorce, it was an important issue to explore. It was very empowering. I realized that even with a divorce I could go on and live my life. I would feel great loss but the idea of being by myself was no longer so frightening. I had spent my whole life wanting to be safe and had given my sense of safety over to men who violated or betrayed me. I finally was really getting the idea that I had the ability and the responsibility to make myself safe. Well, now a few years have passed. We have chosen to stay together and I am hopeful for our relationship. Today my choice to stay is from a place of strength, not fear.

[Jenny] After one and a half years of attempting recovery practices, my husband and I pursued a therapeutic separation that ultimately preceded our divorce. To say the least, we were having a rocky time. I was working so hard to figure out who I was and what I needed. I think that was confusing to him. I think he thought that if he just said he wasn't acting out anymore, everything would be okay. But the relationship had not been okay on most levels for years. So I just kept moving forward in terms of knowing that I needed a life other than being reactive to him. As I stayed fervent in my recovery process, he eventually stopped all of his counseling. Most of our core issues were still unresolved. I had learned so much about healthy relationships that I knew that I could not be in a relationship that didn't practice recovery. I was committed to becoming healed, not only for my benefit, but for the long-term benefit of my kids as well. My spiritual healing was very strong and with trusted friends for support, I knew what I needed to do. I never thought I would ever be divorced or be the one to file for one. In my marriage my husband was always the one threatening to divorce me! While I was scared, I made the decision from a position of strength.

. . . .

Although Jenny chose to divorce her husband after a therapeutic separation, many couples reenter their renegotiated marriages successfully. In my professional experience I have seen more often than not that therapeutic separation does not result in divorce. For many couples, structured time out with terms and goals often secures their coupleship.

It is important that you do what works for you. Do what you think is healthiest for you. Your best determination will come from a place of strength, not from fear or shame or rage.

Am I Crazy to Love Him?

No, you aren't crazy. As angry or anguished as you feel, you may think you are crazy for still loving him. Others may tell you you're crazy. This is a confusing time. Some cosas are so angry because of the betrayal that they can't fathom the thought of still loving the addict. Others may not be quite so angry or stung by the addict's behavior. As angry and hurt as you may be, you are probably still aware that you have some valued history together and that he has lovable traits. In your healing journey it is normal to experience a multitude of feelings and often contradictory ones. You may hate him one moment, love him the next, be enraged another, and then feel sadness.

Don't confuse your loving feelings with not being free to be angry or not having a voice. These feelings are yours—yours to own without having to justify or explain. Remember, though, that while love is often unconditional, healthy relationships are not. To make your relationship work you need to establish conditions. It will take time to sort out the basis of your love, its strength and foundation.

~~~~~~~~~~~~~~~~

Learning the news, whether it's done in a formal disclosure process, a media story, or an inadvertent mishap, can make you feel like your heart has been ripped out of your chest. The intensity and waves of emotion seem relentless and never-ending. Yet when you allow yourself the opportunity to be witnessed, validated, and led by others who have been there and found a path out of this dark time, you will find the strength to take the self-care actions that are a part of your healing. There are a lot of questions at this stage. Your head may feel as if it is exploding or you may be absolutely numb—probably both—but you will find answers. It is my hope that you are already finding direction and will continue to do so as you read on.

Reflective Thoughts and Questions

- How did you initially become aware or suspicious of your partner's behavior?
- What are your thoughts and feelings about further disclosure with a facilitator?
- Have you experienced the dribbling effect? If so, what has that been like for you?
- Have you been, and/or are you willing to be, tested for STDs?
- Would a short-term celibacy contract be helpful to you? If so, explain. Do you see the value of it for your partner?
- What was important for you to hear in this chapter?

 **Chapter Six**

What Do You Tell Your Children?

My kids are asking:

Did I do something wrong?

Do you still love each other?

What's wrong with Dad?

Talking with your children about sexually addictive behavior is undoubtedly a situation that no parent wants to face. Parents seldom want to share their secrets, their pain, or their betrayal with their children. You don't want your children to suffer; you want to protect them from pain. Yet all members of a family are affected by addiction and codependency. Healthy communication and recovery practices make it possible to clear up any confusion your children experience and to create a greater sense of emotional safety.

It isn't just about family; your children already live in a highly sexualized culture. They are ruthlessly bombarded with sexual messages through the media, television, music, and the Internet. Sex represents power and desirability. Consequently, "good enough" parenting involves not only healthy modeling of sexual expression but discussing sexual issues with children earlier than in generations past. But when sexual addiction operates within a family, the need for dialogue about sexuality emerges even sooner and more urgently than parents would usually choose. Kids often sense things aren't right at home. Disclosure to children helps them to understand why.

Children's Reactions

In 2000, two colleagues and I developed a questionnaire that we adminis-
tered to eighty-nine children who have a sexually addicted parent.
(Twenty-two of these children were under the age of eighteen; the others
were of adult age.) We wanted to learn from these children what they knew
about their parent's sexual acting out and how they were told about it. We
discovered that many of the children already knew about the acting out, or
had suspicions about it, before their parents disclosed to them.[1]

As much as parents wish to protect children from their own mistakes
or hurtful behaviors, keeping secrets does not provide the sought-after protection. Sixty of eighty-nine respondents indicated they knew about their
parent's behavior prior to disclosure. Here is a sampling of some of the
responses we received:

> I was surprised that my mother was not aware that I knew.
> I carried this secret with me my entire adolescence!

> I knew. I had read my father's diary. It was quite a shock. I told
> my best friend but I never told anyone else.

> Sure. I would rather have not known about any of this. I don't
> think any of us who have had this experience want to know
> this stuff. But that is impossible because in my case I was living
> in a house with two addicts: my father who was a sex addict,
> and my mother who was addicted to him.

> I don't know which part is the most unfair, that he is doing
> what he does or that he doesn't know I am like the fairy
> princess who has to keep the knight's honor clean.

> I knew my dad had this woman friend; he would have me with
> him in the car sometimes when he called her. And I just knew
> he shouldn't be talking to her the way he did.

Of twenty-nine respondents who were asked directly if they were glad
they were told about their parent's behavior, twenty responded affirmatively.
Yet they also said they did not like the actual moment of learning it was
true. When questioned further, they said they did not want their beliefs or
suspicions to be true. At the time of the disclosure, many experienced

anger: anger for the pain to the other parent, anger for the embarrassment, but predominantly anger over their lives having been turned upside down. They were often fearful of the financial ramifications.

> *I felt like I wanted to punch them. But I just sat there.*

> *My dad was going on about his being a sex addict and treat-ment and Steps and other stuff that I couldn't care less about, and the word "bankruptcy" came up because at the time we were being sued, and that really struck a chord with me. What did that mean for me? Would I lose my chance to go to college?*

For many of the children we evaluated, the term *sex addiction* created a picture of their parent being a pervert or a child molester. They frequently found themselves in fear of a parent whom they had previously trusted.

> *I felt sick, horrified. What are other people going to think?*
> *Can I be left home alone with him?*

Confusion was a predominant feeling the children experienced with the disclosure.

> *I was only seven! I was too little to understand. And now we had to move and I had to leave my friends. That is what I understood. The last thing I needed was to feel different from other kids.*

> *I was really too young (eleven). I didn't know much about sex and it was foreign. I really couldn't imagine my dad doing the things he did and that was hard for me.*

> *This made my relationship with my dad very awkward when I didn't find it that way before. I felt very uncomfortable being left alone with him.*

The children often became compliant or reached out to emotionally take care of their parent(s). Even when they knew what their parent did was not okay, they felt a need to be protective of one or both of their parents.

> *I knew my dad was being forced to tell me. If he didn't tell me, my stepmother would have. She was really angry and was*

divorcing him. He was crying and so embarrassed. I didn't know what to do or feel—mostly I felt sorry for him. He really was my only safe parent, and I knew what he did was supposed to be bad, but how could I be angry? I was more scared I would lose him.

I felt like I had to defend and protect my dad.

My mom was crying so hard, I just wanted her to stop. I wanted to do anything to make her feel better.

It is not uncommon for children to take sides. They may blame one or both parents.

Maybe if my mom wasn't always so angry with my dad he wouldn't have done what he did.

My dad is really a good guy so I don't know why Mom is making such a big deal of this.

No one should have boyfriends or girlfriends when they are married. That just isn't the way it is supposed to be. My dad really hurt my mom and that's not right!

Some of the children said they had no awareness of the behavior until disclosure was made to them, and then they were shocked. They said that to hear about the behavior was a negative experience. We don't know if their negative experience was due to the behavior's impact on their lives because the parents were now visibly reacting to the consequences, or the children's confusion as to what it meant about their parent and how they understood the words *sex addiction*. While most addicts and coaddicts would like to believe their children are unaware, in fact, great numbers of children said they either sensed or knew.

While some children were shocked and confused by the disclosure, some found immediate relief and/or validation. They finally understood why they were feeling confused, fearful, or anxious.

I was initially so shocked, my stomach kind of dropped. I was thinking, "I can't believe I am hearing this." It just blew me away and at the same time incredible relief, wow!

I was not crazy. I had known all along!

I think a lot of parents think that their kids don't know. I think that is a huge mistake. We know almost everything our parents do. We aren't stupid. We may not know exactly what it is but we know enough to wonder, "Why is Mom or Dad doing this?" I think disclosure is a good thing.

Rationale for Disclosure to Children

So the question is: why would you even tell your children? There is no discounting the difficulty of your decision to disclose. I know there is a lot to consider: their ages, the setting, the timing, who tells them, and how much to tell. Let me offer four pertinent reasons to disclose to children.

1. Validation

Disclosure validates what the children know. Having their unspoken perceptions validated takes away the craziness of knowing but at the same time not knowing. It diminishes the additional shame and anxiety that comes with secrecy.

2. Exposure

Children may find out anyway. Often other family members, particularly a sibling, or other children in the neighborhood or at school know and may deliberately or inadvertently tell them. Thoughtful disclosure can be offered in a healthy manner to counteract a mean-spirited or otherwise simply thoughtless act. In some cases children stumble upon information about the behavior by reading about it in a newspaper or on the Internet, or even seeing it on television.

3. Safety

It is always the responsibility of adults to protect the interests and welfare of children. While every child needs to be educated on how to protect him- or herself and what to do in the case of suspected or known molestation behavior, this discussion is even more warranted when you believe your partner has an orientation toward children. But do not automatically equate sex addiction with child molestation. The word *addiction* can mislead some people to believe that this person has no control over any aspect of his sexuality. That is not true. Addicts tend to act out in ways that are directly related to their own childhood wounding.

If your partner has been engaged in child pornography or known to sexually act out with minors, your children are at risk, and this warrants asking your children whether or not they have ever been inappropriately asked to do something sexual for or with your partner. But I say this with caution. It is very easy to take your outrage and fear and distort the situation. I strongly suggest you allow a qualified helping professional to assist you with this discussion, including the words to use and the timing. This professional needs to be associated with a reputable, licensed agency to ensure that he or she will be able to respond to the needs of the children.

If your children are at risk, then it is appropriate for limits to be set in place that preclude the addict from being with the children or having supervision when they are together. These boundaries remain in place and are renegotiated with suggested oversight of a professional. At this stage, state social and health services and courts are often involved and will be making the decisions about parental access to the children.

4. Breaking the Generational Cycle

An age-appropriate, open, honest discussion and education on the basics of addiction and recovery will help you end the generational repetition that occurs in addictive family systems. Addiction thrives in secrecy so it is important to model healthy sharing of information in your family. You are showing your children that when something happens and you are scared, ashamed, and confused, the best thing to do is talk about it. When openly discussed, almost any problem can be solved. A healthy discussion conveys the message that "In this family we can talk about the hard stuff, and you will be supported and heard."

Appropriate Age

At what age is disclosure most appropriate? My judgment is that a minimum age of mid-adolescence is advised. Children who are pre- or early adolescent should only be told in situations where the children's safety is at risk or their exposure to the information via another avenue, such as at school, from a sibling, or from the media, is possible. Even though the pre- and early adolescents in our research said they were aware of their parent's acting-out behavior, developmentally their greatest need is a belief in the stability of their family. It is the children's own sense of security that is most challenged at this moment. To have sexual data about their parent prior to mid-adolescence is too confusing for them to be able to derive positive meaning or value from having that information. Certainly, maturity of children varies greatly so the professional involved in your situation needs to individually assess the maturity level of your children. By mid-adolescence, as much as children don't want to be told, the information will validate their perceptions and help them better cope with the family stress.

There are times when your preadolescent children's behavior may be the greatest indicator of the need to disclose. They may be acting out confusion, fear, or anger in aggressive or otherwise destructive ways; or they may demonstrate sexual behavior premature to their development (a nine-year-old hiding pornographic magazines, for example). They may repeatedly ask questions that point to some knowledge on their part (such as "Is Dad working late with that woman again?"). You may see their grades slip. They may revert to bedwetting. They may become socially withdrawn or clingy.

Due to the many variables of the family system, the individual children, and the extent and type of sexual behavior acted out, determination about disclosure for pre- and mid-adolescent children must be made on a case-by-case basis.

Healthy Disclosure

It is likely that your opportunity to tell your children about what's been going on will present itself in a less than ideal setting, but by being prepared you can still make the most of the opportunity. Following these criteria will make your disclosure a healthier experience for the children:

- ○ Disclosure is best facilitated with a clinician or therapist.
- ○ Both parents should be present and participatory.
- ○ Both parents should be in agreement to disclose to the children.

- Both parents should strategize and agree upon what is and is not disclosed.
- Both parents should speak for themselves (the addict and coaddict each speak about their own behavior).
- The parents should speak in generalities, not specific details.
- Both parents should display signs of recovery.
- Neither parent should take on the role of victim.
- Children should not be used as confidants by parent(s).
- Both parents should be clear that it is not the children's responsibility to fix or take care of their parents' needs. It is very easy for the children to become caught in a triangle of choosing sides and then reacting on behalf of the person who is perceived to be the victim-parent at the moment.
- Both parents should demonstrate an ongoing openness for dialogue and discussion with a clinician.
- Both parents should make sure the children know they can have further discussions whenever they need to. To say or imply, "We'll talk about this today and never again talk about it" reinforces the shame of disclosure and the behavior. Disclosure is not a one-time discussion.
- The children should be offered the opportunity to talk to a counselor or therapist.

Talking to children about the real issues is a much more difficult conversation if the addicted person is continuing to act out, or the two of you are simply not in agreement as to what and when to share. Before you disclose to your children, talk to other women in recovery or a skilled therapist; their experience may prove very helpful as you sort through your specific situation. Even if it becomes essential to talk to your children by yourself, be sure to follow the guidelines discussed in these pages, under "Rationale for Disclosure to Children" and "Appropriate Age," and to seriously consider your motivation.

As a parent, always follow this basic rule: Exercise caution whenever you intend to disclose sensitive information to children. Always consider what is best for the children. It is the responsibility of parents and helping professionals to reassure children that the adults are handling things and taking control of this painful situation.

Whether or not the children ask directly, there are crucial concerns that need to be addressed during the disclosure. The words *addiction* and *compulsivity* don't make sense to most children. When appropriate, describe actual behavior in child-sensitive language by referring to unfaithfulness and engaging in sexual behavior that is wrong.

If the children are adolescents or older it can be helpful to convey how the parent's behavior was about gaining control and power to overcome feelings of powerlessness, responding to unhealthy anger, medicating and anesthetizing pain, or bolstering self-esteem, and these became more important than anything else. That is the nature of addiction.

Acknowledge how the addictive behavior and the coaddiction have impacted the family as it pertains directly to the children. Will the children be affected by financial consequences, the possibility of marital separation or divorce, changing of schools and losing friendships, or possibly public exposure?

For example, you may find yourself saying, "As a consequence of the behavior . . .

- ○ . . . I wasn't spending time with you; when I was home, I was preoccupied."
- ○ . . . when I was angry with your father I often took my anger out on you."
- ○ . . . I spent what was family money on nonfamily activities."
- ○ . . . there are legal problems that are public and will create embarrassment for the family."
- ○ . . . I have not been available to model healthy relationship behavior."

Again, it is best for each parent to speak for him- or herself and use language that is age-appropriate.

When children ask for specific details such as who, where, and when, it is advised you tell them that this information has been shared only with their other parent unless the answer has a direct impact on them (the children). An example of such a situation needing greater detail might be when a family needs to move or not see a certain relative on a holiday.

I know you may be gasping as you read this. This is a difficult situation, but keeping the following key questions in mind will help guide you. Remember, age is a significant gauge. Ask yourself:

- What is in the best interest of the children?
- How is it helpful for the children to have this knowledge?
- How will it be hurtful for the children not to know?

A Soft Approach to Disclosure

The following couple took a less direct or what is thought of as a soft approach to disclosure. They recognized the value of sharing but delayed sharing the sexual component for a few years. Should you choose the softer style, you have the option of sharing the message when you believe your child is more developmentally prepared.

> [Coaddict] **My kids were seven and nine when everything came out in the open. They had seen and heard anger and crying, and they were aware their father had been absent a lot. When my husband went to treatment and I started my therapy, we simply told the kids that we had done some things to each other that were hurtful; that we had not been honest with each other and now we were work-ing on that. I thought the best thing I could do for them was to keep a routine to their lives. I used my dear friends for backup, people the kids knew and trusted, during these initial treatment experiences. Their father and I told them that we loved them, that these problems were not about them, and that we were going to try very hard to work things out and have a happy family.**

· · · · · · · · ·

While you may choose not to share information with your kids about the sexual aspect of your partner's acting out, their experiences related to the stress within the family need to be validated and they need to be supported.

Children of all ages witness tears and anger, and they pick up on the stress between their parents. Basic information can easily validate their perceptions: *Your dad and I are sad right now about how we have treated each other. We are working on being kind to each other. There have been lies and secrets and now we are being honest with each other. We love you and we are sorry we have not paid attention to you and that we have lashed out at you when we were angry with each other. Yes, we are having some adult problems, but they are not about you. You are precious to us and we both love you very much.*

In hindsight, the parents in the next two situations wish they had taken a softer approach to disclosure.

> [Addict] Looking back I think my children, who were under twelve, were too young to hear so much about my behavior. I don't think they really understood other than their father had done some really bad things that were causing a lot of anger and anguish. I think their being exposed to the information has influenced their dating relationships. But it is also hard to separate how much they were influenced by the dysfunction of my sex addiction and/or the hostile relationship their mother and I were openly engaged in for a lot of their early lives. Because they had heard and seen so much, they needed to be told something. But it wasn't like a private discussion with the focus being what was best for them. We should have been coached in how to think like that. Or until we could be more civil with each other, it should have been left with saying their parents had some problems and were angry with each other but that we were trying to work it out. Then our efforts should have been in getting into some healthy family routines.

> [Jenny] As I look back, our kids were ten, sixteen, seventeen, and nineteen. In the moment it seemed so appropriate to get all the secrets out. In hindsight, I think their father and I should have dealt with how our behavior had affected the kids' lives, made amends to them, told them

we were getting help, and then delayed the disclosure of
the sex addiction until we had experienced some healing
and stabilized the environment. I can see the risk in this
too; the environment may never stabilize. Nonetheless, I do
think there is a time and place for disclosing the secrets.
We could have been more general in sharing with them
early on and dealt with the specifics later.

. . . .

A Direct Approach to Disclosure

The following are two examples of couples who chose a very direct style
of disclosure and felt good about this approach in their family.

[Coaddict] My husband and I together told our nineteen-
and twenty-one-year-old sons only after their father went
to treatment. They thought he was in treatment for using
pills. And he was. But we knew he was there for sex too.
We didn't tell them a lot in the disclosure to them. But
we told them that he had been having affairs throughout
our marriage, and we wanted them to know because we
didn't want any more family secrets. We both think they
knew he had affairs, and it was important to us that they
heard that there is an addiction component to this behavior. We felt it was our responsibility to educate. My husband did most of the talking. He and I had agreed to that
so they could hear it from him, and not me who had been
this angry wife/mother for so long. We thought they
would just think it was me being punishing. They didn't
ask much. They wanted to know if the last affair was really
over. They wanted to know if we were considering a
divorce. Later, when our younger son was twenty-three,
he came to my husband and said he needed help for his
sex addiction. He actually used those words. He was acting
out on the Internet. Had we not been honest and had we
not made the changes we made in our recovery, I don't

know if he would have come to his father for help.

[Maite] My children, both young teenagers, know almost everything except some matters that involve legal issues. Both of us shared with them when they asked questions as to why we went to recovery meetings. We explained to them that we as husband and wife have problems and we need to heal. And the way to heal is to commit seriously to changing how we relate to each other. If not, we will be too sick to be a good mom and dad.

. . . .

These parents shared to validate the children's experience; they shared to stop the secret keeping; and they shared in hope that it would help prevent the dysfunction in their family from repeating generationally.

Recognizing the Complexity

No doubt this is difficult. The following example shares the complexity of parents doing what they think is the right thing, recognizing how traumatic the information can be, and second-guessing their decision. Ultimately, several years later, they are grateful for the recovery the family as a whole has been able to experience.

[Coaddict] What I remember is my husband and I telling our nine- and eleven-year-old kids. Over the next few weeks and months, our nine-year-old daughter started to wet her bed at night. She was crying a lot. Looking back I see how very traumatic it was. One night, nine years later, we were watching a movie that reminded her of our family back then and she suddenly started to cry. She cried like a baby in my arms and told me she shouldn't have been told so much about our problems. That is true, she shouldn't have, but I also know she shouldn't have had to be with parents who were so unhealthy, who were so dysfunctional in their lives. When I think about the overall big picture, the outcome is good. She and her brother would not only witness our "War of the Roses" years and our struggles in early recovery, but would ultimately come to see us committed to our recovery practices, committed to our family, and living in the truth. Clearly, the decisions around disclosure are hard to make. Would I have done it differently? I really don't know, given that our family is in good shape today. I only know my experience. It is hard to know how best to do it.

. . . .

For some parent(s) what you share and when is obvious, but as you can see, for others it is not so apparent. What complicates the situation is that often you are making an initial decision very early in your own recovery process and, in many cases, attempting to make this decision with a partner who is looking at this situation through different eyes. While age and timing are significant, the setting and how to answer their concerns are important considerations for this to be a constructive experience.

Answering Their Questions

The following is a list of questions children may pose to you during disclosure. Rehearsing how you would answer such questions will make the conversation go smoother.

Do you still love each other?

Children want to know how parents feel about each other. This may be a difficult question to answer. Your answer may be a resounding yes. If this is not the reality, you might say, "I am very angry and I'm questioning how I feel." Or "I do not know how I feel at this time." Parents need to have empathy and be sensitive to their children's needs.

Did I do something wrong?

Children need to be reassured that they are loved and that whatever happens between their parents, Mom and Dad will always love them. Children need to believe and understand that this is not about them or their behavior.

How does this affect my life?

A child's greatest concern is usually whether or not his or her parents will remain together. Perhaps there will be a temporary separation. Perhaps the parents will be home more often and become more involved in their children's lives. If as a parent you are not sure what may happen for your family, you can express your uncertainty and then commit to tell the children when you do know.

Who else knows?

It is important to discuss who else knows. The disclosure itself should not become the family secret. Recovery is not about replacing one secret with another. Recovery is demonstrating healthy boundaries and being discriminating with whom one does and does not share. If other people know, prepare your children with an honest response to the questions and remarks of others.

Are you sorry?

Children need to hear and consequently come to believe that both the addict and the coaddict are sorry for their individual acting-out behavior. Children need to know you are sorry and see you making whatever behavior amends you can. Making amends takes time. Time and healthy new behaviors allow the possibility of genuine forgiveness to occur. It is not appropriate to ask your children to forgive you. Remember, this conversation is really about what is best for them, not about shifting the focus onto you.

What is happening so that things will get better?

Children need reasons to be hopeful, and they need to be told about your recovery plans as individuals and as a couple. They need to know what both adults are doing to help the relationship and the family.

As you consider whether to disclose your situation to your children, you may also find it helpful to hear what some children thought would have improved their disclosure experiences.

> A little humility would have made me feel better about my dad.

> Dad really let Mom do most of the talking. I would have preferred he said more.

Not so much detail.

My stepmom went crazy. She shouldn't have been so angry in front of us.

More resources like reading material about sex addiction.

Questions should be accepted, even welcomed, so the family unit can face the problem in its entirety.

A qualified therapist present would make the disclosure much easier.

A counselor who didn't just work with my dad would have been better.

I should have been taken to counseling again when I got a couple years older.

Ongoing Healing

Discussing the situation will undoubtedly elicit a multitude of feelings for every family member. At the time of the sharing and after, parents and clinicians need to be willing and available to listen and validate the children's feelings. This may be very painful for parents but it is a necessary part of healing for the family. As an adult child responded in her questionnaire:

> *Truth, even if in very small pieces, can lighten the load. Shame is a burden we as children should not have to bear.*

Of course you do not want to cause your children pain, but that ideal is lost in the act of the addiction. Parents must forgive themselves for their behavior, move on in recovery, and learn recovery skills. Those skills begin with honesty to yourself and then to appropriate others.

You may be wondering how much you should update your children during the recovery process.

> [Sara] **Several years after an initial disclosure, my husband's acting out worsened and we didn't tell our children. They didn't need to know the ups and downs of our marriage. But when the day came that we decided we needed a**

separation, we told our three children, now aged nineteen to twenty-five, of their father's escalating sexual behavior and that together we had made the decision to have a therapeutic separation. Then we explained what that meant. In this process, knowing that two of our children were struggling with committed relationships, I decided it was time I shared a secret only my husband knew: that a few years back, in my anger, I had an affair. My rationale in telling them was that it was time for the family secrets to end and to help my kids see how people do hurtful things when they are angry. I didn't expect or ask for understanding or forgiveness; I just needed honesty. Our kids struggled with their own immediate anger, fear, and sadness. But ours was a family wherein the parenting from both my husband and me was strong. All three kids, without offering resistance, accepted what we needed to do to help our marriage.

. . . .

Your children of any age do not need to be kept abreast of the day-to-day progress of either your or your partner's recovery. They need to be allowed to focus on what is most relevant to their lives (such as school, friends, work, or newly created families or careers). Irrespective of age, they need and desire your well-being. Their lives are more secure knowing their parents are attending to their recovery practices. Teens and older children can make sense of the overall picture, but giving them details of the addicted parent's triggers or relapses (unless that information has a direct impact on their lives) violates a healthy parent/child boundary.

Beyond Disclosure

Stopping the possibility of a generational legacy involves more than a candid conversation. It really begins with your recovery as parents. Whether or not they are aware of the sexual acting out, children are much more impacted by the family dynamics. Your children's relationship with the addict may be emotionally distressed as a consequence of his physical absences, his not showing up to events, his lies and broken promises, or his emotional absence or overindulgence at home. Rageful behavior and mismanagement of money create consequences for children. But this isn't just about the addict and the kids. If the two of you demonstrate poor relational skills (such as anger, silence, sarcasm, or inattentiveness), that is also problematic. Your behavior has a direct impact on your children as well. Your anger, depression, using them to communicate for you, not allowing them their autonomy, or using them as your confidant or friend will create long-term problems. The direct hurt children experience is just as often about the unhealthy expression of emotions and poor relational skills as it may be about sexual messages and behavior.

Without recovery for you and your partner, there is a strong likelihood that in a handful of years the stories shared throughout this book will be the stories of your children. History has proven that time and time again, in the throes of living with addictive behavior, whether or not it is recognized as such, children experience emotional abandonment that sets them up to seek ways to escape or numb their pain, often leading to various addictions. I have worked with many mothers who worked incredibly hard to compensate for an absent, distant, or blatantly hurtful father. It's very possible your children wouldn't have many of the strengths they have had you not compensated in some way. But you must also recognize how your own emotional disconnection, rigidity, silenced anger, or other specific codependent behaviors have impacted your children.

Children growing up with addiction often vow, "It will never happen to me." Yet when they meet with life's difficulties, they don't have the emotional maturity or coping skills to live their life differently. Historically, when young people are hurt, confused, and angry, they resort to acting out with alcohol, drugs, and/or sex. They begin to repeat the models they were raised with, all the while rationalizing, minimizing, and denying that they too are a part of the addictive cycle. They act out sexually or, as the Women of the Lodge said, "become the perfect partner."

My intent here is not to scare you, but to help you garner a healthy fear of the insidiousness of the generational repetition of addiction—repetition that is only broken by way of a recovery process. There is a saying, "When addiction exists within a family, look a second time." I would like to rephrase that slightly as, "When recovery exists in a family, look again." You have the potential to stop the legacy of addiction and significantly improve the odds that healthy choices and lifestyle come naturally in your children's development.

More so than words, your style of parenting will have the greatest impact in the long run. Take responsibility where you can. The resiliency of children will be supported when you:

- keep your children's lives on track
- maintain healthy family rituals and traditions
- listen attentively
- develop healthy boundaries
- validate emotions
- model and teach problem-solving skills
- model healthy ways of coping with stress
- protect your children as appropriate
- steer your children toward appropriate resources
- realize the relationship your children have with their father is theirs and not yours
- engage in your own recovery practices

You cannot change the past behavior, but you can influence your children by example in your recovery practices. If you do not have a commitment to change your family system, disclosure alone won't break this addiction cycle. Changing the family system begins with your individual commitment to recovery. Then, at the appropriate time, disclosing secrets to your children can help to break the generational cycle.

It is in recovery that you will find the strength to be the parent your children need you to be. You will probably always feel sad that your children have been exposed to addiction and that your behavior has caused them pain. It is normal to be concerned and fearful of the consequences for your children. With support from others in recovery and with the guidance of skilled helping professionals, you can do your part by taking responsibility and being accountable to your children.

Reflective Thoughts and Questions

- What are your concerns about your children?

- What are your thoughts about whether or not you will disclose your situation to your children and help them move into healing?

- Identify skills and practices you and your partner do that you believe contribute to healthy parenting.

- Identify behaviors and practices you and your partner do that you believe are detrimental to healthy parenting.

- Identify three behaviors you believe will strengthen healthy parenting.

- What was important for you to hear in this chapter?

Chapter Seven

Your Time to Heal

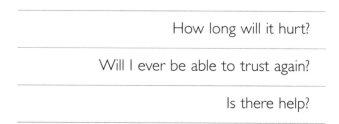

How long will it hurt?

Will I ever be able to trust again?

Is there help?

Your recovery will not be linear; there will be no straight lines. Some women describe it as a crazed meandering through dense clouds. Undoubtedly it is arduous; there will be many ups and downs. You cannot schedule it; there is no timetable for any leg of your journey. It is an expanding process that begins with willingness, from a place of pain (and sometimes relief), and it unfolds differently for everyone. To begin your healing—your recovery journey—you must stop pretending, stop denying, stop minimizing, and stop rationalizing. You may come to recovery angry, defeated, embarrassed, ashamed, or confused, but just come. Remember the wonderful saying, "When you are at the end of your rope, let go." You have held on so long that your arms are tired, your muscles have been stretched and pulled, and your hands are raw. You may feel that if you let go, you will fall. But the Women of the Lodge discovered that it was "hanging on" that caused their pain.

> [Coaddict] When the magazines were not enough, he went to strip shows; when they weren't enough, he bought the girls and took them back to his hotel room. It didn't matter how many of them he had, it was never enough. Now I have had enough. Enough hurting, enough crying, enough bargaining; it is my time to heal.

· · · · · · · ·

Overcoming the Fear of Feelings

The challenge with letting go when you're at the end of your rope is that you quickly get in touch with deeper feelings. For some of you the depth of your pain and anguish or fear is so profound that you don't know how you will survive. The breadth of anger you feel is so pervasive you are convinced you won't have any self-control. The natural response is to scramble for any type of control. Think of the adage, "To make lemonade out of a lemon is great, but to refuse to acknowledge the lemon ever existed is denial"—denial of yourself and your experiences. It is when you own and accept your feelings—whether you feel irritated, fearful, sad, humiliated, or joyous—that you will be able to embrace life, to move forward. To be whole you need to be able to access a range of feelings. Part of your recovery is learning to identify a wide scope of feelings and then learning the healthy expression of those feelings. The following are some initial suggestions to begin this process of owning your feelings.

- **Journal.** Carry a notebook with you. Throughout the day, or at a specific time every day, write about what you've been feeling.
- **Create a feelings list.** Make a list of feelings and carry it with you. Bring it out three times daily and ask yourself what you have been feeling. For example: I am feeling guilty about _____. I am feeling sad about _____. I am feeling afraid about _____. I am feeling angry about _____. I am feeling embarrassed about _____. Share what you are feeling with someone you trust.
- **Affirm your emotional self.** Identify two affirmations that will support you in acknowledging your feelings. For example: "I have the right to my feelings" and "My feelings help me identify my needs."
- **Breathe deeply.** People close off their feelings when they take shallow breaths. Check your breathing throughout the day and particularly at times of vulnerability. Take a deep breath in for three seconds, exhale slowly for three seconds; repeat five times. In time expand this to five seconds, five times.

Learning to own your feelings won't be easy because you have probably spent a lifetime not being safe with your feelings. It is likely that you gleaned your understanding of what to do with your feelings from people who denied them, people who contradicted your perception of reality and generally could not express positive or negative feelings in healthy ways. That modeling then became reinforced in your relationship with someone who sexually acts out. He is not there to listen, to validate, or to offer support. In fact he most often discounts, ignores, and denies your feelings. He rages in anger or walks away in silence. He tells you there is no reason for you to feel the way you do. It's possible he tells you that not only do you have no reason to be fearful, angry, or sad, but in fact you should be grateful.

With so many previous negative experiences, it is likely you have a lot of fears of what would happen should you show feelings. Fears such as:

○ Others won't like me.
○ People are going to be able to see how bad I am.
○ I'll be seen as weak, and that is bad.
○ People will tell me I have no reasons to feel this way.
○ I will be out of control, and that is not okay.
○ I will be vulnerable to getting hurt.
○ People will take advantage of me.

You may be at a stage where you have difficulty expressing your feelings because you have difficulty identifying them. You may not recognize anger as you stand with your fists clenched and arms tightly folded. I have worked with women who had tears rolling down their faces, and when asked what they were feeling, they didn't know. Many coaddicts smile broadly through their fear, humiliation, and anger.

Feelings are cues that signal what you need. If you pay attention to your feelings, you will become more adept at knowing your needs. Feelings also help you determine the boundaries you need to set to provide security for yourself. They are your signals to comfort, safety, discomfort, and danger. A mark of recovery is the ability to know what you feel when you feel it; to be comfortable with your emotional self, and then determine whether or not and with whom you share feelings.

Feelings are most hurtful to yourself when they are denied, minimized, and when they accumulate. Prior to beginning recovery you may have been avoiding your feelings by eating, shopping, working, exercising, drinking alcohol, or taking other drugs. Maybe you did some sexual acting out yourself. The first step is identifying how you mask your feelings. Then pay attention to when you put that mask on.

In the early stages of healing, your feelings will be all over the map and may seem very contrary to each other. You may feel sad and happy at the same time, or sad and angry, or loving and hateful. This is to be expected. You have not gone crazy. It only means you're sad and happy, sad and angry, or that you love and you hate. It's normal to have multiple and even contrary feelings at the same time.

> [Maite] Thank heaven I quickly found a women's group with women in similar situations to me. I didn't feel so crazy. My feelings were all over the place. They would flip: in the beginning sometimes from one minute to the next, in time from one hour to the next, then maybe one day to the next. But whatever I was feeling, the other women accepted me. They understood. They laughed with me; they cried with me; they validated my indignation and anger. It was so liberating for me—me who had been Ms. Perfect, so in control. Not now, and it was great.

> [Jenny] I didn't think the pain would ever go away. For a long time I was mostly numb. I would see other women in my recovery group so full of feelings. And then I started to thaw. And then feelings began to come: pain, raw pain, anguish, shame, loneliness. I was so lonely. Fear ran rampant at all times. Then anger. All of this was so new to me.

· · · · · · · · ·

Like Jenny, sometimes you may wish you could just stay numb. Some cosas do just that, but staying numb can lead to depression, forms of self-medication, and even illness. When you stay numb, the hurt continues to grow. Trust that there are reasons for the depth of your feelings. Whatever you feel, it doesn't mean you are a bad person or wrong. What's important is that you are able to talk about those feelings. You don't have to know the sources of your feelings. But you can open your mouth and say, "I'm sad. I don't know what's going on, but I feel sad" or "I'm so angry, I'm angry at everything." The more you verbalize what you do know and what you do feel, the sooner you'll be able to connect your feelings to their origins.

It is usually early in the recovery process that the pain seems overwhelming, but it will pass if you are willing to identify and own it. Feelings are transitory; they pass. As intense as your pain can be, trying to control and defend against your feelings prolongs the pain. Allow yourself to own them and be with them. A lot of what you are experiencing is the accumulation of many years of unacknowledged feelings related to loss and grief.

Recognizing Yourself in the Grief Process

The many feelings you are having are a natural part of a grief process. Think about the losses you suffered because of your partner's sexual acting out. Some losses may include:

- He wasn't there for the birth of a child.
- He acted out the night before your wedding.
- He had a child with another woman and he didn't tell you for years.
- He hid money to enable him to act out.
- He spent money on other women.
- He didn't show up to a lot of family activities.
- He told lies, lies, and more lies.
- He blamed you for not being sexual enough.
- He was not present when he was with you; his thoughts were focused elsewhere.

The classic grief model encompasses a series of universal emotional reactions. The model always starts with loss, and from loss comes shock. You are numb to what occurred; you disbelieve. From shock you move to denial. You minimize, rationalize; your loss is too painful to acknowledge. In order to get to acceptance, you move through anger. Guilt sets in, and that leads to bargaining. This bargaining is often between you and your God or Higher Power: "God, if you would just make him stop this behavior, I promise I will _____." Then you experience sorrow. You feel too helpless to respond. With progress through these stages, you come to acceptance. Acceptance doesn't imply condoning. You see the reality for what it is, and you transcend that place of reactivity or immobilization to discover meaning from the path you are taking.

When loss is chronic and the likelihood of abandonment looms at emotionally painful times, you are more apt to bypass the shock stage of grief and quickly proceed to the denial stage. If you have made a habit of employing denial to cope with your feelings, you have become so skilled at this that you may have difficulty even identifying a situation as a loss. You may think the following:

- No, it wasn't important to me that my husband didn't get to my awards banquet last night. I really didn't expect him to show up.
- I am used to it. It didn't really hurt.
- I suspected he was out at the strip club, but I told myself as long as he was with his work buddies it was okay.

Anger is a natural response to loss. It is a protest; an attempt to retrieve what is gone or never was. Feeling anger can be a healthy reaction when your rights have been stomped on. It heightens your awareness and propels you to act. Without it you may lack the courage to speak out, to seek a just resolution, and to protect yourself from further harm. If you don't allow yourself to feel indignant when someone hurts you, if you don't know that you are bruised or enraged, who will encourage you to question what your relationship is worth? Who will draw the line and say enough is enough? Who will be your voice? Inability to feel anger is as dangerous as the inability to feel pain and it will render you just as defenseless. Acknowledging pain allows you to address it. When you have been hurt, anger is a natural, valid response. It can be a gift, as it provides a feeling of empowerment. Suddenly you do not doubt yourself. You can do whatever needs to be done.

Anger gives you energy to cope; it reinforces your confidence and offers the strength to mobilize. Anger's vector is always forward—to push away the source of pain. In anger it is easier to forget the other person's needs. All that counts is your pain and your needs, not theirs. The coaddict who has been more in tune to other people's needs than her own can be mobilized by anger to act on her own behalf.

But when you are afraid of rejection, distrust your own perceptions, and are highly dependent on others' approval, you have difficulty owning your anger. You don't want to be angry; you want to be understanding. That's anger avoidance. When you are anger avoidant you find it easier to skip the anger stage of grieving and move straight on to guilt or depression. Inability to identify anger interferes with your ability to move through the grief process.

If you are chronically angry, on the other hand, you may be stuck in the grief process, unable to move from your anger. Anger is your safe place; other feelings are the ones that create greater vulnerability for you. A very important question then is: what would you be feeling if you weren't angry?

Guilt (both true and false) is a natural response to a loss. *True guilt* is a feeling of regret or remorse over something you have or have not done. *False guilt* is the feeling of regret or remorse for someone else's behavior and actions. If you have difficulty separating true guilt from false guilt, you are more apt to stay stuck. As a result, you continue to wonder what you could have done to have made things different: "If I had paid more attention to him . . ." or "If I did what he wanted sexually . . ." or "If I had been home more . . ." The false guilt you carry keeps you stuck in the bargaining stage.

As painful as it is for anyone to wend his or her way through a grief process, many people find a type of psychological safety in their bargaining. To let go of the bargaining and reach a healthy place of acceptance, you have to allow yourself to acknowledge and tolerate very intense feelings. If this is difficult for you, don't despair. In recovery you will develop the ability to tolerate your feelings without engaging in self-defeating or otherwise self-destructive behavior.

Sorrow is a normal part of the grief process where you may get stuck. When you think that you aren't worthy, you are apt to succumb to the power of defeat and experience a more chronic state of depression rather than move on to acceptance.

When you are grieving, it is not the time to be judgmental or critical about what it is you are feeling. You've been wounded and you're hurt; your feelings are legitimate.

Acceptance comes as a result of having been able to experience each step of the grief process. Acceptance does not mean what your partner has done is okay or not hurtful. It means accepting the reality of his behavior and its impact on you, your relationship, and your family. Finding meaning for yourself from this experience is significant in your healing process.

Review the dynamics of loss and grief—shock, denial, anger, guilt, bargaining, sorrow, and acceptance—and identify where you are more apt to get mired in the process. While shock and denial are often the first stages of grief, you will find that you will slip in and out of the other feelings, frequently revisiting them. Depending on your defenses, you are also more likely to stay in some stages longer than others.

Getting through the grief process takes time, but people who actively engage in their recovery find that the pain gradually diminishes. In times of intense feelings, you need to take deliberate steps to lessen your external stresses. Be aware that you are in a vulnerable emotional state, and it is going to be very important for you to identify and practice self-care behaviors. That means you need to be eating healthy, getting some exercise, resting properly, and taking advantage of a support system. This is no time to take on added responsibilities. Make more time for yourself. Stay aware that you are vulnerable. There is no specific time frame allotted to complete your grief process. Don't put expectations or shoulds on yourself. With the help of others in recovery and/or a professional, you'll find you're able to work through your grief in your own time. It is a passage that does not last forever. Now is the time to treat yourself gently and with kindness.

How Long Will It Hurt?

I liken the process of grieving over losses to peeling an onion. You do it one layer at a time, and in the process you cry a lot. You may cry until your eyes swell shut and your bones ache. One day you think you are doing okay and the next day you feel devastation again. The losses are so deep: the ability to trust, your dreams, your confidence, the sanctity of your marriage bed, the blow to your pride. The pain often comes in waves. At times numbness may move in and out. This is very common as the truth unfolds. Numbness is protective and temporary. You will be able to experience a wider range and greater depth of feelings as you feel safer.

[Coaddict] The pain comes and goes as I'm in recovery. It's true the pain is not like it was in the beginning, and I often feel as if I'm moving to different levels of pain. Sometimes I feel overwhelmed because so much of my life I've stayed away from anger and sadness. I used to just put my feelings in a drawer and move to a happier me. I know it was a mask, but learning how to swim in anger and sadness makes me vulnerable and I don't like it. My recovery support and practices help me embrace the pain and take care of myself.

. . . .

Your pain is both deep and wide. Sadly, we haven't invented a healthy remedy to make it go away quickly. Quick fixes only lead to a deeper, longer fracture later. While feelings don't disappear, the intensity of them will decrease if you give voice to all of them. They also lessen when your partner does his part and works on repairing the damage. Whether or not he joins you in the recovery process, your pain will lessen when you accept the reality of what has happened. It lessens as you own your pain, your shame, and your anger. You need to live with the pain, accept its reality, and practice healthy behavior until the hurt begins to ease.

It may be helpful to think of grief as a hurricane-force wind. If you stand rigid, lock your knees, support your back with a broom, and keep your feet together, the wind will surely blow you over. Conversely, if you stand and face the wind with balance and flexibility, with space between your feet, knees bent, and leaning into the wind, you may sway like a palm tree on the beach, but you will find your strength and durability. Peace comes by walking through the pain, not around it. The process of grieving and attending to your losses will take months, and you will periodically find yourself back in the grief process when a specific issue is triggered—even years into your recovery journey. The depth and span of your suffering is strongly influenced by the degree of grief you allow yourself to experience in early recovery.

It is crucial that you have a support system, people you can talk with regularly about these feelings. Talking, rather than keeping the feelings inside, takes the power out of the feelings. It is essential for you to find other people who understand your circumstances and to listen to their stories too. Eventually you will be better able to share your story. Receiving validation from others lessens your pain.

Accepting Powerlessness and Recognizing Unmanageability

In the Twelve Steps of the COSA program, the First Step, "We admitted we were powerless over compulsive sexual behavior and that our lives had become unmanageable," addresses coming to a recognition of your own powerlessness around the addiction and seeing how your life has become unmanageable. For many, *powerlessness* is a difficult word to digest. You may say, "Sure, I am powerless," and see that as being a victim or down in a bitter defeat. Try thinking of it differently. Think of powerlessness in terms of the many ways you have attempted to control the addict or the behavior—ways that in the long run haven't helped; the acting out continues. Accept that you are powerless over other people, places, and things, but remember you are not powerless over your actions in your recovery. By acknowledging and accepting your powerlessness over the behaviors of your partner, what happens is that you let go of thinking you have the answers for what is his addiction.

Now this is scary because you may be thinking, "But I don't want to give up the fight, I want this relationship to work." You aren't giving up the fight; you are giving up the illusion that you can control the addict's behavior. In letting go, you have the potential to receive. Read on. This will make more sense in time.

For the time being, focus on surrendering control of your partner and his behavior. Begin by asking yourself:

- In what ways do I try to control him?
- Do I lie or make excuses to cover for him?
- Do I check through his personal belongings?
- Do I yell? Threaten? Plead? Demand?
- Do I avoid sex?

○ Am I sexual when I don't want to be, in ways I do not want to be?

○ Do I throw out his stash or monitor email messages, purchases, or mileage?

○ Do I try to avoid or limit his access to the object of his addiction(s)?

○ Do I give him the silent treatment?

In the long run, have any of these behaviors made a difference?

The confusion and pain you experience due to his behavior leads you to become increasingly focused on your partner. In this process, you may fail to recognize how your own behavior creates chaos and is hurtful in your life. In your recovery, addressing this unmanageability is about addressing your behavior. That is where your power lies.

[Coaddict] I was with my husband in a treatment setting; I knew that not only was he out of control, but I too was out of control. I was in a constant state of rage or immobilized with fear and bounced back and forth like a teeter-totter. I also remember thinking how much I was acting crazy like my mother, who was someone I did not want to be. I couldn't control it. I told myself I didn't want to behave this way, but it was a knee-jerk response. I was acting obsessive, spying on everything about my husband's life. I was raging. I was controlling. I was preaching. I look back now and I had more addictions than he did. I was addicted to control. I was trying to control everything so I would be okay. I was addicted to my own anger. I felt so self-righteous in my anger. I was addicted to food; it brought me solace. And what I know today is that I brought all of those issues into the marriage—my previous history with a mother who was an addict, and then sexual abuse. It only got worse with this hidden addiction of my husband. Then I added my addiction to religion. I used religion in an attempt to manage and to control what was happening, reading scripture excessively, trying to manage and control with the pontificating. I believed if he just got onboard all would be okay. As he got more out of control, I moved into more high control via religion, more involvement with Bible studies, church, more doing stuff than being spiritual. If I was just a good enough, holy enough wife, he would be okay. For which there was some reinforcement in the church I belonged to: "If the wife is good enough, he will fall in line."

. . . .

Think about how your denial, preoccupation with the addict, your lack of self-care, lack of healthy boundaries, and your defenses have contributed to the pain and confusion.

- What toll have these problems taken on you physically? Describe physical symptoms such as loss of sleep, headaches, gastrointestinal problems, back pain, weight gain, or weight loss.
- What effect has there been on your physical appearance? Are you obsessive about your appearance? Do you take less pride in your grooming and dress?
- What effect has there been on you sexually? (Did you have an affair, engage in sex acts that you didn't want to, avoid sex?) Has this behavior affected how you feel as a woman?
- What effect has there been on you emotionally? Are you depressed? Angry all the time? Are you displacing your feelings? Numb?
- What effect has there been on you spiritually? Are you reluctant to seek a spiritual path? If so, what is that reluctance about? Do your religious beliefs interfere with asserting yourself?
- What effect has there been on you intellectually? Do you think you are stupid? Incapable? Forgetful? Preoccupied?
- What effect has there been on your parenting? Are you being overprotective? A super-parent? Distancing? Rageful? Inattentive? Neglectful? Too enmeshed?
- What effect has there been on your friendships? Do you find

yourself lying or making excuses for your partner's behavior, his absences, his ogling, and his sexualized comments? Are you isolating?

○ What effect has there been on your work? Have your attendance and performance been impacted? Are you working overtime? Are you changing jobs frequently?

○ What effect is there in the area of responsibility? Are you being overly responsible or irresponsible?

○ What effect has there been on your daily routine? Are you "dancing as fast as you can" with busyness? Are you feeling the stress of perfectionism?

[Coaddict] I would rehearse what I was going to say to him when he walked through the door, but the minute I saw him all of those thoughts flew out the window and I'd start ranting and raving. There were times I'd be sitting at home imagining what he was doing, making incessant phone calls to locate him. There were nights I'd replay his phone message to me for hours while drinking wine and calling every motel in the city.

[Coaddict] I was sleep deprived, I was forty pounds over-weight, I flipped from crying to rage on a dime, and my husband's latest affair was just exposed on television. A friend suggested that maybe, just maybe, I needed some help. I simply couldn't keep going on pretending while my life was falling apart on every level.

[Coaddict] He kept asking me to go to the therapist with him, and I was so self-righteous. My husband was so earnest in his recovery. He was like a different person. He was becoming this considerate, accountable man. For three years I hung on to my martyrdom, my anger, my shame. I was becoming more and more cold. It was as if I wanted his old behavior back, the way I egged him on.

> But he wouldn't engage like the old days, and I saw
> myself getting sicker and sicker. Thank heaven one day
> I really was tired of being sick and tired.

. . . .

Has there been a turning point that makes you aware your life is becoming unmanageable?

Boundaries, Boundaries, Boundaries

No boundaries, walled boundaries, damaged boundaries—everything but healthy boundaries. Boundary violation and distortion is a given for cosas. Beginning in childhood and setting you up to be a good coaddict, you have become someone who will not recognize or challenge behavior that hurts you. It is possible that as a child you had no way to defend against boundary invasions. When you live with boundary violation and distortion, it erodes your esteem and creates confusion about who is responsible for what. It sets you up for becoming a victim and/or victimizing others. Living with an addict only reinforces boundary violations because addicts are masters at trampling on boundaries. In time, as your esteem is battered, your boundaries sustain major damage.

> [Jacque] I had heard that word "boundaries," but in reality
> it meant nothing to me, as I had so few. I let myself be
> talked into doing things I didn't want to do sexually. I
> allowed myself to sit and listen to him tell me everything
> that was wrong with me. I was truly a doormat. I felt so
> poorly about myself that I just wouldn't stand up for
> myself with any self-respect.

. . . .

A boundary is a limit, an edge that defines you as separate from others—a separate human being, not someone else's possession. While people readily recognize physical boundaries, we also have emotional, sexual, relational, intellectual, financial, and spiritual boundaries. Emotional boundaries define the self: our ideas, feelings, and values. We set emotional boundaries by choosing how we let people treat us. Our spiritual development comes from our inner self. Only we know the spiritual path for ourselves. We have sexual boundaries: limits on what is safe and appropriate sexual behavior. We have a choice about whom we interact with sexually and the extent of that interaction. We have relationship boundaries. The roles we play define the limits of appropriate interaction with others. Our intellectual boundaries offer us the opportunity to enjoy learning and teaching. They allow us to be curious and inspired.

It's important to establish boundaries that are flexible but within limits; they can shift appropriately in response to situations: out for strangers, in for those you are intimate with; out for those you don't feel safe with, in for those you trust. For example, you may not find it acceptable for a stranger to give you a hug, but you are willing to receive a hug from a family member. It is not okay for an acquaintance to expect to stay at your house while on vacation, but that might be an appropriate expectation from friends or family members. Boundaries should be fixed enough to preserve your individual self, yet open to considering new ideas. They are firm enough to uphold values and priorities, and open enough to communicate your priorities. Boundaries convey that you have determined certain behaviors are inappropriate in the context of certain relationships.

Codependent women find it almost impossible to protect or defend themselves when it might upset their partners, particularly when the partner is threatening or is dangerous. You back off; you retreat. In recovery, you need to learn to strike a balance between showing respect and concern for others and showing respect and concern for yourself.

> [Coaddict] I was so afraid to say that I needed things to be a certain way for me in this relationship. He started attending these groups, but I just wanted him to tell me what he was going to do differently. I wanted him to be different because I didn't know if I could really live and be on my own. I had two kids and there was no child support from their father. But I listened to other women start to say it was important for me to respect myself and not to stay in my fear. So little by little I started to say

what I thought and what I felt, and then the biggie—
what I needed. With that, I was setting boundaries.

. . . .

When codependent women are being harmed or attacked, they tend to
want to analyze the situation rather than take cover. Let me share with you
a riddle that stumps many coaddicted women: "If you are standing under a
window and someone starts dumping garbage on top of your head, what
do you do?"

Long pause.

Then the woman replies tentatively, "Ask them to stop?"

The answer and the appropriate response is, "You get out of the way.
You move."

This isn't the moment to ask why, it's the time to take care of yourself.

While a lack of boundaries sets you up for being a victim, it can also set
you up to be hurtful and intrusive to others. Going in either direction is an
act of being boundary-less. You are not protecting yourself when you are in
a victim stance. You also lack boundaries when you fail to respect the
boundaries of others. Healthy boundaries reinforce your inner worth and
value, and support your integrity and self-worth.

> [Sara] A lot of my problems with boundaries had to do
> with my being uncontained. I'd flip from totally walled
> boundaries to being boundary-less. And when I did, I was
> hurtful to others. I had this wall of silence where I literally
> said nothing. When I finally spoke up to my husband, I
> preached and ranted! Certainly his behavior toward me
> was abusive, but I was abusive too, in other ways. And
> then having no boundaries, it was like I was leaking all
> over. I was telling everyone what was going on with him
> and others. I called his family and told them. I told his
> coworkers. I even told the hairdresser, who didn't know
> either of us.

. . . .

Maintaining boundaries that prevent you from being retaliatory can sometimes be challenging. Yes, you have the right to be angry, even outraged, but being boundary-less only inflames greater chaos and drama.

Developing boundaries means knowing your physical and psychological comfort zone—your safety zone—and knowing what you like and don't like. It is having a sense of your own self separate from others. Your ability to protect yourself psychologically and physically is linked to the durability of your boundaries. They are mechanisms that bring safety into your life by establishing healthy control. As you strengthen your boundaries you gain a clearer sense of control of yourself and your relationship with others; they empower you to determine how you'll be treated by others. They are statements about what you will and will not do, acting as limits for what others can and cannot do to you. By setting boundaries for yourself, you are exercising your inherent power to declare that you are a separate and independent individual, not a possession or extension of anyone else. This skill is vital to defining who you are and how you will be treated.

You don't set boundaries to punish another person; you set them to honor and protect yourself. It is up to you to decide how you want to live and what you can and cannot live with. It is up to you to set boundaries that help you feel safe and confident so you can heal. This takes time, but you can do it.

Saying No, Saying Yes

Boundaries enable you to embrace both the words *no* and *yes*. While the words are not usually verbalized within boundaries, they are the underpinnings. When you adopt a victim stance while being belittled, harshly criticized, or being raged at, to say nothing or to remain in the situation is in essence saying, "Yes, I deserve this" or "Yes, I am helpless and must endure." Saying no to this behavior is saying, "Stop, you are disrespecting me" or "I will listen to you when you speak more respectfully to me, but not now." And if he doesn't stop, say, "I am willing to talk about whatever it is you are angry about at another time when you can speak to me differently. Right now I am going in the other room and you are not to follow me." By saying, "No, this behavior is disrespectful," you are saying yes to yourself.

If you are out to dinner with your partner and you perceive him being preoccupied with other women in the restaurant, setting a boundary in which you honor yourself would be saying no to the situation. You would also be saying yes to yourself by telling him something such as, "I am uncomfortable with your interest in the other women; please refrain from looking in their direction and engaging in conversation with them."

If your relationship with the addict is one where he controls the money, you are saying no to this dynamic and yes to honoring yourself and a more mutual relationship around money when you say something such as, "I need to have my name on all of our bank accounts and on our stock portfolios."

On the flip side, if you are lacking containment and you find yourself raging at someone, you rein in your boundary-less behavior by saying no to yourself: "No, I am not entitled to be abusive toward another," and "Yes, I will honor my self-respect and find another way in which to tell him what I am thinking and feeling."

In your healing, explore what the words *no* and *yes* have meant to you. Consider how your inability to say no or yes have been hurtful to you. Challenge your beliefs about the meanings that might underlie these words. Does saying no mean you won't be liked? Does it mean you aren't a nice person? Does it mean people will avoid you? Does saying yes prevent you from being rejected? Does saying yes make you feel lovable? Does saying yes help you avoid uncomfortable feelings? While the words *no* and *yes* are small in size, in recovery they are powerful and are crucial to having healthy boundaries.

Early Recovery Boundaries

In early recovery the boundaries you set around the addict's behavior will help stabilize your situation. These boundaries state what is and is not acceptable behavior on the addict's part. You have probably already begun to discern what you deem to be unacceptable behavior. Now it's time to communicate those healthy boundaries. By failing to do so—not owning your reality, your truth—you are treating yourself with the same disregard your partner has shown you.

Some women in recovery have found it helpful to set boundaries such as these:

- He must stay in therapy for me to stay in the marriage.
- I will not engage in sex acts I find demeaning, repugnant, or uncomfortable.

- When my husband makes sexual remarks under the guise of humor, I will tell him I find that behavior offensive.
- He cannot assume I will be sexual, but must ask me if I would like to.
- I will not engage with him sexually until we both have been tested for HIV and other STDs and have waited long enough to be assured of our safety.
- It is not okay with me for him to take women to lunch alone, business or personal.

If you and your addicted partner are working with a counselor who is experienced in addressing these issues, you will both probably be asked to identify what we refer to as *nonnegotiable* and *negotiable boundaries*. Examples of nonnegotiable boundaries cosas may establish in relationship to their partners might be:

- You must stay in your aftercare for at least one year.
- You will have no work–related travel for the next six months.
- You won't go on the Internet.

As you can see, there are time frames for two of the above nonnegotiable boundaries. All three examples are boundaries that can be renegotiated at a later time. They are initially being set to provide greater stability when in crisis.

Having a discussion about boundaries and coming to an agreement about what is negotiable and what is not often stabilizes the relationship enough to allow both of you to deal with the confusion of pain and recovery. Just as you have laid out your nonnegotiable points, the addict can do the same. Undoubtedly you feel justified in your reactive behavior, but when your behavior is abusive your partner is entitled to have some boundaries as well. It doesn't mean that you cannot be angry, but it does require a level of respect. As hard as that may be to swallow, as much as you may want to hurt him as you have been hurt, it doesn't help to ease your pain or rectify the injustices.

Examples of his nonnegotiable boundaries might be:

- When you are angry it's not okay to hit me.
- It is not okay to threaten to take the kids away from me.
- You must attend therapy at least once a week.

These boundaries are emotionally laden and are best worked out with a counselor. Honor them as a commitment to your recovery.

If your partner is not pursuing recovery, you will most likely want to strategize how you will present these limits to him. It can be helpful to rehearse this conversation ahead of time so you are more confident.

Setting boundaries means taking responsibility for yourself and reclaiming the power you have given away. It is letting others know what is acceptable to you and what is not. Learning about boundaries takes time. Be patient. Get feedback from other recovering women and/or a counselor. They will have a perspective you may not have.

Freeing Yourself from the Mental Frenzy

One of the biggest challenges wives and partners of sex addicts face is preoccupation and ruminating thoughts. Ruminating is a cognitive attempt to control the situation and/or to avoid the overwhelming emotions of the situation at a time when you are trying to make sense of it. "If I can picture it, I can figure it out." "If I can say the right thing, I'll stop his behavior/ punish him/hurt him." This mental vigilance is a form of traumatizing yourself. You can be so consumed in your mind-set of preoccupation and rumination that it feels as if you are going crazy with the various images. To get out of your head means getting in touch with the feelings you are carrying. Freeing yourself from that state requires a willingness to begin to show and share those feelings, recognizing that you are the one keeping yourself trapped in this mental frenzy. It begins by accepting that preoccupation doesn't help your situation and only keeps you trapped in defeated thinking.

Let me share with you how some of the Women of the Lodge addressed this.

> [Jacque] I journal because I need to get it out of my head. Putting my thoughts and feelings down on paper has been a great tool for me. I catch myself and STOP—STOP—STOP. I see this as my scared little girl inside of me, and I speak to her. I thank her for sharing, for telling me how scared she is, but I tell her that I am doing well now and can take care of myself in a way I haven't been able to before. It's

like setting limits with your child. I set limits with myself. I just stop. Sometimes it just does not work, so then I call another cosa in my group and tell her I am struggling.

[Maite] I use the Serenity Prayer.[1] Over and over and over. Today it truly is not a problem for me.

[Sara] Oh, this has been a big one. I can get going in my head and that takes on a life of its own. One time on our way to the airport to take a trip, I had been thinking about things and suddenly I insisted he give me some details about what he did when he was with this last woman. I got focused on the sex act itself. Well, he refused to be specific. I got more and more mad, furious. By the time we arrived at the airport I refused to go on the trip, threw him his suitcase, and raced away in our car. He got on the plane and called me later. I was sure he would apologize. He called to let me know that I had thrown my own suitcase at him and he had my things. Today when I start down that road of ruminating and obsessing, I just say, "Take a hammer and hit yourself on the head because the only person you are harming is you."

· · · · · · · ·

As Sara said, "This has been a big one." Obsession and ruminating are major challenges. I don't know that I've ever worked with a cosa who didn't struggle with obsessive thoughts. Vanessa found some answers in the use of a practice she called the God Box.

[Vanessa] I use my God Box. I pray. Left to my own devices I will only ruminate and obsess. I was introduced to this concept by other recovering women who told me that they keep an actual box for this purpose. Mine sits on a shelf. So when I get into my fear and realize it, I put it down on paper and say this, "I turn it over to you."

> **And sometime during the day I will make sure it gets to the God Box.**

. . . .

Many women in recovery use a God Box; others refer to this as their Worry Box. It can be as simple as a shoebox or as fancy as a specially chosen decorative box. It's designated as the repository for those thoughts you know you can no longer carry and still maintain your health. You simply write down your thoughts and put them in the God Box. In this way, you turn your worry over to your Higher Power.

Ruminating and preoccupation are immobilizing. As natural as this behavior is, remember you are only hurting yourself with it. It is as if you are drinking poison and hoping the other person will die. When you find yourself ruminating or projecting, ask yourself, *What can I do about this right now? Is there action I can take? A decision I can make? Something tangible I can accomplish at the moment?* If so, do it. If not, let the problem go for the moment. You can do that with the help of prayer, deep breathing, meditation, and support. Keep your head where your feet are—together in the present. Then get focused on other aspects of your life. Get ready for work, make needed appointments, exercise, or finish a project. With specific recovery practices and support, you can quiet your obsessive thinking.

Building Trust

Your partner can verbalize his intentions for fidelity; he can be honest in the moment. But the only guarantee is that there are no guarantees. This issue confronts every coaddict who is new to recovery. Of course you'd like reassurance; you want to be able to trust that you're getting the truth, and it's very frustrating to know that you don't have control over that. Women become more trusting of their partners when they see them engage in recovery practices, when they see a commitment to continuing therapy or participation in self-help groups. Trust comes when that commitment to recovery practice translates into changes in behavior, such as sobriety, fewer angry outbursts, less controlling behavior, consistency in behavior, dependability, and accountability. Time plus change in behavior will be the building blocks to developing trust in your relationship.

[Therese] Time, sobriety, and working the program will help me to have more trust. I don't expect to ever trust completely again. But I can live with that. It isn't as tough as it sounds; maybe I just have less illusion about the human condition.

. . . .

When Therese says she can live with no absolutes of trust, that is only possible because of her recovery. She can live with no guarantees because she is accepting of the gifts of recovery. For so many women, life in early recovery means living in limbo and ambiguity. It is hard to keep moving forward when the future of your coupleship is not totally within your power. But it never is and never was. The illusion may feel secure, but again, it's an illusion. Recovery will lead you to restoring or developing your self-esteem, improving communication, and trusting yourself to do what is right for you. It is in your recovery process that you will choose to be account-able for your own health, practicing relational skills of knowing and speak-ing your feelings, thoughts, and needs. You speak to be accountable for yourself; you listen to better know your partner. You learn to set healthy boundaries wherein you do not forsake your own esteem. You learn to trust in your own perceptions, your own internal voice—a voice you discounted or minimized for years.

[Maite] It doesn't matter if I trust him, I trust myself. If I have a feeling, an intuition, or something doesn't feel right, today I make sure I say it. Before, it was about not trusting me, not just him. I would be too quiet. It's not okay now not to be heard. He is on his journey and I see him going to his therapy and his meetings, doing his exer-cise, and that is helping to assure me that he takes care of himself.

[Jacque] In early recovery I had this great need to know. I thought if I was up on everything that was going on in his mind, heard about every thought in his addictive think-ing, and knew about how he dealt with every temptation,

I would be able to control the situation. Later I learned
that this is a part of my own illness. Today I look at his
commitment to his Twelve Step program, attendance at
meetings, and a change in attitude as signs of recovery. I
have found I may come to trust certain things one hundred percent, but other things will not be so clear.

[Jenny] I am not in control of what will happen, and I
learn to give my fears to God.

. . . .

These women are practicing the act of "letting go." Letting go is a spiritual concept.

André Gide wrote, "One does not discover new lands without consent-
ing to lose sight of the shore for a very long time."[2] Letting go, relinquishing
the need for control, the need to be right, and the need to be all-knowing
means you genuinely accept in your heart that holding on to old behavior
holds no promise; it does not work and it does not help. For many, a willingness to be in this in-between state only becomes doable with the
alliance of a spiritual path. Chapter 8, "Finding Your Serenity," will give you
the opportunity to reflect on how spiritual practice can be significant to
your healing.

Your Sexual Relationship

While some couples insist their sexual relationship has been strong aside
from the addiction, when both partners are in recovery, the emotional and
relational tools they learned will enhance and change the previous experiences to one of greater intimacy. As chapter 5 described, a celibacy contract
is strongly advised in early recovery and before a sexual relationship is
resumed.

[Addict] Our initial sexual relationship started with me
bringing her into my addictions, so in recovery our sex life
had to start all over. I had to learn the basics of holding

hands; then we had dates where we did fun things together. We went to ball games. We hiked. During those times we held hands, we kissed on the lips, small kisses. We touched knees. We talked about little things and big things. Then we talked about how we felt after the date. Some of this sounds silly but it was great.

. . . .

The steps this addict described allowed this couple to develop a friendship; it inspired a sense of loving romance into their marriage. It created safe environments to be together and converse. It allowed both partners and the coupleship to grow intimately.

Like many women who have been socialized to feel sexually shy, this next coaddict is more focused on her partner's needs than her own.

[Coaddict] I always accepted what he thought made me feel good sexually. So while I had the physical part down, I needed to learn to tell him what I liked. I had to take risks by speaking up and taking ownership of what made me feel good versus focusing on his needs. He had to deal with his insecurity about thinking he was supposed to know what pleasured me and that somehow there was something wrong if I redirected him. We read books together about healthy sexuality and I think because we both really wanted to have this part of our relationship better, we stayed with it and today it is much better.

. . . .

In the recovery process this cosa learns to take more ownership of her sexual desires and needs, and her partner has the opportunity to share rather than to control the experience, creating intimacy.

In the past, addiction overshadowed any healthy sexual experiences, and you were likely responding to the socialization of who you are and how you are supposed to act sexually. The addict did not have healthy sexual esteem in his active addiction, and it doesn't suddenly exist just because he has quit acting out. Now, in recovery, you both bring a vulnerability to this intimate experience. You are still experiencing the feelings of a relationship that has been seriously hurt.

> [Coaddict] **My husband acts scared of being sexual with me. I can feel his tentativeness, his anxiety, and then I get anxious and frustrated. Then we get in this pattern of not even trying to be sexual.**

. . . .

This is a tentative time when unspoken thoughts and feelings sabotage the reconnection. Keep communicating.

At any point in the recovery process where sex is being avoided, it is time to again consider an agreement for a therapeutic sexual time out. During this time you're working as a couple to identify and address the barriers and resistances to sexual intimacy.

It is possible that one or both of you may experience a phenomenon of the addictive cycle called *sexual anorexia*. Sexual anorexia is a dread or self-hate of one's sexuality. Yet the term is used broadly and may also be defined as a fear of intimacy to the point where the person has severe anxiety surrounding sex.

> [Addict] **In my addiction I was nonsexual with my girl-friend but completely out of control with one-night affairs, prostitutes, phone sex, massage parlors, and the Internet. I am in recovery today, meaning I don't do those things anymore but I still avoid my partner sexually. It is not about her. Maybe her not pushing me to be sexual is about her, but I hate what I have done, that whole part of me, and when I try to be sexual with her I am impotent or I ejaculate prematurely. I am like a scared young boy. Not exactly the vision of a sex addict, is it? Ever since I was a child I have felt that I am bad for feeling sexual and should be punished.**

. . . .

The extremes of living with addiction are often reflected by switching to polar opposite behaviors. As the addict may experience sexual anorexia, you may fluctuate in your behavior, being flagrantly sexual in an attempt to combat your severe dislike of your sexual self to blatantly avoiding sexual behaviors. This is similar to the binge/purge cycle of a bulimic where he or she overeats and then purges the food. It is also possible to simply move to one side of the continuum and stay there in a more purely anorexic, deprived state. Irrespective of the pattern, binge or purge, recovery involves learning and valuing healthy sexuality and addressing the loss and trauma issues that underlie this severe reaction to one's sexuality.

> [Coaddict] As much as I hated knowing he was sexual with others, in some ways I was relieved to not be sexual. I had never liked that part of me. For years I wouldn't confront him about what I knew he was doing because then he wouldn't ask much from me.

. . . .

Undoubtedly, the key to healthy sexuality for you and the addict begins with emotional healing. When there is so much anger, shame, and pain, you need to be realistic and patient in your expectations. Conversations about what is satisfying and emotionally safe for both partners need to occur and keep occurring throughout your coupleship. As you build your adult-to-adult relationship around spiritually and emotionally healthy guidelines, the physical aspect of your relationship can become a more enriching experience.

Facing Relapse

What if he acts out again? Reengaging in the behavior after some recovery practice is referred to as *relapse*. Unfortunately the possibility is always there, and relapses occur for many in the recovery process. In a treatment process or a Twelve Step program, the addict will have defined for himself what sexual sobriety entails, and that will vary depending on how he acted out. It could mean he will not use the Internet to access sexual sites, or it could mean he'll not use the Internet at all. He could determine that he

can still masturbate or that masturbation is not allowed. He will have identified what is a part of his addiction cycle, and he will be accountable for
what triggers him to act out.

Most women find that with some time in recovery, they look at any
relapse in its overall context. What was the behavior? How did the addict
respond to having a relapse? How quickly did he tell you and others to
whom he is accountable about the relapse? In what ways was he accountable? What is he doing to prevent a future relapse? Is he asking himself what
he needs to do or address in his recovery that he was not attending to or
previously addressing enough?

One woman became aware her partner was watching sexual videos and
masturbating. He told both his Twelve Step sponsor (a chosen mentor in his
Twelve Step program) and her within a couple of days of his relapse. In her
mind he was being accountable by quickly owning his behavior and having
some insight into what triggered it. He also had a plan to handle the trigger
differently should it occur again. She expressed her disappointment, fear,
and anger about his behavior, but determined that it was his to address and
that she would stay focused on her recovery.

Therese was confronted with her husband's relapsing when he began
using pornography again and then sought out women at a massage parlor.
He had been having relapses about every four months that involved
pornography on the Net, but this behavior was a major escalation from that.
By then he had been in recovery for a few years, and his relapses were like
binge drinking—periods of being dry and then a short period of acting out
on a cyclical basis. This relapse led to a therapeutic separation for the couple.
The consequence here appears more severe, but in the overall context, they
both saw this relapse as a threat to his long-term recovery and their marriage, and they felt a therapeutic separation would help them better address
their individual recovery issues.

You have choices about how you respond to known relapses. How you
think you will respond and how you actually respond may vary. That is
most likely dependent on your history with the addict and how much
more you are willing to tolerate. You may feel there is no room for any
relapse or the relationship will end, and that is your bottom line. Women
whom I have worked with had the greatest difficulty with relapses that
included other people or that had legal ramifications. Relapses that include

masturbation, viewing X-rated videos, or attending a strip joint may be more forgivable. But all relapses are serious because they create distortion in your relationship; they set up a disconnection between the two of you and may trigger escalating behavior on his part. It may offer some comfort to believe you know exactly how you'd handle a relapse should it occur. Yet I suggest you not try to problem-solve and don't live in the future of "what ifs." If you are in your own healing process, you will have the tools to address a relapse should it occur.

As the addict may experience relapse, coaddicts do as well. Coaddiction recovery is not always as identifiable as bottom-line behavior may be for the addict, but you will find it helpful in your healing to recognize the reengagement of self-defeating thoughts and behaviors as your own relapse. In coaddiction relapse, you return to a pattern of behavior, such as resuming your detective behavior, saying yes to situations when you really want to say no, or verbal raging.

What would your relapse behaviors be?

Remember that recovery is a process; you are learning new ways of thinking and relating. This process takes time, so you don't need to be harsh on yourself.

Asking for Help

You have probably been coping on your own or with the advice and direction of family and friends. Hopefully the time has come for you to let go of your fears and shame and be willing to get help from a professional or recovery program that specifically addresses your issues. This means you recognize that your best efforts don't have the power to change him, you don't like your own thoughts and behaviors, and you recognize how your life is being impacted. This is a journey where your relationship is in jeopardy and your foundational beliefs about your self-worth and value are in question. Depression, anxiety, and a host of self-defeating coaddictive behaviors are governing your life. Perhaps your own addictions have come to light. Signs of post-traumatic stress may become apparent, as well as the role of childhood wounding and trauma repetition.

You deserve the opportunity to work with someone, privately or in a group, who can lead and support you. Professional and self-help resources are out there. Look for a therapist who has specific training in how to work with families impacted by sex addiction. Most will have CSAT (Certified Sex Addiction Therapist) training available through IITAP (the International Institute for Trauma and Addiction Professionals) or be affiliated with SASH (the Society for the Advancement of Sexual Health) or specific treatment programs. Begin by asking around for names of therapists who have experience working with your issues. Talk with others who have struggled with the same problems and who have sought the help of a professional. Find out what they valued or did not value about their choice of therapist before you call for an appointment. If it is difficult to find a therapy group, perhaps you already have or know a counselor who, with a little encouragement and effort on your part, would be willing to start a group focusing on cosa issues. It only takes two clients to begin a group.

Be open to exploring specific Twelve Step programs for partners and spouses of sex addicts. S-Anon and COSA groups are more prevalent than the lesser-known Codependents of Sex and Love Addicts Anonymous (COSLAA). The focus of these groups is specific to partners of sex addicts. Recovering Couples Anonymous (RCA) is also a viable Twelve Step program for couples to attend together. Because these meetings are held primarily in larger urban areas, and thus unavailable to some, many women will need to find a program of recovery in the Twelve Step programs of Al-Anon, Codependents Anonymous, and Adult Children of Alcoholics. Al-Anon offers a strong basis for "staying on your side of the sidewalk"—taking responsibility for yourself without being preoccupied with your partner's behavior. The latter two groups will help you focus directly on codependency and family of origin issues. Twelve Step meetings are peer led with no professional facilitation and no fees. Confidentiality and anonymity are strongly reinforced. They are structured on the traditions and recovery steps of the original successful model of Alcoholics Anonymous.

See pages 237–240 to find a list of Web sites that will be helpful in seeking professional and/or self-help services.

While a group may not be conveniently located and available in your area, many cosas involved in Al-Anon, AA, or other Twelve Step group experience have initiated the formation of a Twelve Step cosa model using materials readily available from the COSA national office.

[Jacque] In the beginning I drove two hundred miles round-trip to find a cosa group. After several months in both this group and in Al-Anon in my hometown, I started a cosa group in my own community. I practically ran to a group looking for hope and help with how to live with this problem. I was looking for connections with others who would validate my feelings, women whose lives looked like mine.

[Coaddict] For so much of my marriage I was the crazy one, and I think others thought that too. I was the one who went searching in my car to bar after bar, made scenes in public places, got hysterical over little things. I was angry all the time. I had given my life over to the addiction. In my groups I can recognize my own craziness and see it for what it was. Clearly I needed some help. I found a Twelve Step group for co-sex addicts. Today I focus on my behavior. In essence, I stay on my side of the sidewalk.

. . . .

Reflect back on the women who introduced themselves in chapter 1. In their journeys all of them found a place in a group. Some of them entered a specific therapy group for spouses and/or partners of sex addicts; others connected in a Twelve Step group. Initially the only thing they knew about these groups was that there would be other women and possibly men there who had spouses and/or partners who identified as sex addicts.

[Therese] I couldn't believe that I was so desperate that I would take myself to this group of people who supposedly had the same type of problems I was having. How could that be? When I felt my whole family disintegrating, with pressure from my counselor I was willing to do anything that might take away my horrendous pain. To think that life is full of so many hidden secrets. And then I began to hear others and realized they were the mirror image of

me. My pain was at least temporarily set aside as I felt both shock and relief to know I was not alone.

[Vanessa] I was so scared, confused, and uncertain of my marriage. I was intimidated by the words "sex addiction." How strange to be intimidated. After all, sex addiction was what I was living with. I found myself driving around in any and all directions, not sure why I was going in the direction I was. I finally had the sense to pull the car over, stop, and try to figure out what I was doing. Odd, but in essence, it's what I needed to do with my life.

[Sara] I walked into the group room full of anger and fury about what my husband was doing. I was in absolute terror about my future and the future of my family, both financially and emotionally. The fear was overwhelming. I was in horrible pain about the choices and mistakes I had made, the shame about our situation. I knew I didn't know all of the facts. I would go through more shocks, hurt, shame, and outrage. And it was in that room that I would find a way out of my shame and pain.

[Jenny] Here I was walking into this group of women who had partners or husbands like mine. Men who flagrantly, yet deceivingly, had been with other women in lots of different ways—women in massage parlors, women at work, even women who were supposedly friends. I had been living in a capsule for so long, drifting at sea, being tossed around in a storm. I was ready to no longer be alone.

. . . .

I cannot emphasize enough the healing power of a group—whether it is a self-help group or therapy group—of women who have experiences similar to yours. In both Twelve Step groups and therapy, confidentiality is strongly adhered to. I know you probably feel ashamed and angry and don't want to be exposed. You think this is a private issue and may be concerned about your family's anonymity. Yet it is in the group experience that many women heal to a degree they never imagined possible. In the group they come to realize their healing journey is a gift to themselves that will take them through life and its ultimate challenges.

Even though you have read how many women found answers in a group setting you may still find yourself procrastinating. "Yes, but . . ." "Yes, but I have child care problems." "Yes, but I have transportation problems." Or "Yes, but I am very well known and visible in my community and couldn't possibly expose myself like that."

Stop. Take a deep breath. Prioritize your well-being, as it affects every aspect of your life. I know you don't want to keep living with stress and shame. Perhaps your unwillingness to reach out to others is because you don't want to intrude; maybe you think you've imposed enough on those people closest to you. Your fear of being burdensome is an aspect of your codependency and is detrimental to your welfare. You deserve better; you deserve more. If child care is a concern, think about asking a family member or trusted friend to sit with your children. If transportation is your problem, seek out community resources or public transportation. A Twelve Step member will often offer to help you get to a meeting. If you maintain a high profile in your community and you feel that the visibility of participating in a group would greatly impact other areas of your life, know that the anonymity at Twelve Step meetings is sacred, and confidentiality is required in therapy with a professional. Also, here in the United States there are specialists in the sex addiction field working with many high-profile individuals and couples. But it is mostly fear and shame that will keep you away. As you allow your reality to be acknowledged, the fear and shame will lessen.

~~~~~~~~~~~~~~

Your time to heal has come. It won't happen all at once; it will be a process. There will continue to be obstacles to overcome, pain to face, and work to do. Yet on your journey of healing, you'll gain the strength to walk through the pain. You'll learn to own your voice, identify your feelings, and grieve your losses. You will come to terms with your powerlessness over your partner's addictive behavior and recognize where your personal power lies.

It lies with your own behavior and your choices. The work you'll do—establishing boundaries and letting go of the need to control—will be a freeing experience that increases your sense of who you are and what you need and want. This will give you the courage to be the person you want to be, who you truly are. You will feel your value and worth and come to embrace the need for self-care, knowing it is an act of self-love. You deserve that. And you don't need to do this alone. Addiction and coaddiction are about isolation, disconnection from self and others. Recovery is about connection. Allow others to be a part of this journey.

Reflective Thoughts and Questions

- Do you agree that it is your time to heal? What does that mean to you?

- How would you describe yourself in the grief process?

- To what degree and how do you identify with being powerless?

- Where does your power lie?

- In what areas of your life do you recognize aspects of unmanageability?

- Which boundary violations do you identify with?

- What are some important boundaries that will help you at this time in your recovery?

- What can you do to lessen your ruminating and preoccupation?

- Do you find yourself preoccupied by wondering if you can trust your partner? "If so, how can you let go of that mental frenzy long enough so that recovery practice and new behaviors can take effect?"

- Do you recognize any present barriers on your part to a healthier sexual relationship?

- What self-defeating thoughts and behaviors would you identify as relapse indicators for you?

- Have you been willing to ask for help? Do you need more assistance?

- What was important for you to hear in this chapter?

Chapter Eight

Finding Your Serenity

Can I ever forgive him?

How do I find peace?

With every tear that you shed and every outcry of rage you release, more room is opened in your heart for forgiveness and a sense of peace to enter. As you progress in your own journey of recovery, you will likely contemplate forgiveness and what that means for you. You will develop a deeper connection with God or a Higher Power. And you will discover your own spiritual path. These are all ways to support your healing process.

Forgiveness

Women have been taught that they owe it to others to forgive their transgressions. But there are no "shoulds" here. The addict often asks for your forgiveness soon after you've heard the news. Frequently women who immediately offer forgiveness to their partners are engaging in what we refer to as *cheap* or *false forgiveness*—an act that deepens the denial process by promoting an illusion of closeness when nothing has changed, has been faced, or has been resolved. You may want to dismiss the injury to yourself and the relationship for the sake of protecting it. Your record and habit of being overly compliant and going to great lengths to avoid conflict is entrenched. In her book *How Can I Forgive You?* Janis Spring eloquently describes cheap forgiveness as trying to preserve a relationship at any cost, including sacrificing your integrity and safety. On the surface you may act as if nothing is wrong, but inside you're bleeding out. Silencing your anguish and indignation only silences your heart and soul.[1]

False Forgiveness

To avoid disrupting the relationship with expectations or boundaries, cheap forgiveness may come readily to you. Perhaps a deep fear of conflict and anger, the fear of rejection and abandonment, or the strong need for outside approval fuel your desire to quickly forgive. With a smile on your face, you remain in the relationship without voice and with impoverished expectations. Or you leave the relationship only to reengage in another, repeating your pattern. Once again, you don't ask, you don't expect, and you don't operate from a place of esteem or worth, but from a place of defeat or silent defiance.

> [Therese] I was so busy doing what I thought was right. I thought I forgave my husband. I said the words; I smiled. Well, there is no right here. Of course I knew I was hurt. I was angry, but I was working so hard to not be angry. I thought that made me look bad and I wanted him to be the bad person; after all, his behavior was the problem. I just couldn't tolerate being out of control with my feelings, which is how I feel when I'm angry. So I smiled and talked forgiveness and then silently punished and controlled him as much as I could. I was still living inside his addiction.

> [Maite] Before recovery I did a lot of false (controlled) forgiveness. I pretended to forgive, but I kept a secret file with all the information about his lovers and acting-out behaviors just in case, and I would gossip about his behavior with others.

> [Jenny] Prior to my beginning any specific recovery, I had a lot of years of false forgiveness. Mostly it was just going numb and trying to breathe. But after recovery began and I really understood what we were both dealing with, he would badger me by telling me I had to forgive him because, after all, he was changing. But it was badgering, and it was not a lot different from his old behavior. A bit

> softer in volume, but the tone was still a threat to me.
> Somehow it was like if I would say the words, "I forgive
> you," then I didn't have the right to have any limits or
> ask for things to be different.

· · · · · · · · ·

You won't get to a place of heartfelt forgiveness without being emotionally honest. When you say you forgive but you have not claimed your voice, not grieved your pain, and not owned the injustice, then you're only talking the talk but not walking the walk of recovery.

I worked briefly with a woman who was not willing to stay in the therapy process or to ask her husband to look seriously at his behavior. They had been married for twenty-five years, and during all those years he blatantly acted out with other women, flaunting them in her face. She spent all those years in the act of cheap forgiveness. She didn't believe her husband's repetitive sexual acting out was addictive, but even more she didn't think he had any responsibility for his behavior. She frequently caught him in his lies and deceit, and she forgave him time after time after time. She thought, *He really does love me; it's just those other women.* Her vision focused only on his woman of the moment. She was convinced that as long as the other women stayed away, she and her husband were just fine. He did love her; it was just that those other women came in as if from outer space and captured him against his will.

Forgiveness and Recovery

Being able or willing to forgive is not the focus of recovery. If you have just become aware of the nature of your partner's behavior, you are still grieving significant losses. Forgiveness at this point would be very premature and most likely false—again, cheap forgiveness. The process of true forgiveness begins with acknowledging that a wrong has been done to you. Then you can grieve; you can own the feelings associated with those wrongs, and that certainly means owning your anger and pain. You pursue your own recovery, set boundaries, and decide which behaviors in the relationship you can and cannot accept.

Whether or not the relationship is sustained, the act of forgiving is about your own healing; it is about letting go of resentments, preoccupation, and controlling behavior. Far too often when there is a separation or divorce the cosa holds on to her resentments. I've met many women years later who are still consumed with resentments pertaining to their previous partner. This negativity in their life that comes with obsessive resentment darkens every other relationship, be it with their children, friends, coworkers, or new partners.

Forgiveness is a moral right, not your moral obligation. Love does not obligate you. Ultimately, forgiveness is remembering and letting go. It is about being true to you. So don't put a timetable on this. Don't put any "shoulds" onto yourself. Forgiveness is made possible with your commitment to your own recovery practices.

It may offer you some peace of mind while you are in this journey to have a framework for forgiveness. Only in knowing what that means can you put it into a healing perspective. Think about the following aspects of forgiveness.

When you forgive, you no longer build an identity around something that happened to you. You realize that there is more to you than your history with your partner. The past is put into its proper perspective as one part of who you are in the present.

When you forgive, you recognize that you no longer need your grudges and resentments, your hatred, your self-pity. You don't need these negative emotions as excuses for getting less out of life than you want or deserve. You do not need them as a weapon to hurt those who hurt you or to keep other people from getting close enough to hurt you again. You no longer want to punish the people who hurt you. You realize that you truly do not want to even the score; forgiveness is the inner peace you feel when you stop trying to do so.

> [Coaddict] I found my way to forgiveness when I began to set boundaries and tell my boyfriend what I needed from him. I asked for very specific things, and when he responded positively it softened my heart. I asked him to talk to the children, who were seventeen and twenty. I knew they knew a lot, but technically it was still all a big secret. I was looking like the bad guy because I was so

angry and depressed. So together we sat and talked to them. We did that with some guidelines from a counselor. It took a lot of courage and I am grateful. I asked that he change departments at work and he did that. He didn't want to but he did it anyway. I was just too upset all of the time to know he was working next to one of the people he acted out with. I asked him to change his cell phone number. I asked a lot of things and he actually did them. That was all part of the process, but I think his willingness to hear me and to respect my requests helped make it possible for me to begin to forgive.

[Sara] Forgiveness is the most challenging thing of all. Well, forgiveness and trust. I have learned over the years that forgiveness is a process totally about me, not about another person. It's about what I want for myself. In the Big Book of Alcoholics Anonymous it is suggested that what you want for yourself, you pray for for your enemy. I believe that forgiveness is manifested through prayer for their well-being. That is how I have come to forgiveness.

[Maite] Real forgiveness started for me when, through education and being in therapy groups with addicts and coaddicts, I was able to see this as a disease, a compulsive disorder that affected his brain and hijacked his will and his soul and, in that process, mine too. The losses, craziness, and fears are real and painful but they can be explained, and I put them in another context. It is not about me or even him. As I call it, it is a cancer of the soul, our souls. We are a wounded couple, a lot alike, thirsty for healing. That was the beginning of compassion, true compassion, and a lot of grieving for me, for him, for our families, our losses, our lives. It was not about judging; it was about getting control of a disorder that was destroying us, not only during crisis, but on a daily basis. Soon after that I started having glimpses of the gifts of the pain, and that was the beginning of my new spirituality.

[Vanessa] Coming from a highly religious background, I think I had a warped viewpoint of forgiveness; high levels of judgment were a part of the formula followed by mandated forgiveness, which simply meant bury it. Operating from this misguided viewpoint of forgiveness just made me more toxic. I would forgive him verbally and then throw it back in his face at the first sign of trouble. It fed my superiority and confusion. It also kept me in a dangerous place of denying the resentment. You can't heal from what you don't own. I first had to experience the pain rather than medicate it through busyness or helping others. As a perpetual happy-face codependent, I had to get to the root of my anger and do some releasing. It was very hard work, considering it was buried so deep. But a wonderful freedom comes from congruence and authenticity! Upon experiencing and feeling honest emotions, I was then able to release it.

A very valuable tool for me to come to a place of genuine forgiveness with both my husband's acting out and my father's raging behavior was to start seeing them in their own woundedness; realizing they were not participating in these behaviors to be mean to me, but because they were broken. Hurt people, hurt people. In one of my groups, we were led through a visualization in which we got in touch with our inner child. Then we were to see our abuser as a child as well. In the exercise we introduced the two pure little children and I visualized them walking off together hand in hand, unfettered by the pains that drove their adult actions. It was a beautiful way for me to see them for who they were at their core rather than simply by their actions. This was another step to letting go of the resentments and anger I was carrying and to

> honoring the soul instead of continuing to focus on the
> behavior. To this day I find this exercise very helpful
> when I can't seem to get past a behavior that disturbs me.

· · · · · · · · ·

It may be easier to appreciate what forgiveness is by recognizing what forgiveness is not. The following thoughts may be helpful to you as you sort through your feelings and come to terms with the role of forgiveness in your healing.

Forgiveness is not forgetting what has happened. Your past experiences and pain have a great deal to teach you about not being victimized again and about not victimizing others. Forgiving the people who hurt you does not mean you condone or absolve them of their behavior. You are not saying that what was done to you was acceptable or unimportant or was not hurtful. It was important, it hurt, and it has made a difference in your life. Forgiveness doesn't erase what he has done. He is still responsible for the harm his behavior has created.

Forgiveness doesn't mean you are never angry again about what occurred. What happened to you was not right; it was not fair. For that you may always feel anger. You have every reason and right to be angry. But you want to get to a point where your anger no longer interferes with how you care about yourself or how you live your life.

Forgiveness doesn't happen by making a one-time decision. No matter how sincerely you want to let go of the past and move on with your life, you cannot just wave a magic wand or flip a switch and blithely make the past disappear in one moment.

> [Jacque] What he did was not okay. I hated him for it. I
> trusted him because I wanted so badly for him to be my
> knight in shining armor. Now I know I blindly trusted.
> It's been a couple of years now in recovery for both of us,
> and I have forgiven him. My ability to forgive him came
> as I found my strength. I set boundaries I had never pre-
> viously had. I owned feelings I have spent my life avoid-
> ing. As I started to take care of me and think about me,
> I insisted on recovery practices for the marriage that I

hoped would ensure our relationship. As he moved forward in recovery, I could be more compassionate to who he was. But during this time I did not focus on wanting to forgive him. That wasn't even in my realm of thinking. I was just trying to make sense out of what had happened in my life. I didn't want to live with self-loathing and pain. I came to understand us in a way I hadn't before and could see how we were a perfect match for each other. We were both in search of wholeness, which ultimately has only been found in our recovery. From that strength of being more whole, I could come to the place of forgiveness.

· · · · · · · · ·

Forgiveness doesn't mean reconciliation. Sometimes you fight against any form of forgiveness because you think that means you have to stay in the relationship. Reconciliation is a choice. You may choose to leave the relationship, or he may opt out. Whether or not the relationship survives, the recovery process is your opportunity to let go of self-defeating thoughts, feelings, and behaviors; to learn new relational skills; and garner esteem from within. Too often the relationship ends, and even if that is your choice, you stay angry and depressed and continue to act in ways that erode your esteem. That does not have to be you.

[Jenny] After some time in recovery there was this quiet acceptance. I didn't know if I forgave him, but I quit hating him. I started to see him differently. He was no longer this monster to me. Yet I chose to divorce after a couple of years of us working a recovery program. Not letting him back into my life in a committed relationship had nothing to do with forgiving or not forgiving him, it had to do with boundaries. I found we had too little foundation and I could feel no love. I can get philosophical at times about what our journey together was about. I go in and out of times when I feel anger about the years we spent together, being hurtful toward ourselves and each other. I still have to deal with him around our kids, and I

find myself judgmental and critical—I am not perfect by any means. I realize I am human. How is that for self-forgiveness? Today I am more at peace than ever, not because I am not with him anymore but because I chose to quit hanging on to my resentments and my wounds. I also decided to quit being the victim. That was amazing. What freedom it gave me to be genuinely more loving to myself and even to him.

[Coaddict] Here he was crying, pleading with me to stay, to not leave. He did appear to be sincere. I believed him in the moment, but I had heard some of this before. The counselor told me that he believed him. I thought the counselor was telling me I was supposed to forgive him. But I needed time. I needed to see different action. I will say my anger has quieted. For now I stay focused on what I need to do for me, knowing that it will be of help to us re-creating a different relationship. As for forgiveness—I think I love him, and there are things I respect about him, but I will just see where this healing journey leads me.

. . . .

Self-forgiveness

In addition to forgiving your partner, you need to look at forgiving yourself for any behavior that has hurt others and your behavior that has hurt you. You may have been unavailable to your children or close friends because you were caught up in the throes of preoccupation or depression. You may have had a revenge affair or hurt yourself with negative self-talk. You may have lied and covered up for the addict. You need to forgive yourself for ignoring your suspicions, for making unfair comparisons by idealizing his lover and degrading yourself, for discounting your own perceptions, for tolerating the abusive behavior, and for making peace at any cost. The list can seem endless. You are human and you deserve acceptance for who you are in your humanness.

[Jacque] Even more helpful to me in my recovery than coming to forgive my husband was coming to forgive myself. I have been able to forgive myself for my sexual acting out, for how my fears allowed me to stay a door-mat and not be confrontational, for how I would back down from my ultimatums, and for how I would berate myself and doubt myself. Oh, I had beaten myself up so much of my life. It is nice to get to a place where I don't do that any more and, even more so, have incredible compassion for why and how I did those things to myself.

. . . .

To get to a place of self-forgiveness you begin by stopping your negative self-talk, such as "I should have known better, I'm so stupid." You aren't stupid; you shouldn't have known better. Self-recrimination will only make you feel worse. You were scared, operating from a place of low esteem; you may simply have not known how to protect yourself, honor yourself, or express your feelings any differently. It's so much easier for women to extend compassion to others than to themselves. So pause, be reflective, and extend that courtesy to yourself. Self-forgiveness comes by taking baby steps; it doesn't come all at once, but you too can get to this place of self-love that other women have gotten to.

[Coaddict] I have had to forgive myself for a lot of my behavior that was hurtful toward myself. A biggie for me was that I felt like I prostituted myself to him in doing sexual things I didn't want to do just to keep him happy or to keep him from getting angry. Today I accept that that behavior came from being scared, not having a strong sense of my own worth. I don't want to ever be in that place again.

[Vanessa] I cannot stress enough how important the con-cepts of self-forgiveness and self-love were to me. Until I

truly forgave and loved myself, I had no capacity to give
the same gift to someone else.

. . . .

With forgiveness you can look at your partner apart from his behavior
and weigh the good and the bad. You can look with empathy toward yourself and how you contributed to the impairment in the relationship. You
can give up the need for revenge, stop obsessing about what has occurred,
and reengage in your own life.

> [Coaddict] **Forgiveness took time—time for me to heal;
> to come to my own rescue; to sort out all the confusion,
> control, and obsession; and to let go. It also took the help
> of a counselor. For me, forgiveness had many prongs. I
> had to forgive my parents, my abuser, my husband, and
> most importantly I had to forgive myself. Forgive myself
> for not being perfect, for not protecting myself, for not
> getting help and into recovery sooner.**

. . . .

For you to heal it is necessary to have a commitment to healing; forgiveness will then take care of itself. Forgiveness is something that you come to
gradually over time in degrees. Ultimately, it is your own powerful spirit
that will heal you.

Spirituality: Where Is Your God?

Infidelity and all that comes with it doesn't leave you much time or energy
for the emotional work required to build or maintain a connection with God
or a Higher Power. You may not be the least bit convinced that a spiritual
solution is the answer. You may have little practice in allowing God into your
life, or you may be questioning your faith. So how does spirituality fit into
this picture? Consider the fact that the problems you are facing may be so
debilitating that human power alone is not sufficient to handle them.

It's possible your entire life has been about reacting, surviving, and keeping vigilant watch over outside forces. You've found your esteem through others; you've been trying to please, accommodate, and take care of others. However, discovering your true self cannot be done solely from the outside. Healing changes the course of your search for serenity from the outer world to the inner world.

Becoming whole requires a journey into and through the darkness of the wounds of childhood. When you begin to experience the world as less frightening, when you know you can take care of yourself, and when you know you have the inner resources to make it, you do not have to live in hypervigilance any longer. You can say no to your shame. By doing these things, you move beyond the confines of the past on a course of spirituality in the present. As this happens, you will realize you cannot rely on your partner to make you whole, and you can and will be okay with or without him.

You deserve the opportunity to make that inward journey. In *A Dialogue with Hasidic Tales,* Maurice Friedman relates the Hasidic belief that if you want to change from one reality to another, you must first go through a "between-stage" in which you must morph into a blank slate. During this between-stage you will experience a "holy despair," which happens when you know that no other help will come except that which is from a Higher Power. When you accept that you cannot be the Higher Power yourself, it is the turning point of your recovery. When you come to believe that the Higher Power is all around you and also within you, that marks the turning point of your spirituality.[2]

[Jacque] **My spirituality was compartmentalized. Like the rest of my life: broken, separate, not flowing. I grew up Catholic, went to church, and followed the rules, but it was something I had to do. Prayer offered me no solace. They were just words to repeat. The weekend my husband told me he was leaving was the weekend of Easter. I felt as if I were in a slimy pit with slick walls and no way to climb to the top. I was truly alone with no one to tell, no one to talk to. I listened through my pain to the inner voice that said, "Go to Mass." I hauled myself off to church and cried through the entire service. I'm sure the priest**

thought I was nuts. It may sound funny, but I could feel the presence of God, perhaps for the first time in my life. I think I was so raw, so empty, I had finally hit bottom and there was an opening in my armor to allow God into my life. I had let go because I felt I had hit a wall; there was nothing left. By finally finding God, I had an ability to turn my life and will over.

The Serenity Prayer has become so valuable to me. Sometimes I journal and use each line of the prayer as a starting point. It helps me sort out, sift through, and give up to God. I love my God Box too. I learned about it from another cosa. Whenever I am struggling with an issue, thought, or obsession, I write it down and put it in the box. It actively helps me let go, and it works! I know God is present; I can hear and I can listen. A therapist once asked me where I thought God was when I was being abused as a child. At first I said clearly God was not around. But really when I think about it, God can't stop the evil in the world. He must have been present. I'm still alive, fairly normal, and not mentally insane. He protected my spirit, kept me whole, and led me to recovery. God had to have been there protecting me and my psyche.

Spirituality for me is different from going to church. For me, spirituality is finding God in the everyday around me: in nature, in the breath of wind, in my dog's smile. I look to God when I get cut off in traffic and say, "Oh well, God must not want me to get there now." And I used to have road rage! Obviously, I had a lot of anger, and the only place I felt safe getting it out was raging at other faceless, nameless drivers around me.

I have learned to pray about anything and everything, to seek God's guidance, and, more important, to thank God for my life.

* * * * * * * *

Most women I work with, such as Jacque, come to find an acceptance and peace in their lives as they embrace a God or a Higher Power. Some women exercise faith in a Higher Being through their religious practice or at their house of worship; others find theirs through their Twelve Step involvement.

[Maite] Before recovery, my spiritual life was about a God out there whom I had to please in order to be loved—a lot like my relationship with my parents. Since recovery, I've learned about other spiritual practices, especially Zen Buddhism. I meditate several times a day, I trust my inner guidance, and I am learning to let my husband and kids trust theirs. I look for the sacred in everything, especially inside myself and in others. As a woman in my culture, I am the spiritual compass of the family. I'm looked up to and valued as such; therefore, as I heal, my family heals too.

[Sara] My ingrained religious practices just weren't work-ing; they were too judgmental, too fear-based, and involved too much magical thinking. My religion was more about having a formula; if you do A-B-C, then D will happen. But it doesn't work that way. It was in Twelve Step pro-grams that I learned spiritual principles, such as showing up, service, and unconditional love. In Al-Anon, I would show up and not talk. I couldn't talk because the pain was too great. I went for months and months. They wel-comed me. They supported me. I felt the love. I had never in my life felt unconditional love. What I was learning gave me a chance to live in the present—spirituality was freedom, a bigger plan that was not up to me to control. And I desperately needed something I wasn't trying to control. This spiritual path worked. There's a Twelve Step saying, "It works if you work it," and I just did my best to work it even when I was totally skeptical, which I was.

My inner knowing is my best companion. I don't have
to deny it, hide it, or explain it to be able to fit into any
intellectual or religious group, as I did before. Today I
think of the addiction as a privileged journey of losses,
pain, fear, and grieving to teach me to let go of my
attachments to outside persons and things, and to go into
my soul in order to find my wholeness and my divine,
universal connection to everything and everybody. That
is the gift.

. . . .

Sara was learning what Gary Zukav, author of *The Seat of the Soul,* says:
"Your soul is not a passive or theoretical entity that occupies a space in the
vicinity of your chest cavity. It is a positive purposeful force at the core of
your being."[3]

[Jenny] My faith saved me. I hurled myself into reading
scripture and listening to sermons and Christian music on
the radio. I joined recovery Bible studies. All of this gave
me the courage and a foundation to come out of denial
and into reality. I came to realize that instead of asking
for what I needed and wanted, I was covertly trying to
manipulate others to get what I wanted. As soon as I confessed that I had been trying to control the situations and
the people in my household, God was faithful to give me
strength to trust Him. Every time things worked out fine!
God revealed to me that feelings of unworthiness separate
us from Christ. I had to accept all of myself before I could
let Christ accept me. I had to find out that there was a
part of myself that I was denying.

[Co-addict] I feel several things from my culture are helpful and they are closely related to my Catholic/African-
Indigenous mix. The most important one is having faith in
a universal Higher Power that is in charge of everything. I
am not alone. There are guiding beings, seen and unseen,

to help me when I need it. I know the pain and darkness
are not forever. They are only challenges that make me
stronger as a person and purify my soul. With patience
(Let Go) and faith (Let God), everything is possible.

[Vanessa] The key for me was moving from my rigid
religious upbringing to an authentic relationship with a
loving God. I have studied Jesus, Buddha, shamans, and
saints, and have come to believe that a true connection to
your Divine is paramount to your journey. It was about
finding quiet in my soul and learning the gifts of "being"
in all circumstances. Self-love, forgiveness, peace, and
equanimity are all keys to healing that I can only find
when this part of my soul has been ignited. To me, surrender is impossible without God. Releasing my control
and pain was only possible when I had a powerful, loving
God to give it to. That represented true healing to me. I
no longer deny or hold on to my pain because I now
believe that something greater than me will look after it.
I truly connected with my Divine by working through
years of religious indoctrination to establish a connection
within myself and my God. This allowed me to find the
powerful gifts of surrender and forgiveness, which has
resulted in peace. To genuinely resonate with peace and
love in my soul was a path to healing.

· · · · · · · ·

Even if you don't come from a background where you were introduced
to a Higher Power, or you do not have a history connected to a specific
faith, be open to the possibility. These women found incredible direction
and peace in their spiritual practice.

The Spiritual Path

For a path to enhance the evolution of your spiritual well-being, it must be
creative, not destructive; progressive, not regressive. It must stimulate and

enhance, not stifle, your spiritual well-being. In *The Teachings of Don Juan,* Carlos Castaneda writes, "Look at every path closely and deliberately. Try it as many times as you feel is necessary. Then ask yourself, and yourself alone, one question: Does this path have a heart? If it does, it is good; if it doesn't then it is of no use."[4]

Many women in recovery develop a spiritual path in their relationship to nature, song, or meditation. Julia Cameron, author of *The Artist's Way,* has instructed millions of women on the practice of daily morning free writing, which she calls Morning Pages.[5] Daily free writing or journaling can be grounding, centering, and a wonderful form of meditation. Other contemplative pursuits, such as physical activity, singing, and connecting to nature, will also still and free your mind.

> [Jacque] **Walking has become my time of contemplation. In my walking I find silence. I find beauty in my path. There is a stillness in which I go within.**

> [Coaddict] **Bicycling has been the time I feel a physical and personal strength, and in that time I am able to feel my feelings and gain a sense of direction. I take these wonderful moments in my ride to stop in some incredible scenic places and just be still.**

. . . .

Think about meditation literally. Many women in their fear and anger have metaphorically developed hardened or closed hearts. The closed heart cuts off the flow of the blood to itself and other body parts. The clinical term for this is *atherosclerosis,* a process by which plaque builds up and interferes with the flow of the coronary arteries. Famed heart specialist Dr. Dean Ornish, in his studies in India, recognized the connection between unresolved anger and fear (closed heart chakra and closed coronary arteries) and found that diet, exercise, support groups, and meditation could reverse heart disease without invasive procedures.[6] In many languages, cognates of the word *spirit* mean *breath* or *to breathe.* Meditation allows you to open your heart and lungs. It offers the opportunity to clear your mind and be present with the here and now.

It doesn't matter which spiritual path you take (Christianity, Judaism, Islam, Mother Earth, or others) or what form it takes (prayer, song, nature, meditation), what's important is that you keep moving forward and growing on the path you have chosen.

Questions you may want to consider:

- If you practice a particular faith, how can it support you in your healing process?
- If you have no specific faith or religion, what spiritual practice might you try?
- What form of spiritual practice appeals to you? Are you willing to try it?
- Do you find sound or silence conducive to a sense of spiritual connection?
- Have you established, or could you establish, any personal daily rituals?

Author Brian Seaward, in his book *Stand Like Mountain, Flow Like Water,* speaks of the path using the metaphor of a mountain climber seeking the summit. He says, "To stand on a mountain peak epitomizes the expression 'I have touched the face of God.' Yet the trip of life doesn't end at the mountaintop. One only stays long enough to enjoy the view and become inspired before beginning the descent. There is no one best route up the mountain, only several paths each offering different experiences." He goes on to quote author Glen Clark: "If you wish to travel far and fast, travel light. Take off all of your envies, jealousies, unforgiveness, selfishness and fears."[7]

There are no porters on the spiritual path; you have to carry your own baggage. The ultimate question in addressing spiritual growth becomes, *How can I best nurture a relationship with a Higher Power?*

As a woman, you may feel that society often expects you to operate at a higher ground; you are supposed to be understanding, forgiving, and spiritual. In an attempt to be a "good" woman you try to skip over the emotional work and go directly to the spiritual realm. Or you attempt to find inner peace and harmony from an intellectual understanding, or you throw yourself into volunteer work to demonstrate your spiritual intent. While any sincere effort can be extremely valuable, you cannot singularly will yourself to a higher plane. You cannot skip any steps. You cannot be a spiritual person unless you apply yourself to the necessary work. To grow spiritually you must walk the walk.

Practicing spirituality means that you:

- do the footwork
- are present, being in the here and now
- stay attuned to your inner guidance
- be authentic
- put forth the effort
- let go of the attachment to the results
- believe in divine guidance and the choice it offers
- engage regularly and repetitively

As you grow spiritually, you will learn to trust that life will continue to unfold as it must.

> [sara] I practice staying in touch with a loving God on a daily basis. It begins in the morning for me with a meditation reading from one of those many day-by-day meditation books. My God is a loving, not punishing God. I believe the more love you feel toward others is the essence of God. Accept people for who they are with their imperfections—now that doesn't mean sacrificing myself to a victim role, but that means letting go of judgment of both others and myself and loving myself with healthy boundaries.

Your spirituality acknowledges and does homage to the spark of divinity within you; it is an approach to life, an attitude. When lived, practiced consistently, and acted on consciously, it reinforces your commitment to personal transformation. This manifests itself most clearly in your attitude toward life. Your personal spirituality is a blend of your purposeful intent to be authentic and trust your intuition. Authenticity and intuition are hallmarks of your recovery. From this foundation follows a willingness to continue learning from life.

"I cannot separate what I conceive as Spirit
from my concept of God.
Thus I believe that God is Spirit."

Maya Angelou[8]

Reflective Thoughts and Questions

• What does forgiveness mean to you?

• Do you think you have engaged in cheap or false forgiveness?

• Have you forgiven yourself?

• Is faith or a belief in a Higher Power an important part of your life today? If so, describe.

• Is spirituality an aspect of your life you are willing to explore more as it relates to your recovery process?

• What was important for you to hear in this chapter?

Chapter Nine

The Women of the Lodge

Change takes time. Recovery is a process.

Trust and give voice to your reality.

Begin your healing journey.

Living in a society of instant gratification, instant coffee, instant breakfast, and even instant money from the ATM, it's easy to want to show up at a therapist's office or Twelve Step meeting and expect an instant solution to all of the problems that come from living with sex addiction. But recovery is a process, not an event. It is a process with no guarantees about the relationship, but a process that does guarantee a journey to self-love and self-care.

You no longer have to tolerate the hurtful. You can trust your own perceptions and give voice to your reality. You can move forward in truth. Secrets disappear and the potential for connectedness with self, others, and the universe is fully there. You deserve to continue your life free of fear, confusion, denial, and shame. You deserve to believe in your preciousness and to have it honored from within and by those you invite into your life. This is possible when you allow others to be a part of your process, as did the Women of the Lodge. These women found a path; they have tools and they have faith. Let's continue with their stories and hear how their journeys have progressed.

• THERESE •

Why would I need my own recovery? After all, he had
the problem. Now I just shake my head at my thinking I
was so much better than him. Recovery and group has
been my life blessing.

I certainly knew that my husband needed help, but
I've had a hard time realizing that I needed help too. I
believed I was entitled to say and do whatever I wanted.
After all, I was the victim. When he started his recovery,
I wanted him to change, but I didn't like him asking me
to change. I found that I was jealous about him giving his
time to his recovery. I actually became more obsessive
about whether or not he was on the Net once he was in
recovery. I was shameless in my sleuth work trying to trap
him. He seemed to feel better about himself, but I actually
became angrier. I was interpreting everything to be about
me. He owed me now. What was he going to do for me?
What was he going to do to assure me that he wasn't
going to look at other women? I wasn't giving him any
support, although periodically for the sake of being nice
I would go to one of his therapy sessions. I did not want
to talk in front of those people. I had nothing to say to
them. Then things began to crumble even more when our
fourteen-year-old got into trouble with drugs and sex. I
thought we were going to lose her. One night she was
almost raped. I also knew that my husband was in a serious relapse. I drove myself to see his counselor. As much
as I had set out to catch him in a relapse, when he actually
had one I let go of my entire ego. For the first time I
realized I didn't have the answers; I wasn't in control; I
was a mess.

I was so scared and numb I simply did what his
counselor told me and showed up at a group with other
women. For several weeks I didn't talk, I just cried quietly.

They gently accepted me, my tears, and my silence. I so respected these women; they were angry, they cried, they laughed. Feelings were everywhere, and yet they could talk about them. Slowly I began to talk about myself. They wouldn't let me talk about my husband. I came to really understand that his behavior was not about me. I heard that early on but didn't truly understand it. Now I understand we were a match for each other. Pornography was his answer to his fears; it was his fix and it became addictive. My addiction is my codependency—my lack of a strong sense of knowing myself, deriving my self-esteem from how we looked, and having control over my feelings but not being honest about them.

Today I work hard at recognizing and talking about my feelings. I'm aware when I mask them and can even laugh at myself for how readily I use my defenses. I don't think I can say I like showing my vulnerability but I do it. And of all the people, it is my husband who most understands and accepts me. When I show him this part of me rather than my controlling side, he meets me where I am. Mostly I get scared. I get scared of the unknown more than anything real. So I work a lot at staying in the here and now. I don't schedule all of my time or the family's time. And after months now, I can say it works. I have time to be spontaneous, to be available to others, to listen to myself. I am not running from myself anymore. And better yet, I like myself more. I like my husband more. I like life more.

I realize I have been scared a lot of my life—certainly long before my marriage started. Mostly I have been scared I'm not good enough. I always acted like I was above everyone else and separate from them. By the time I got to my first group I was so humbled. I felt like I was crawling out from some deep hole in the ground. Maybe others didn't see this superiority of mine, but I knew I had been hiding behind it all of my life.

Today I am proud, truly proud to be accepting and available to all the women as they come through the doors of the Lodge. As different as we are, our underbellies are the same. I have been in group with a lot of different women and I have very strong friendships with some of them. I respect all of them for just showing up. I know how hard that is. Recovery is very humbling.

In the long run I don't know what all of this means for my marriage, but I'm hopeful. I know that being quietly angry and playing the martyr is not going to make our marriage work, and I already feel so much better about myself, him, and us. I actually believe my marriage is better today than it ever was.

. . . .

When your partner uses pornography to act out, as Therese's did, it is common to rationalize that your situation is very different from cosas' whose partners' acting out involves flesh-and-blood people. Whether it's pornography, cybersex, or other behaviors such as voyeurism or exhibitionism that don't involve actual bodily contact with others, the process of holding yourself apart and different only increases the likelihood that you will miss the opportunity to heal from your pain. Or you could miss the opportunity to join your partner in a coupleship based on mutual healing and recovery, as Therese almost did. While Therese came slowly to the realization that there were an incredible number of gifts for her in the recovery process, she also came to realize she had fewer differences and much more in common with the other Women of the Lodge than she anticipated.

• VANESSA •

When I first found out my husband had exposed me to an STD while I was pregnant, I took his minimal disclosure as yet another call to action in my life. Let's just buckle down and fix this. We both entered our respective Twelve Step programs and therapy. I was happy to have some other cause to focus on, another project I could fix. This attitude changed approximately three months later when I found his First Step document. The level of infidelity detailed in it was shocking! I was enraged and I turned into this evil, vindictive woman bent on making him pay. The next few months were hell for both of us. I felt my life was crumbling. It was impossible to be the perfect wife, perfect mother, perfect work-addicted employee, and perfect friend to all the needy people I had surrounded myself with, while my foundational belief system was being shattered in every way. It was a crisis time in my life, and luckily I chose to look at my own stuff—my work addiction and issues—and make some changes. It was such a hard year but pivotal to my recovery. I quit my high-powered job, became a full-time mom, and dug into recovery in a serious way. My life was forever altered by that decision.

My don't talk/denial training was so ingrained I found it very difficult to share the dark side of my life with people. Twelve Step programs helped a lot because they were a safe place to share with others undergoing similar experiences and pain. Initially I found it very difficult to discuss this with my friends, partly because I had spent so much time selling my perfect life to myself and others. I had a new awareness of how emotionally shut down I was as I realized that, even though I had a ton of friends, I had become very proficient in becoming close to people by listening to all their problems and encouraging them to share their issues but disclosing very little about myself. It was a very big step for both me and my husband to come out. It was so important for me to start breaking my childhood rules—don't talk, don't feel—by telling on myself and becoming vulnerable with safe people.

In my recovery I would come to confront my father about his raging behavior. I would let go of my need to be in control. I would let go of my perfectionism. I would embrace my beauty and that inner child who needed nurturing. I would learn to trust myself. My husband and I worked hard, not without relapse and pain. We were truly finding some happiness when another bomb dropped—I was diagnosed with aggressive ovarian cancer. Now this would be a true test of recovery.

I cannot tell you how valuable all those trite adages of recovery became to me during this time: One day at a time. Let go and let God. You're never given more than you can handle. Those incredible lessons became lifelines for me, and I became vulnerable in a way I had never known. I was so broken; I was truly fighting for my life. I finally learned to reach out, to ask for help. In the darkest time of my life, I actually found what it was like to seize life. Looking at my son, I really understood how important it was to seize every single moment. I believe that recovery was instrumental in saving my life because my physical death sentence became a spiritual and emotional growth period. In facing death, I became more alive. I believe my husband walked with me on this journey. In an act of solidarity he shaved his head so I wouldn't be bald alone while I underwent chemotherapy. My many friends supported us with vigils of prayer and friendship before every major treatment, whether it was surgery, chemo, or major testing. He was there for every one of those, seemingly invested in the whole process. But the Jekyll and Hyde of addiction was clearly at play again. One year after my diagnosis (and bleak prognosis), he was called to come clean to me at an intensive treatment center. Apparently the whole time he was holding my hand through cancer, he was also engaging in sexual relationships with escorts, having affairs with other women, and soliciting sexual relations with adventurous couples. As I sat in the therapist's office listening to his full disclosure, still bald from the chemo, I felt a part of me die inside. I had never felt such brokenness, such blatant and deceptive betrayal, in my darkest hour. It was then that I knew my recovery journey was far from over. I had some serious relationship/recovery decisions to make.

Right or wrong—there can be no second guessing—I made the decision to stay. And though I labored over that choice with therapists, I realize looking back that I was simply not strong enough to leave at that time. I was only then starting to look at what drove me to be in such a hurtful relationship. Until I cleaned up the baggage in my soul, I would never be able to truly look at the dis-ease in our relationship. I was still operating inherently from that place of not good enough.

The good news is we both went to new levels of healing. Things seemingly smoothed out. We engaged in therapy where I focused on my childhood issues. Then another painful life event occurred. My sister, who had been in remission for many years, found out she was now dying of her cancer. She was in terrible pain and needed constant assistance. I faced my sister's death and my own mortality with a new level of healing.

. . . .

Vanessa continues her recovery practices and in that process she grows emotionally and spiritually, her cancer disappears, and she physically heals. She is finally at a place of calm in her life and she is feeling strong in her marriage when, to her surprise, her husband decides to leave the marriage to be with another woman.

I wish that I could share with you a "happily ever after" ending that I spent most of my life fantasizing about. Alas, though recovery has been one of the greatest gifts of my life, it did not have the ability to save my marriage. Addiction is cunning and baffling; it's a prickly thing that

takes a lifelong commitment to avoid relapse. After seven
years in recovery together, my husband went back out.
I pray for him as a human being and the father of my
child. I have finally learned the meaning of letting go. It
is through the hardships I have encountered in my life
that I learned about the need to surrender, to live in the
now, and to focus on me and a journey of self-love. I
make a commitment daily to operate from a place of
gratitude, authenticity, and congruency so that I can truly
live life and strive to make a difference in this world.

. . . .

Sadly, even with recovery practice, there are no promises of marital bliss.
Vanessa's husband made various choices along his path and in his journey
he wasn't honest with her about his feelings or his behavior. He made the
choice to leave the marriage. Steeped in her recovery process, Vanessa
would come to an inner peace, knowing that her recovery is not based on
being in this marriage.

This journey of healing has been painful and arduous.
It has also been so rewarding and life-changing. And it's
far from over; recovery is a journey, not a destination.
Every day I look into my soul for toxic messages and
unhealthy behaviors. Every day I look for the beauty in
every moment, for the joys of my relationships, and for
the gifts of my recovery. I live the paradoxes. My spiritual
and emotional paths are so rich and authentic. I talk, I
feel, and I love. I know that this is yet another step on my
journey and that I have lots more to learn. I also know
there is no happily ever after, but there can be peace and
joy in the moment. And now is all we really have.

. . . .

• MAITE •

As a woman who strongly identifies with her culture, Maite has chosen, in her recovery, to confront the rules of silence that fuel addiction as well as the societal rules of being a Latina. With the support of other women, she embraces a newfound freedom to let go of social and familial constraints and find intimacy with herself and her husband.

I have found I need support and I need therapy, not as a punishment for his behaviors but as a way of understanding and healing. I deserve recovery too. I spent a lot of years in my good/perfect/saint role: someone who saw herself as better than my husband in my saintly behavior. Like many Latinos and Latinas, I am a very proud person. But I see how this disease affects everyone involved. I see it affect coworkers, family members on both sides, and friends. It certainly affected me. It pains me to see women who don't want to be in recovery for themselves, who choose to hang on to that false pride, who prefer to stay in the "better than" thinking. Not for me, no longer. Before recovery I had walls of fear to control and protect me from others. Today in my recovery I have the gift of knowing I don't need to control. In fact, by letting go of my controlling behaviors I have found a freedom I've never known. In that freedom I don't have to hide my fears or my shame; I feel love for myself and my husband. And I've learned about boundaries. I've discovered that boundaries are about honoring and respecting me and others physically, emotionally, intellectually—the spiritual sacred spaces—living honestly and with integrity.

In my family and in my culture, everyone is into everyone else's business. I was trained never to question authorities or loved ones, even when my intellect or my intuition knew my truth. Enmeshment brings a lot of abuse. If someone has a pain, I am supposed to cry. If you have a need, I am to meet it. If you are fat, I am to be fat. If a neighbor is sad, I am supposed to be in mourning too. That is no longer okay with me. Today I am learning I have the right to say no, I have the right to my own feelings, I don't have to caretake to be a good human being.

I am fortunate because my husband wants recovery. He doesn't want to keep living his secret life. But I know I can have my recovery with or without him. I am no longer willing to live with the dishonesty, the lying, and the craziness where I doubt myself when the truth is not spoken. Now my healthy self knows what it knows and I honor it. It doesn't matter who gets upset.

My husband is a businessman and many people know us. I used to participate in everything. People in our community, people in our family, and people in other families asked us for all kinds of help, from money to jobs to assistance with visa paperwork for new immigrant families. I used to give money, time, write letters, and lots of things to anyone when asked. Now I say no when I want to. I don't think I have to do what they want in order for me to be a good person. I know I am a good person. We have a good, economical life so I thought I was obligated to caretake our many family members, friends, and employees. I gave and gave and gave, and it was never enough. I felt guilty, angry, and used. Now I choose. Today I find myself saying no to anything that interferes with my spiritual life, my interior life.

Today I have much laughter in my life. By not trying to control and manipulate everything and everyone, and by not being vigilant about the rules of perfection, it's so much easier to find the laughter and humor in everyday life. Laughter gives me a freedom to be myself, to know my feelings, to be imperfect, to let go of judgment, to find serenity. I don't live a role anymore. I wear fun, colorful clothes. At times I know my kids might prefer I be a bit less colorful, but I simply find humor in that as well.

My kids have the typical young adult challenges, but my recovery tools have made me a better mother.

In addition to being with other women in recovery groups, I make a point of socializing with some of them outside of group. We go to movies, we go to the mall, we have coffee, and we spend a lot of that time laughing. I don't live all bound up in other people's expectations— my husband's, my family's, or my culture. I have come to a place in my recovery where I love myself. I nurture my body, my spirit, and our relationship. As difficult as reality can be and as frightening as honesty sometimes is, living in truth has been so freeing. As for what happens in my marriage, for now we each practice our recovery. Learning to communicate has been vital and at times still awkward. I think I sometimes overwhelm my husband with my openness. I'm sure that it's shocking, given that early in our marriage I learned to be very silent. There is no hiding from each other. I trust that whatever it is, if we talk about it, it will be okay. When I feel like I just want to attack him, I ask myself, "What are my intentions?" Healthy intention is not to make him feel bad, not to control or manipulate, but to seek the truth. The truth is the path to healing. Living in reality is necessary. He is a mirror of my reality; when he lies or just doesn't tell me something then the reality gets distorted. I am not preoccupied with his recovery, but I know he has to be in recovery for us to be a couple. We love each other no matter how sick we are, but we need to heal this sickness.

We are not the perfect family; perfect is an illusion, perfect is crushed, and perfect is not real. The fairy tale is not there. Today we are a family—a family with a lot of love and a lot of good communication. I take care of my recovery and my husband takes care of his.

. . . .

After years of seeking the help of multiple therapists who basically told her the problem was in her head, Maite challenged the gender and cultural teachings that had been so strongly ingrained into her being: your needs are not important, discount your perceptions, defer to the man, don't question, look good at all costs, never complain. This was quite a fight for her, but while waging it she found a path that led to self-love, self-care, and true joy by living in the truth. And in that process, her husband joined her in the journey.

• JACQUE •

When my husband and I finally named what was happening in our lives, I wanted to know everything there was to know about sex addiction and what to do about it. I wanted it all tied up in a neat little box so I could have control of my life again. I wanted a promise that we would work it out. I wanted recovery for us, not so much for me. Little did I know that what I really needed was to let go completely and give it all up to see what would come back to me. I would ultimately need to walk through my life with a sifter to bring the fine and delicate pieces of my life back together and to toss away the chunks that really didn't work for me (the control, resentment, anger, fear, lack of trust, and misplaced trust) no matter how much I hung on to them. I felt so broken I wanted to be with others who maybe knew how it was, if that was possible.

I found other women who had walked in similar shoes. I listened and began to talk about my experiences. I had so much shame about my behavior, our behavior, and my husband's behavior. But I felt such acceptance and love from these other women. I wanted what I saw some of them had: a voice. They could talk about their feelings. They had a sense of how to take care of themselves. They were struggling for sure, not knowing what was totally

real in their own relationships, confused about whether or
not to go or stay, and angry about the betrayal, the consequences. Together we would heal. I had a lot to learn
about the power of being with other women and how to
be good to myself in a nurturing way.

In spite of the incredible struggle to confront and
change old beliefs and behaviors, I discovered so much
about me. But I can't say it came easy. My insides often
screamed in protest of what I had to let go of to get to
a greater place of wholeness. I discovered the only way to
trust again was to learn to trust myself. I learned to be
honest in all areas of my life. I learned nothing could ever
be the same again. All of my interactions would be different because I was different. I learned to let go completely,
to trust in God. I learned the power of supportive women
in my life. I learned to trust women. I learned to speak up
for myself in an empowering way. I learned to share the
hard stuff: the pain, fear, anger, and resentments. I learned
to tell on myself, my mistakes and fears. I learned the
power of laughter and fun. I learned to listen. I learned
to honor myself as a woman; to hold on to that and never
let it go. I learned I am controlling and judgmental, not
perfect. I learned to honor that part of me too. I learned I
needed more work on my abuse. I learned to trust therapy.
I learned I couldn't do it on my own, no matter how hard
I tried. I needed the group. I needed therapy, I needed a
sponsor, and I needed friends.

Much of my recovery has come from being willing to
talk about the sex abuse in my childhood, from grieving
the loss that came with not being able to have children,
and from breaking my denial about how men have chronically abused me. I have worked to transition from sex
abuse victim to survivor. I read numerous books, but one
in particular, called *The Courage to Heal*,[1] spoke to me, and
I spent the next year working the exercises. I felt such

shame the day I purchased it. I wanted to hide it and pretend I was buying it for someone else. Then I told my
parents about the sexual abuse my brother performed on
me for four to six years. I have no real memory of the
time frame other than knowing about when it started and
about when it ended. I do have some specific memories,
and through my recovery I have discovered I have a very
strong case of post-traumatic stress disorder related to the
abuse. I also used the incredible therapy tool of EMDR
[eye movement desensitization reprocessing] to lessen my
anxiety and reframe loving beliefs about myself as well
as allowing myself to be heard, allowing myself a voice,
allowing myself to grieve, and then to be held safely by
wonderfully caring women.

I learned to "do" recovery, to have a plan as to what
my recovery could look like. I was looking at me and not
living in reactivity to my husband. I would go to meetings
and share. I found the courage and support to start my
own Twelve Step group for cosas since I lived in an area
where there were no groups. I learned that I am a part of
the whole, that my part is just as important as any other
woman in the group. I feel whole and believe in myself.
I quit feeling less than, and I stopped comparing myself
to others: I stopped competing. I have begun to use the
other half of my brain, to allow my artistic side to rise to
the surface, to let what was there flow in the way it was
intended. I listen and accept feedback. I discern what will
and will not work for me. I've stopped defending myself,
stopped giving my power away, and stopped giving myself
away. I hold myself as precious. I experience the power of
women, the power of tradition and ceremony.

I have had to get therapy to help me get to a place of
healthy anger. I have ripped up my share of Kleenex. I
have beaten the bed. I also kick things, and I walk hard,
and I air box. I have a great time with my anger and it's

empowering. But having been a major peacekeeper in my life, I can still go there when I get scared. And my husband's anger can scare me. So I always work at boundaries, knowing whose stuff is whose. I don't take on his blaming. I am not willing to be abused. Today I recognize it early on and I have learned to stick up for myself verbally and remove myself from the situation if that is necessary.

My best boundary is in knowing I cannot do his recovery. Today in his work he still travels some so I talk about any fears I have. I no longer bury my head in the sand. If he chooses not to follow his recovery plan, then I really believe it will be a short amount of time and I will know. And then I am free to make my own decisions. Today I stay because I feel hope for us. I feel hope because I see a change in behavior. We communicate so much better and so much more than before. I am more trusting of myself with him, more willing to be genuinely vulnerable and he so with me. Today I have learned to ask for assistance to allow people to be of support.

In the early stages of our relationship I had this desperate need not to be abandoned. The love I had for him morphed into not wanting to be alone. As we moved into our recovery and I began to value myself, to get my own esteem. I knew I didn't want to be in a relationship if he could not be present with me. I do remember what it was like to love him with heart and want to be with the kind, loving, fun man. And as he got working more and more on his recovery, I know this man, this man in recovery, is a man I do want to be with; he's kind, caring, fun, adventuresome. I was wounded long before I met my husband and he was the product of woundedness before his sex addiction. We are two wounded people tapping into our strengths and learning to be in this world in a way we never were before.

. . . .

Jacque has worked hard in her recovery and, as you have just read, she talks about herself more than she talks about her marriage or her husband. This is what she takes to her marriage now, her recovery. With two therapeutic separations behind them, she and her husband are together and both of them are actively engaged in their recovery processes.

• JENNY •

For so many years I lived in denial and fantasy, beginning my marriage with a façade of seeing myself as righteous, capable, and having the world by the tail, yet having an inner world of self-loathing, terror, and confusion. After fifteen years of marriage and my husband acting out his many addictions, I was operating at a minimal level, experiencing severe depression and two nervous breakdowns. It was at this time that I began to seek my spirituality in Jesus. I prayed and prayed for my circumstances to change, but it wasn't until I took the Lord at His word that things did start to change! "There is none righteous, no, not one." I guess that meant me, but I thought I was so much better than my husband. "Take the log out of your own eye before you try to remove the speck from your brother's." Wow! It was *me* that I needed to ask the Lord to change!

This was hard. I saw myself totally as the victim and he an abuser. I began to be present with my prayer and came to realize that I had things I needed to address about myself. The style of my prayers changed. I asked for direction. I asked for courage and strength.

A few years into my spiritual journey, when I started to pray, "Lord change me," is when my husband actually began to change. At first his acting out became worse. Finally after a heartfelt disclosure he started looking for treatment centers. At this time I knew nothing about sex addiction. I was so naive that I didn't even know what a treatment center was. He said he was going for his drug addiction, but he took painstaking steps to pick out just the right one, and today I believe it is because he knew his sexual acting out was controlling him and severely hurting his family.

At the encouragement of the treatment program staff, I began therapy with a specialist in sex addiction so I could focus on my codependency issues. While I was scared, I was nonetheless eager and willing to discover why I was in the situation that I was in. The focus was a lot on understanding the way in which we were raised and how we relate to others in relationships. It explored trauma, abuse, neglect, and abandonment. I didn't know what was wrong with me or even what had happened to me in my life, but I was willing to look at anything in my life that needed changing, *anything*. The scriptures told me, "Know the truth and the truth shall set you free." I knew I wanted to be free but I wasn't sure what I wanted to be freed from. I just knew I wanted to get out of the hell that I had been living in. This is where I learned about codependency and co-sex addiction. And that I, too, had a dis-ease.

I would discover the shameful self that I had been trained to cover up and eventually forgot was there. It was buried alive, always nagging to come out, and actually coming out sideways in everything I did: how I related to my children, what I thought and felt about myself, and how I related to my husband. Judgment, condemnation, and control oozed from the pores in my skin.

I was working with a therapist to address my childhood history and my addiction to a sex addict. That is when I joined a support group at my church with other women whose partners acted out sexually. I also joined a codependency group at my church. The individual therapy would keep my head above water. It was in group I felt the validation I needed to move from a victim mentality, a childlike person, to trusting myself and asking for what I needed. It was in group that I would learn how to connect with other people and not be so afraid of them.

I have no doubt that the single most powerful tool I had in my healing was my support groups. Without those women I could have never experienced the love and acceptance that Jesus wanted me to experience. I had never been comfortable in groups and didn't make friends easily. I was afraid of people, especially women. But in the group I learned to trust safe people; I learned to tell my story. I learned to confront my husband and I learned to tell him what I wanted and needed. I acquired incredible courage and conviction. As I healed spiritually I began to heal emotionally and relationally as well.

Then I was led to another group where I would go deeper into my recovery process and I could be more explicit about my abuse and my marriage. It was here I would work a lot on how much I was dissociating, not able to stay present. This had been going on for years. It was here I allowed myself to be seen, meaning I was able to share the self-loathing I often felt. And it would be in this group that I would become open enough to receive from others, to receive their caring, and with that, to come to really accept my worth. This healing process was essential for me because it helped me shatter the toxic shame that I carried. One of the more profound experiences I had in this group was that no matter what I had to say about what I had done or about what had been done to me, I experienced a sense of unconditional love and acceptance from the group. The facilitators would guide me to look deeply into the eyes of each group member. They'd have me hold that gaze for a significant amount of time before looking to the next person. This process helped to turn the lies that caused me self-hatred and

shame into the truth of acceptance and my true value
given to me by my Creator.

I would come to realize that my healing was the most
important thing in my life, and to believe that my husband
was standing in the way of my being able to fully heal. I
decided I could not be with such a controlling and fearful
husband. I wasn't strong enough to survive that, and I was
committed to my healing. I really didn't know how I could
support myself. I had not worked outside of the home in
years. But I put one foot in front of the other, I prayed,
and I was practical. After a couple years in recovery, as
scary and financially difficult as it was, I chose to divorce.
I didn't see my husband's recovery behavior as consistent
with mine, and our differences were too great. I am not
very confident in myself when it comes to relationships
today, but I think that will pass. I know I am still fragile;
neither life nor recovery has been easy. But today I also
feel my strength. I am grateful for what I have with my
children; I recognize that I am smart. I am learning how
to have fun, how to take care of me, and how to know
and honor my feelings. Each day I feel stronger within.
I can actually feel my insides smile—this is a long way
from my depression and nervous breakdowns.

· · · · · · · · ·

Ultimately, Jenny's faith led her into a recovery process, and as she said,
it gave her "the courage and foundation to come out of denial and into
reality." She was readily able to embrace how the teachings of the Bible,
together with her therapy process, offered a path to healing. Like many
cosas, she prayed, bargained, and pleaded with her God, and in time Jenny
heard and listened. She approached therapy willingly, she followed direction, and she read widely about codependency and trauma. As scared as she
was of allowing herself to open up to other women, she came to blossom
in their strength and support.

• S A R A •

Sara came into recovery as a cosa after ten years in Al-Anon. It is very likely her participation in a Twelve Step program led her to trust in the group process and believe in the power of sharing with others with similar experiences.

> I came to this group to meet other women with husbands who were acting out. I was so angry—angry that this is where I was in my life. I was not sure what I was hoping for. I had one foot ready to head out of this marriage, yet I came and am forever grateful for that.
>
> Today when I think about my recovery, I see it so far in three levels. My first level began in Al-Anon; that was the beginning of my path. My husband had just gotten sober, but I was having trouble sleeping and eating, I was worried about money, and the kids were acting out. There wasn't a corner of my life that was peaceful. The concept of being responsible for the results of my own life despite what happens to me was a beginning, a big beginning.
>
> The second level was the recovery more connected to sex addiction. Here again I was in crisis, not just from the knowledge my husband had been continuing to act out sexually and it was addictive, but I now had breast cancer. Also at this time three of my family members and friends passed away. While all levels of recovery begin with crisis, at this stage the crises were so much more deep, threatening, and terrifying. I needed to be led, supported, and confronted. I knew enough that I knew I couldn't do this alone. I sought out several professionals—counselors experienced in addressing codependency, sex addiction, and loss. I found medical help I trusted. Together they were my team; they helped me put one foot in front of the other. I was hurting and scared, and I needed to call upon every internal strength I had at a time of incredible

brokenness. I listened to my host of guides, I followed direction, and I honored myself.

I had so much loss—loss of illusion, loss of health, loss of family and friends—and so much fear. I grieved and grieved, moving up and down and through all of the stages they talk about—anger, sadness, bargaining, guilt— sort of like in staccato fashion, with a lot of starts and stops. I would come to understand the generational repetitions in my family. This would offer me a framework to understand I wasn't crazy, I wasn't defective. I was simply wounded, and from that I could heal. I would put into practice healthy boundaries. I would learn to take down my walls and to be vulnerable but hold on to my integrity and esteem. I would also learn to listen and, more important, to hear. I learned better communication and problem-solving skills. I would constrain that part of me that wanted to lash out in my pain. I would also lighten up and not take myself so seriously all of the time. I practiced gratitude and laughter in my life a lot at this stage.

The third level of recovery, which would come within two to three years of beginning what I call level two, was to know myself differently than ever before. No matter what on earth happens to me, I will be all right. My being all right is not about his sobriety with alcohol or sex. I know I can get through whatever is there in front of me. I trust myself. Never again is it okay for someone to mistreat or abuse me. I realize when we first got together we were both desperately in love and saw ourselves as soul mates, star-crossed lovers. Then my love became conditional in the height of our addictions. Today I can say I love him, and I love him forever. Now that does not mean he can live with me forever. If he acts out and doesn't do anything about it, that is mistreating me. The way I see it, we both have warts and bumps. His warts don't mean he is throwing me away. I realize today

I had my husband on a fairy-tale pedestal from the day we met; then, with his acting out, he crashed down from that pedestal. Today I am very aware of his faults and they can irritate me, but now I don't need him to be an illusion for me.

Being in recovery means every day belongs to me to express who I am in each thing I do. It means when I make the inevitable mistakes in that day, I have a way to set my conscience straight, no matter what the rest of the world says or thinks about my behavior. I know my heart and I know who and why I love. It is because of honesty and trust in my judgment and motives. I know my job is not to save anyone. I can't. I don't want to interfere with their beautiful but sometimes painful path. I do take great delight in being of loving service in this world. I sometimes quake in my boots from fear, but I know it can be shared with God and my trusted friends. I swirl and delight in the delicious joy and challenge of life. I play. I cry. I hurt. I laugh. I am beginning to trust that what I put out into the universe comes lovingly back to me. I am in partnership with those I choose, including my spouse. If any relationship becomes toxic for my well-being, I will be there for myself and take care of this precious life of mine.

People ask me how I live with knowing he could relapse. Well, there have been relapses and he could have more. I hope he doesn't. What I do know is that whatever comes about, it is not about me. His behavior is not about me. And I will handle whatever comes my way. Nothing is guaranteed.

When old habits and fears arise, there are friends whom I talk with through situations, disagreements, and challenges. Being in recovery means reaching out for this support when I feel myself lapsing back into the old patterns that made my life so miserable. My recovery friends are willing to call me on my stubbornness and control issues, or point out when I'm being self-righteous or self-centered.

If I were to name the one area I need the most work on today it would be jumping to an emotional response. When I'm feeling hurt or threatened, I threaten back. I have never stopped working on this overreaction. I know why it's so hard to overcome: because I used it to survive when I was a child. When my spouse and I have a really heated argument, or worse, a disagreement that never gets expressed, my mind will sometimes jump to thoughts of leaving and finding a more peaceful life. But I recognize that is old behavior, fear-based behavior. Today I use my tools to work through feelings, to communicate, to own my needs, and to value them. We talk. We listen. We work toward the win—win.

My greatest strides have come with being with other women in recovery and Twelve Step groups. It is a privilege to be able to go and tune up. The truth is what I recovered. I don't need to hide anymore.

. . . .

As Sara said, she came to the Women of the Lodge group incredibly angry, but her Al-Anon experience had taught her that she would be safe with other women. In that safe environment she vented and ultimately owned her own shame and fears. She was able to make the connection and see how her early life abandonment was perpetuated in her adult relationships with men. The internal shift that propelled her life into one of laughter, connection, and peace occurred when she recognized that her healing was predicated on the commitment to no longer abandon herself.

The Invitation

The personal crises that Therese, Vanessa, Maite, Jacque, Jenny, and Sara experienced led them to pursue recovery specific to living with sex addiction. Therese began her journey a couple of years after her husband had begun his. Vanessa embraced recovery after being exposed to an STD while she was pregnant. Just when Maite was ready to leave her marriage, she and her husband began their recovery journey. Jacque and her husband began their journey together as he was walking out the door to be with his girlfriend. Jenny began recovery when her husband sought treatment for his drug abuse and when his sexual behavior was also addressed. Sara and her husband began theirs when she discovered a book on sex addiction in his car.

It may be discouraging to read about women who put their heart and soul into the healing and recovery process and still their relationship or marriage did not survive, as is true for two of the six women of the Lodge. Yet in spite of the present-day outcome of their relationships and what their partners did or didn't do in recovery, all of these women continue their healing journey. While their relationship problems got them into a recovery process, they stayed to heal themselves. This journey transcended the issues of betrayal and deceit and became one of personal healing never before imagined. They learned to trust their perceptions, listen to their feelings, recognize their needs, and establish respectful boundaries. They addressed their childhood trauma issues, recognized the signs of generational repetition, developed esteem, and found their voices.

It was a long road paved with an overwhelming amount of internal dialogue such as "How could he? Why am I not enough? How will I live? How will I manage?" But these women discovered an inner strength they had never before experienced, and in that strength they found esteem; the skills for genuine emotional intimacy, joy, and laughter; and inner peace.

Although others have walked before you, this is your very own unique journey. You are to be congratulated for coming this far, reading this book, and facing your truths. It takes courage, and you have it within you. It is important that you focus on the present and not try to project the outcomes. As much as you would like to know in terms of absolutes where your journey will take you, there are areas outside of your control: your partner's behavior, thoughts, and feelings. You didn't cause his behavior; you can't control it, nor are you the answer to his problems. But there are also areas of your life that you have the power to affect, and those are your behavior, your thinking, and what you do with your feelings. This is when the Serenity Prayer becomes a staple in your life:

> *God, grant me the serenity*
> *To accept the things I cannot change,*
> *The courage to change the things I can,*
> *And the wisdom to know the difference.*

To be suspended in the unknowing is initially a stage of despair, but with the support of others who have been there, you will find you will walk through it with far greater grace and a sense of empowerment. With recovery it becomes possible to get to a place of genuine acceptance of the unknowing as a natural part of life.

The choice in front of you today is either to continue what you have been doing in your coaddiction or to dig in and embrace a path where you find your voice and honor your needs. This means having a willingness to share honestly and let go of all your defenses and pretenses.

〰〰〰〰〰〰〰〰

The journey of self-discovery will offer you many gifts. You don't have to live in the shadow of someone's addiction or be controlled by anyone else's behavior. You can learn to trust yourself—in essence, to listen and trust "your worms." This is your opportunity to learn about healthy boundaries, who is responsible for what, and what gives you a sense of safety. As you begin this journey, remember that it's all about honoring and respecting yourself. You, like the Women of the Lodge, can move from immobilization or reactivity to a life of hope, greater esteem, and greater choices. While no one can walk the road of recovery for you, there are others who have traveled a similar path who will assist you. When all seems dark, these women will shine the light that helps you to continue moving forward. As you begin your healing, you will find an inner strength that allows you to transcend the pain; you will learn to trust in yourself and find meaning from the experience.

You don't have to come to recovery knowing what you want for your relationship; you don't even have to be in a relationship. You don't have to come eagerly. In truth, I suspect that you will come haltingly; you will be angry, sad, and very confused. I simply encourage you to come and begin your journey.

We are sisters and together we heal.

Reflective Thoughts and Questions

- Underline or highlight the parts of the women's stories with which you identify.
- What can you take from the different women to inspire your own healing and recovery process?
- What you are willing to do for yourself in your healing process? Be specific.
- What gifts are you already aware of receiving in this healing process?
- How has your ethnicity and/or culture influenced your story?
- What potential gifts do you see for yourself as you continue?
- What was important for you to hear in this chapter?

Recommended Readings

Sex Addiction

Carnes, Patrick. *Contrary to Love: Helping the Sexual Addict*. Center City, MN: Hazelden, 1994.

———. *Don't Call It Love: Recovery from Sexual Addiction*. New York: Bantam Books, 1992.

———. *Out of the Shadows: Understanding Sexual Addiction*. 3rd ed. Center City, MN: Hazelden, 2001.

Carnes, Patrick, David Delmonico, Elizabeth Griffin, and Joseph M. Moriarty. *In the Shadows of the Net: Breaking Free of Compulsive Online Sexual Behavior*. 2nd ed. Center City, MN: Hazelden, 2007.

Delmonico, David, Elizabeth Griffin, and Joseph Moriarty. *Cybersex Unhooked: A Workbook for Breaking Free of Compulsive Online Sexual Behavior*. Phoenix, AZ: Gentle Path Press, 2001.

Earle, Ralph, and Gregory Crowe. *Lonely All the Time: Recognizing, Understanding, and Overcoming Sex Addiction for Addicts and Codependents*. New York: Pocket Books, 1989.

Ferree, Marnie. *No Stones: Women Redeemed from Sexual Shame*. Camarillo, CA: Xulon Press, 2002.

Kasl, Charlotte. *Women, Sex, and Addiction: A Search for Love and Power*. New York: HarperPerennial, 1990.

Laaser, Mark. *Faithful and True: Sexual Integrity in a Fallen World*. Grand Rapids, MI: Zondervan Publishing House, 1996.

———. *Healing the Wounds of Sexual Addiction*. Grand Rapids, MI: Zondervan Publishing House, 2004.

Weiss, Rob. *Cruise Control: Understanding Sex Addiction in Gay Men*. Los Angeles: Alyson Books, 2005.

Weiss, Rob, and Jennifer Schneider. *Untangling the Web: Sex, Porn, and Fantasy Obsession in the Internet Age.* Los Angeles: Alyson Books, 2006.

Coaddiction

Adams, Christine. *Love, Infidelity, and Sexual Addiction: A Codependent's Perspective.* Bloomington, IN: Authors Choice Press, 2000.

Carnes, Patrick, Debra Laaser, and Mark Laaser. *Open Hearts: Renewing Relationships with Recovery, Romance, and Reality.* Phoenix, AZ: Gentle Path Press, 1999.

Carnes, Stefanie, ed. *Mending a Shattered Heart: A Guide for Partners of Sex Addicts.* Phoenix, AZ: Gentle Path Press, 2008.

Corley, M. Deborah, and Jennifer P. Schneider. *Disclosing Secrets: When, to Whom, and How Much to Reveal.* 3rd ed. Tucson, AZ: Recovery Resources Press, 2004.

Hall, Laurie. *An Affair of the Mind: One Woman's Courageous Battle to Salvage Her Family from the Devastation of Pornography.* Wheaton, IL: Tyndale House Publishers, 1998.

Laaser, Debra. *Shattered Vows: Help and Hope for Women Who Have Been Sexually Betrayed.* Grand Rapids, MI: Zondervan Publishing House, 2008.

Lusterman, Don-David. *Infidelity: A Survival Guide.* Oakland, CA: New Harbinger Publications, 1998.

May, Alice. *Surviving Betrayal: Hope and Help for Women Whose Partners Have Been Unfaithful; 365 Daily Meditations.* New York: HarperCollins, 1999.

Pletcher, Claudine, and Sally Bartolameolli. *Relationships from Addiction to Authenticity.* Deerfield Beach, FL: Health Communications, 2008.

Potter-Efron, Ronald. *Angry All the Time: An Emergency Guide to Anger Control.* 2nd ed. Oakland, CA: New Harbinger Publications, 2004.

Schneider, Jennifer. *Back from Betrayal: Recovering from His Affairs.* 3rd ed. Tucson, AZ: Recovery Resources Press, 2005.

Schneider, Jennifer, and Burt Schneider. *Sex, Lies, and Forgiveness: Couples Speaking Out on Healing from Sex Addiction.* 3rd ed. Tucson, AZ: Recovery Resources Press, 2004.

Spring, Janis, with Michael Spring. *After the Affair: Healing the Pain and Rebuilding Trust When a Partner Has Been Unfaithful.* New York: HarperCollins, 1996.

Weiss, Douglas, and Dianne DeBusk. *Women Who Love Sex Addicts: Help for Healing from the Effects of a Relationship with a Sex Addict.* Los Angeles, CA: Discovery Press, 1993.

Codependency

Beattie, Melody. *Beyond Codependency: And Getting Better All the Time.* Center City, MN: Hazelden, 1989.

Bradshaw, John. *Family Secrets: The Path from Shame to Healing.* New York: Bantam Books, 1996.

———. *Healing the Shame That Binds You,* Deerfield Beach, FL: Health Communications, 1998.

Carnes, Patrick. *The Betrayal Bond: Breaking Free of Exploitive Relationships.* Deerfield Beach, FL: Health Communications, 1997.

Carnes, Patrick, with Joseph M. Moriarity. *Sexual Anorexia: Overcoming Sexual Self-Hatred.* Center City, MN: Hazelden, 1997.

Katherine, Anne. *Boundaries: Where You End and I Begin.* New York: Simon & Schuster, 1991.

Mellody, Pia, with Andrea W. Miller, and J. Keith Miller. *Facing Codependence: What It Is, Where It Comes From, How It Sabotages Our Lives.* New York: HarperCollins, 1989.

———. *Facing Love Addiction: Giving Yourself the Power to Change the Way You Love.* New York: HarperCollins, 1992.

Spring, Janis, and Michael Spring. *How Can I Forgive You? The Courage to Forgive, the Freedom Not To.* New York: HarperCollins, 2004.

Whitfield, Charlie. *Boundaries and Relationships: Knowing, Protecting, and Enjoying the Self.* Deerfield Beach, FL: Health Communications, 1993.

Other

Bass, Ellen, and Laura Davis. *The Courage to Heal: A Guide for Women Survivors of Child Sexual Abuse.* New York: HarperCollins, 2008.

Carnes, Patrick. *A Gentle Path Through the Twelve Steps: The Classic Guide for All People in the Process of Recovery.* Center City, MN: Hazelden, 1994.

Duerk, Judith. *Circle of Stones: Woman's Journey to Herself.* Novato, CA: New World Library, 2004.

Helpful Resources

Adult Children of Alcoholics (ACA)

310-534-1815
email: info@adultchildren.org
Web site: www.adultchildren.org
A Twelve Step program for those who grew up in alcoholic or otherwise dysfunctional homes. Literature and online forums can be found on the Web site.

Al-Anon/Alateen

888-4AL-ANON for meeting information
757-563-1600 for Al-Anon Family Group Headquarters
email: wso@al-anon.org
Web site: www.al-anon.alateen.org
A Twelve Step program for family members and friends whose lives have been affected by another person's abuse of alcohol.

Alcoholics Anonymous (AA)

212-870-3400
Web site: www.alcoholics-anonymous.org
A Twelve Step program of recovery from alcohol abuse.

Codependents Anonymous (CoDA)

602-277-7991
email: outreach@coda.org
Web site: www.codependents.org
A Twelve Step program of recovery from codependence.

Codependents of Sex and Love Addicts Anonymous (COSLAA)

860-456-0032
Web site: www.coslaa.org
A Twelve Step support group for the recovery of family members, friends, and significant others whose lives have been affected by their relationship with someone addicted to sex and love.

COSA

763-537-6904
email: info@cosa-recovery.org
Web site: www.cosa-recovery.org
A Twelve Step program for those involved in relationships with people who have compulsive sexual behavior.

Families Anonymous (FA)

800-736-9805
email: famanon@familiesanonymous.org
Web site: www.familiesanonymous.org
A Twelve Step support group for anyone whose life has been adversely affected by another person's addictive behavior. Literature and referrals can be found on the Web site.

International Institute for Trauma and Addiction Professionals (IITAP)

866-575-6853
email: info@iitap.com
Web site: www.iitap.com
A resource site for finding a certified addiction specialist in your area.

Overcomers Outreach (OO)

800-310-3001
email: info@overcomersoutreach.org
Web site: www.overcomersoutreach.org
A Christ-centered Twelve Step support group for persons with compulsive behaviors as well as their families and friends.

Recovering Couples Anonymous (RCA)

510-663-2312
email: wso-rca@recovering-couples.org
Web site: www.recovering-couples.org
A Twelve Step program focused on the recovery issues of the couple itself. Both partners (addict and coaddict) are encouraged to attend.

S-Anon

800-210-8141
email: sanon@sanon.org
Web site: www.sanon.org
A Twelve Step support group for persons who have a friend or family member with a sexual addiction.

Sex Addicts Anonymous (SAA)

800-477-8191
email: info@saa-recovery.org
Web site: www.sexaa.org
A Twelve Step program for those who want to overcome their sexual addiction or dependency.

Sexaholics Anonymous (SA)

866-424-8777
email: saico@sa.org
Web site: www.sa.org
A Twelve Step program for those who want to stop sexually self-destructive thinking and behavior. Literature, books, and a phone network can be found on the Web site.

Sex and Love Addicts Anonymous (SLAA)

210-828-7900
email: generalinfo@slaafws.org
Web site: www.slaafws.org
A Twelve Step program for those who desire to stop living out a pattern of sex and love addiction. Information, referrals, conferences, and phone support can be found on the Web site.

Sexual Compulsives Anonymous (SCA)

800-977-4325
Web site: www.sca-recovery.org
A Twelve Step program for anyone with a desire to recover from sexual compulsion. Information, referrals, phone support, and conferences can be found on the Web site.

Sexual Recovery Anonymous (SRA)

212-340-4650
email: info@sexualrecovery.org
Web site: www.sexualrecovery.org
A Twelve Step program for those with a desire to stop compulsive sexual behavior. Online referrals, literature, and support can be found on the Web site.

Society for the Advancement of Sexual Health (SASH)

706-356-7031
email: sash@sash.net
Web site: www.sash.net
Information for professionals and recovering people regarding therapists, treatment centers, support groups, and written materials.

Notes

Chapter One: You Are Not Alone

1. C. S. Lewis, *Collected Letters of C. S. Lewis,* vol. 3 (New York: HarperOne, 2007), 758–59.

Chapter Two: In the Face of Truth

1. Patrick Carnes, *Contrary to Love: Helping the Sexual Addict* (Center City, MN: Hazelden, 1994).

2. Adaptation of the closing line of Act III of *The Mourning Bride* by William Congreve, first produced in 1697: "Heav'n has no rage, like love to hatred turn'd, Nor Hell a fury, like a woman scorn'd."

3. Elisabeth Kübler-Ross, *On Death and Dying* (New York: Simon & Schuster, 1997).

Chapter Three: His Behavior Is Not About You

1. Benjamin Franklin, *The Autobiography of Benjamin Franklin* (New York: Touchstone, 2003), 55.

2. Wilt Chamberlain, *A View from Above* (New York: Signet, 1992).

3. Al Cooper, ed., *Cybersex: The Dark Side of the Force* (Philadelphia: Routledge, 2000), 120.

4. Harvey Milkman and Stanley Sunderwirth, *Craving for Ecstasy: How Our Passions Become Addictions and What We Can Do About Them* (San Francisco: Jossey-Bass, 1987).

5. Michael Lemonick, "The Science of Addiction," *Time* 170, no. 3 (July 16, 2007): 46.

6. Patrick Carnes, *Contrary to Love: Helping the Sexual Addict* (Center City, MN: Hazelden, 1994).

7. Terrence Real, *I Don't Want To Talk About It: Overcoming the Secret Legacy of Male Depression* (New York: Simon & Schuster, 1998), 35.

Chapter Four: You Didn't Get Here by Accident

1. Patrick Carnes, *The Betrayal Bond: Breaking Free of Exploitive Relationships* (Deerfield Beach, FL: Health Communications, 1997), 26.

2. Euripides (c. 485–406 B.C.)

3. Maureen Canning, *Lust, Anger, Love: Understanding Sexual Addiction and the Road to Healthy Intimacy* (Naperville, IL: Sourcebooks, 2008), 98.

Chapter Five: Learning the News

1. Jennifer Schneider, M. Deborah Corley, and R. R. Irons, "Surviving Disclosure of Infidelity: Results of an International Survey of 164 Recovering Sex Addicts and Partners," *Sexual Addiction & Compulsivity* 5 (1998): 189–217.

Chapter Six: What Do You Tell Your Children?

1. Claudia Black, Diane Dillon, and Stefanie Carnes, "Disclosure to Children: Hearing the Child's Experience," *Sexual Addiction & Compulsivity* 10, no. 1 (2003): 67–78.

Chapter Seven: Your Time to Heal

1. The Serenity Prayer was written by Reinhold Niebuhr (1892–1971): "God, grant me the serenity to accept the things I cannot change, the courage to change the things I can, and the wisdom to know the difference."

2. André Gide. French critic, essayist, and novelist (1869–1951). Source of quote unknown.

Chapter Eight: Finding Your Serenity

1. Janis Spring with Michael Spring, *How Can I Forgive You? The Courage to Forgive, the Freedom Not To* (New York: HarperCollins, 2004).

2. Maurice Friedman, *A Dialogue with Hasidic Tales* (New York: Human Science Press, 1988).

3. Gary Zukav, *The Seat of the Soul* (New York: Fireside, 1989), 31.

4. Carlos Castaneda, *The Teachings of Don Juan: A Yaqui Way of Knowledge* (New York: Washington Square Press, 1985), 82.

5. Julia Cameron, *The Artist's Way: A Spiritual Path to Higher Creativity* (New York: J. P. Tarcher/Putnam, 2002).

6. Dean Ornish, *Dr. Dean Ornish's Program for Reversing Heart Disease* (New York: Random House, 1990).

7. Brian Seaward, *Stand Like Mountain, Flow Like Water* (Deerfield Beach, FL: Health Communications, 1997), 56–7.

8. Maya Angelou, *Wouldn't Take Nothing for My Journey Now* (New York: Bantam Books, 1993): 33–4.

Chapter Nine: Women of the Lodge

1. Ellen Bass and Laura Davis, *The Courage to Heal: A Guide for Women Survivors of Child Sexual Abuse* (New York: HarperCollins, 2008).

About the Author

Claudia Black, M.S.W., Ph.D., is one of the most recognized women in the field of addictive disorders; she is a renowned author and trainer internationally acknowledged for her pioneering and contemporary work with family systems and addictive disorders. She has always brought heart and soul to her work, beginning with her seminal work with children of alcoholics and adult children in the late 1970s. She has shared her message of understanding and hope in all corners of the world from Iceland to Australia, China to Mexico, touching the lives of women and men, young and old. For over thirty years she has been enthusiastically received as she has trained thousands of addiction specialists and mental health practitioners in issues related to family violence, multi-addictions, relapse, anger, depression, and women's issues.

Since 1998 she has been a clinical consultant for The Meadows Treatment Center in Wickenburg, Arizona, specializing in the treatment of trauma and addictive disorders. She is past chairperson of the National Association of Children of Alcoholics, and presently serves on its advisory board. She also serves on the advisory council of the Moyer Foundation, helping children in distress. In 2004 she was the recipient of the Distinguished Alumni Award from the School of Social Work at the University of Washington.

Deceived is Claudia's fifteenth book. She has also produced several audio CDs and over twenty DVDs related to addiction issues.

Claudia thoroughly enjoys her life in the Pacific Northwest with her husband and two Westies, Quinn and Katie. Her moments of solitude are found in the Grand Forest and kayaking on Puget Sound.

For more information on Dr. Black's other materials, her presentation schedule, blog, and newsletter, visit her Web site at www.claudiablack.com or email info@claudiablack.com.

Also by Claudia Black, Ph.D.

Books

Anger Strategies
Changing Course
Depression Strategies
Family Strategies
A Hole in the Sidewalk
It Will Never Happen to Me
It's Never Too Late to Have a Happy Childhood
"My Dad Loves Me, My Dad Has a Disease"
Relapse Toolkit
Repeat After Me
Straight Talk

Games

The Stamp Game

CDs

Emotional Baggage
Imageries
Letting Go Imageries
Putting the Past Behind
A Time for Healing from Abandonment and Shame
Trauma in the Addicted Family

DVDs

Anger
Addiction in the Family
The Baggage Cart
Breaking the Silence

Children of Denial
Double Jeopardy
Healing from Childhood Sexual Abuse
The History of Addiction
Issues of Recovery
Legacy of Addiction
The Process of Recovery
Relapse: The Illusion of Immunity
The Relationship Series
Roles
Shame
Sound of Silence
Triggering Effect
What Do I Say to My Kids?

To order books, games, CDs, and DVDs, contact:
Mac Publishing
PMB 346, 321 High School Road NE, Suite D3
Bainbridge Island, WA 98110-2648
800-698-0148 Toll free
206-842-6303 Voice
206-842-6235 Fax
www.claudiablack.com

To arrange a speaking engagement with Dr. Black, contact Claudja Inc.
800-698-0148 Toll free
206-842-6303 Voice
206-842-6235 Fax
info@claudiablack.com